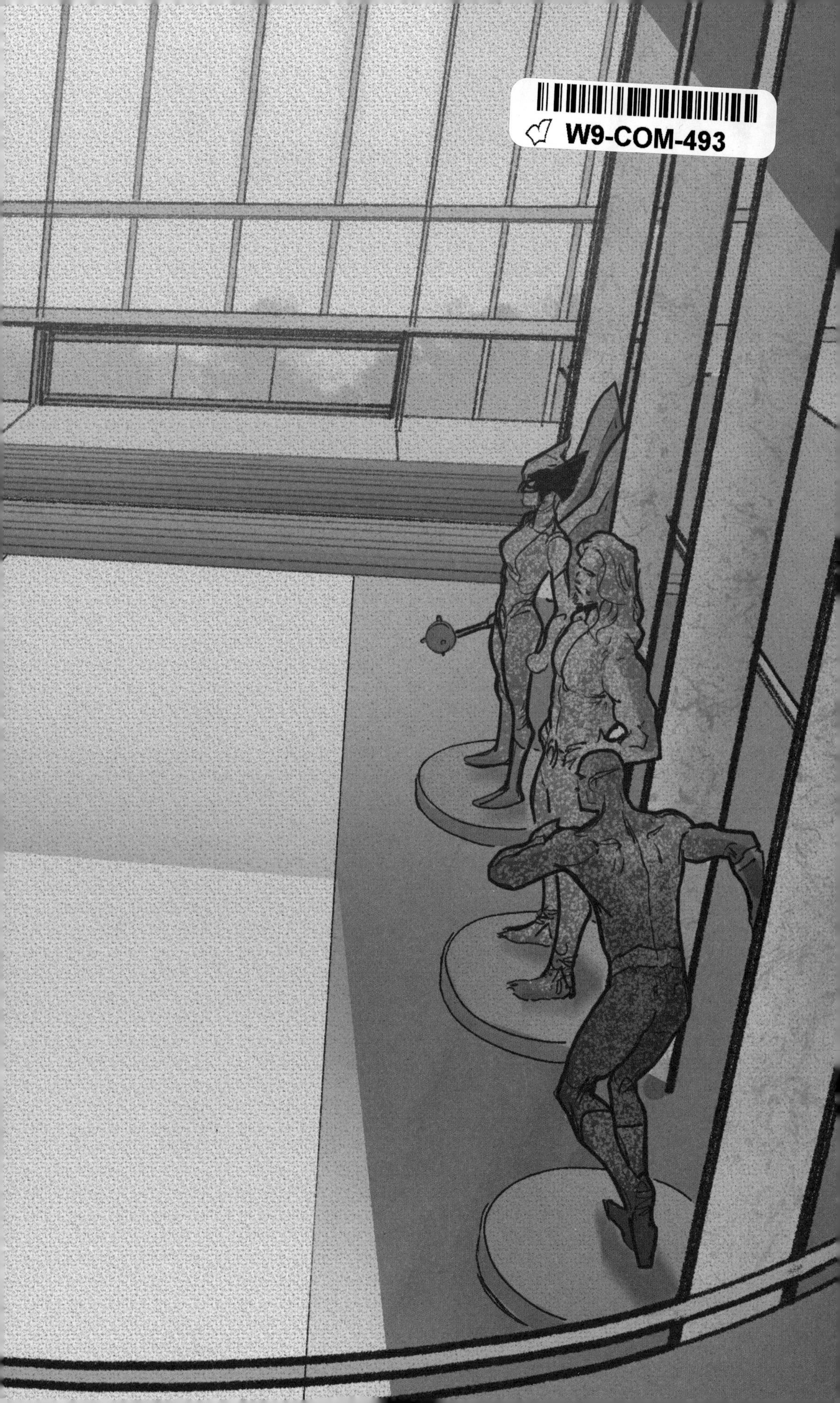

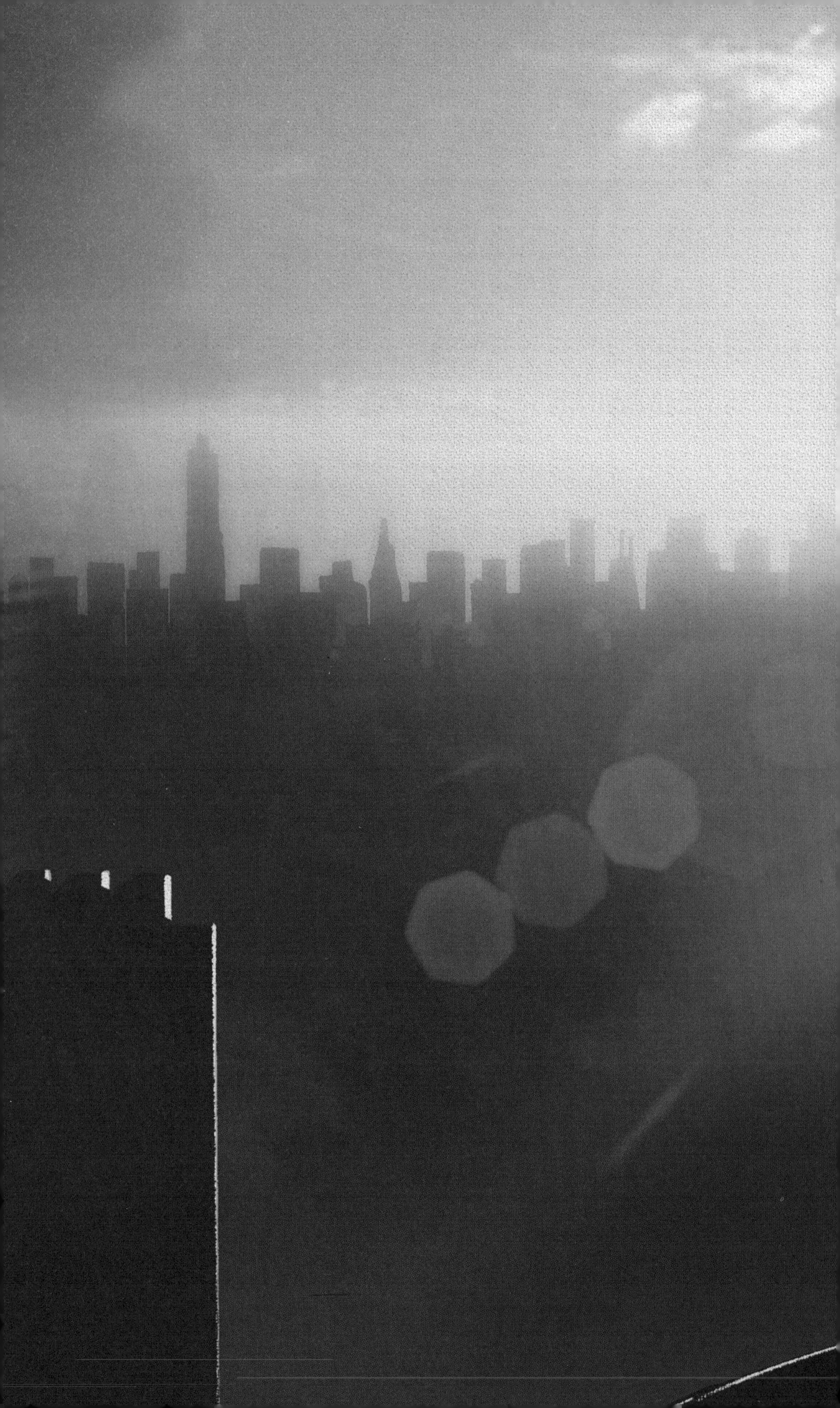

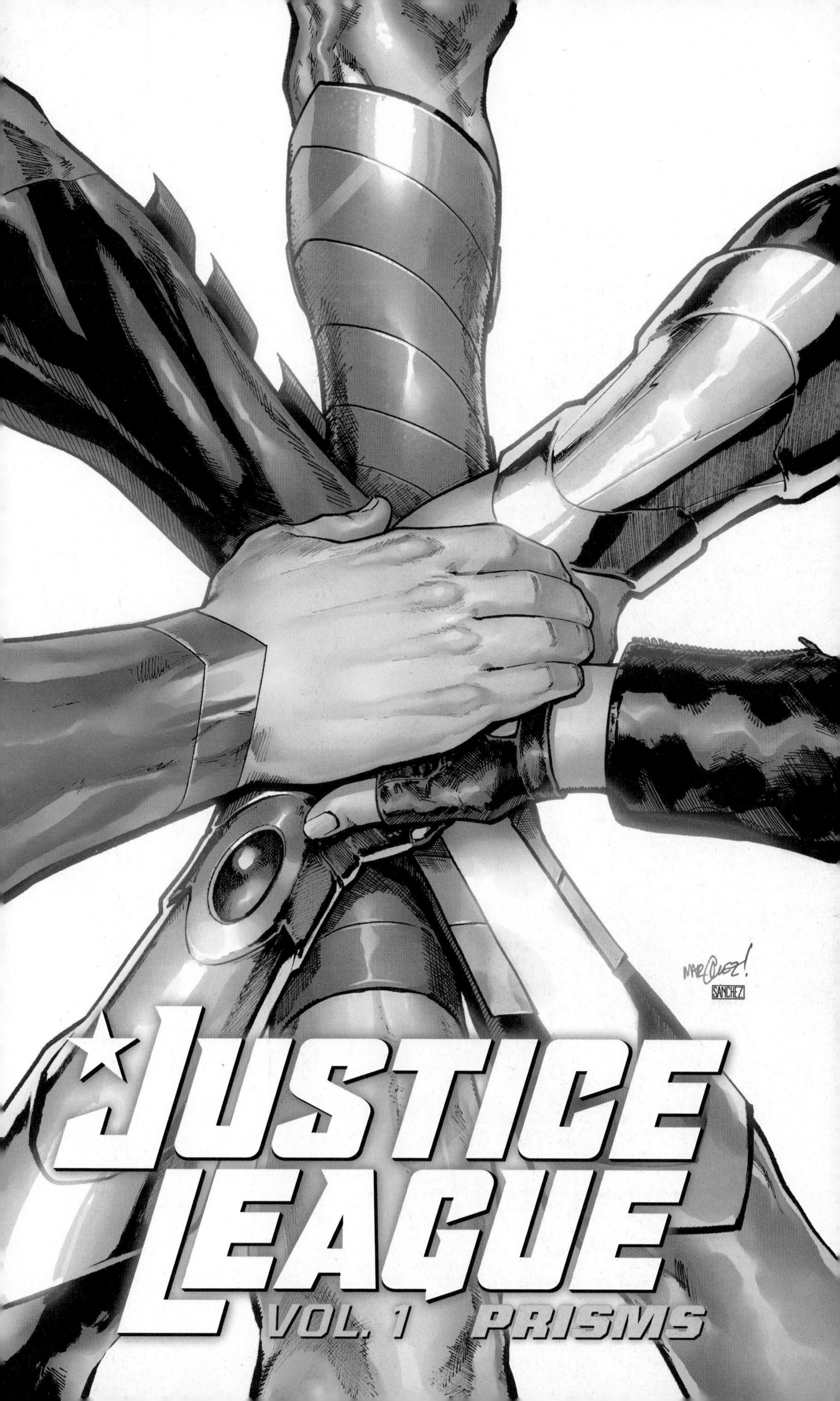

JUSTICE LEAGUE
VOL. 1 PRISMS
MARQUEZ!
SÁNCHEZ

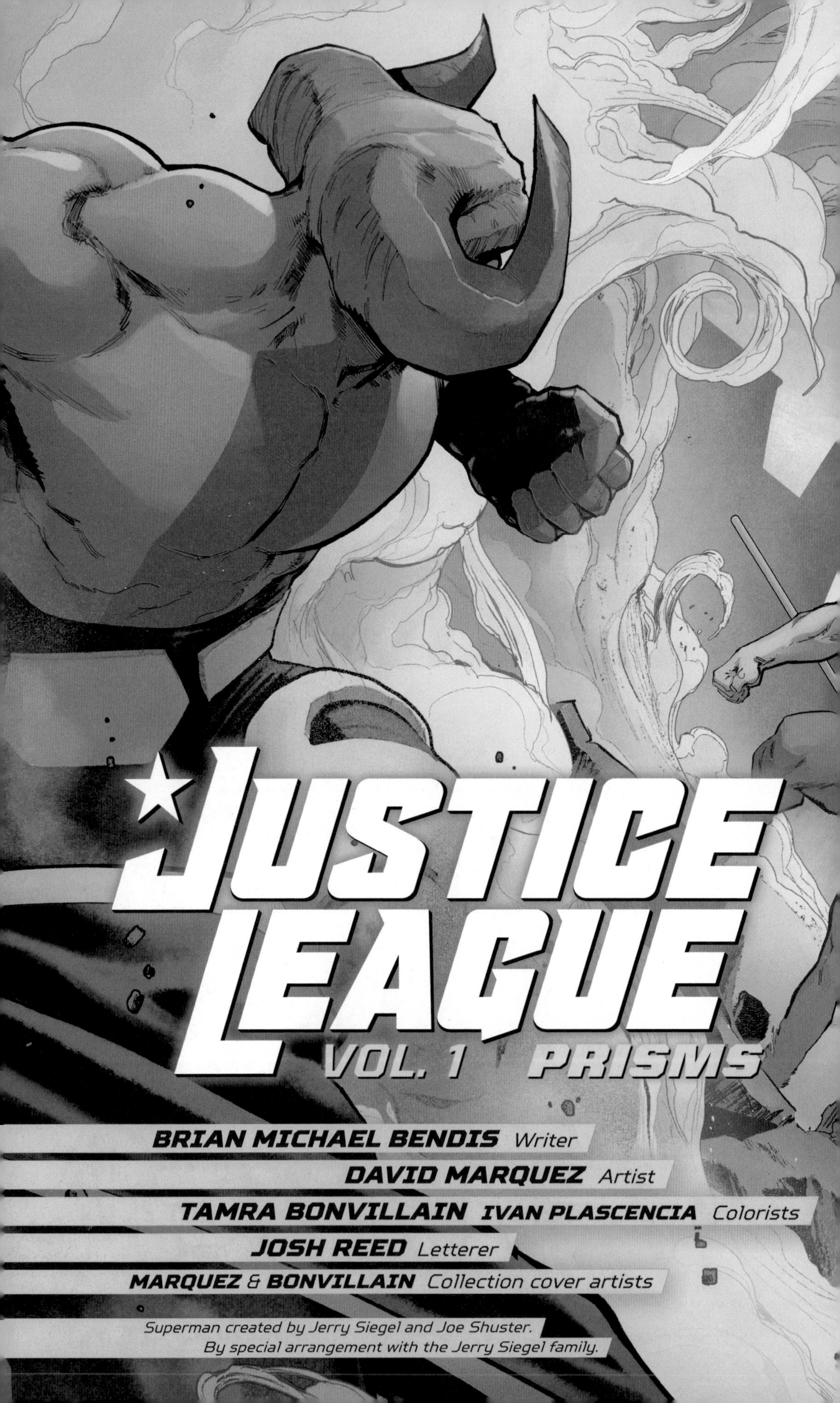

JUSTICE LEAGUE

VOL. 1 PRISMS

BRIAN MICHAEL BENDIS *Writer*

DAVID MARQUEZ *Artist*

TAMRA BONVILLAIN **IVAN PLASCENCIA** *Colorists*

JOSH REED *Letterer*

MARQUEZ & BONVILLAIN *Collection cover artists*

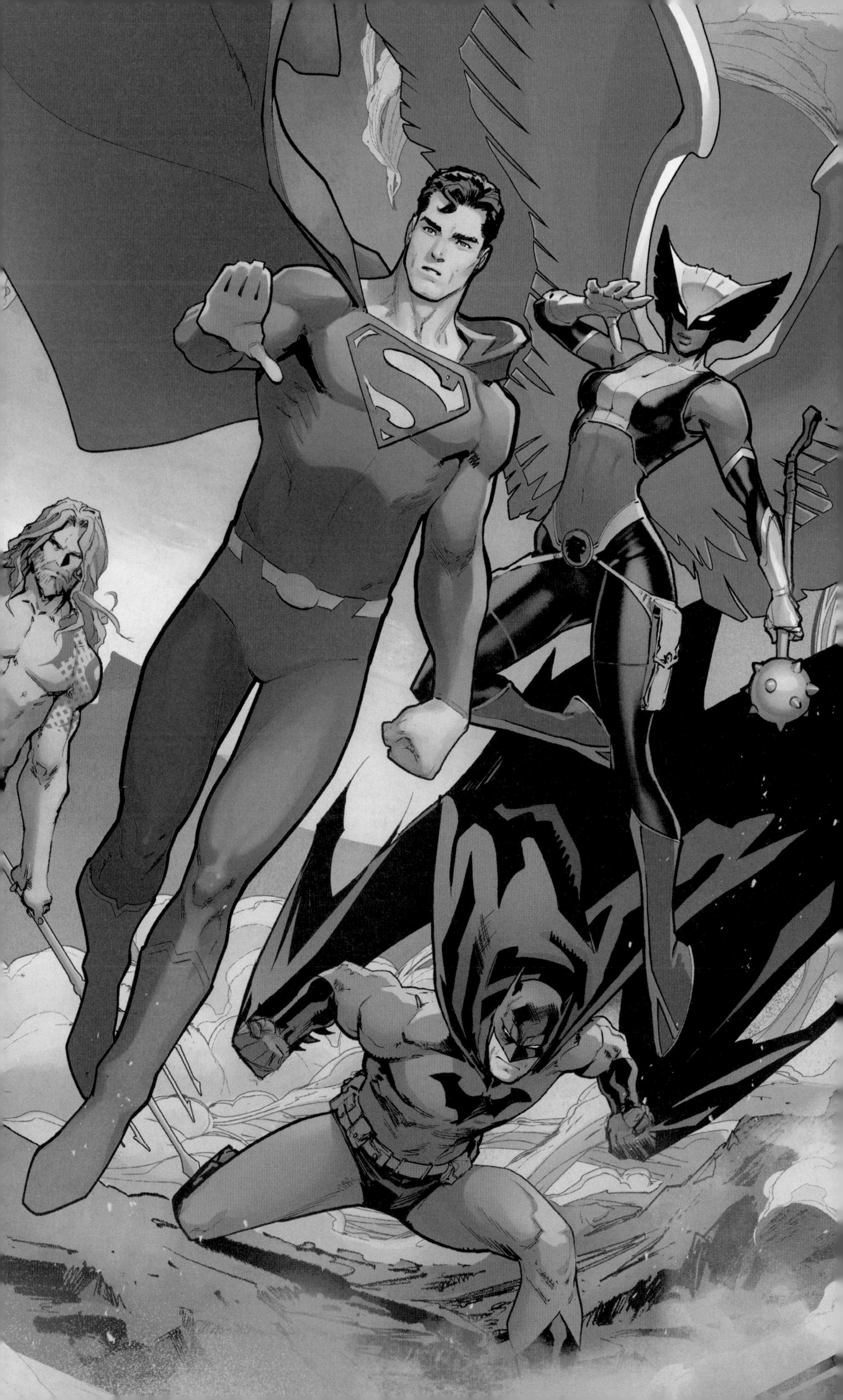

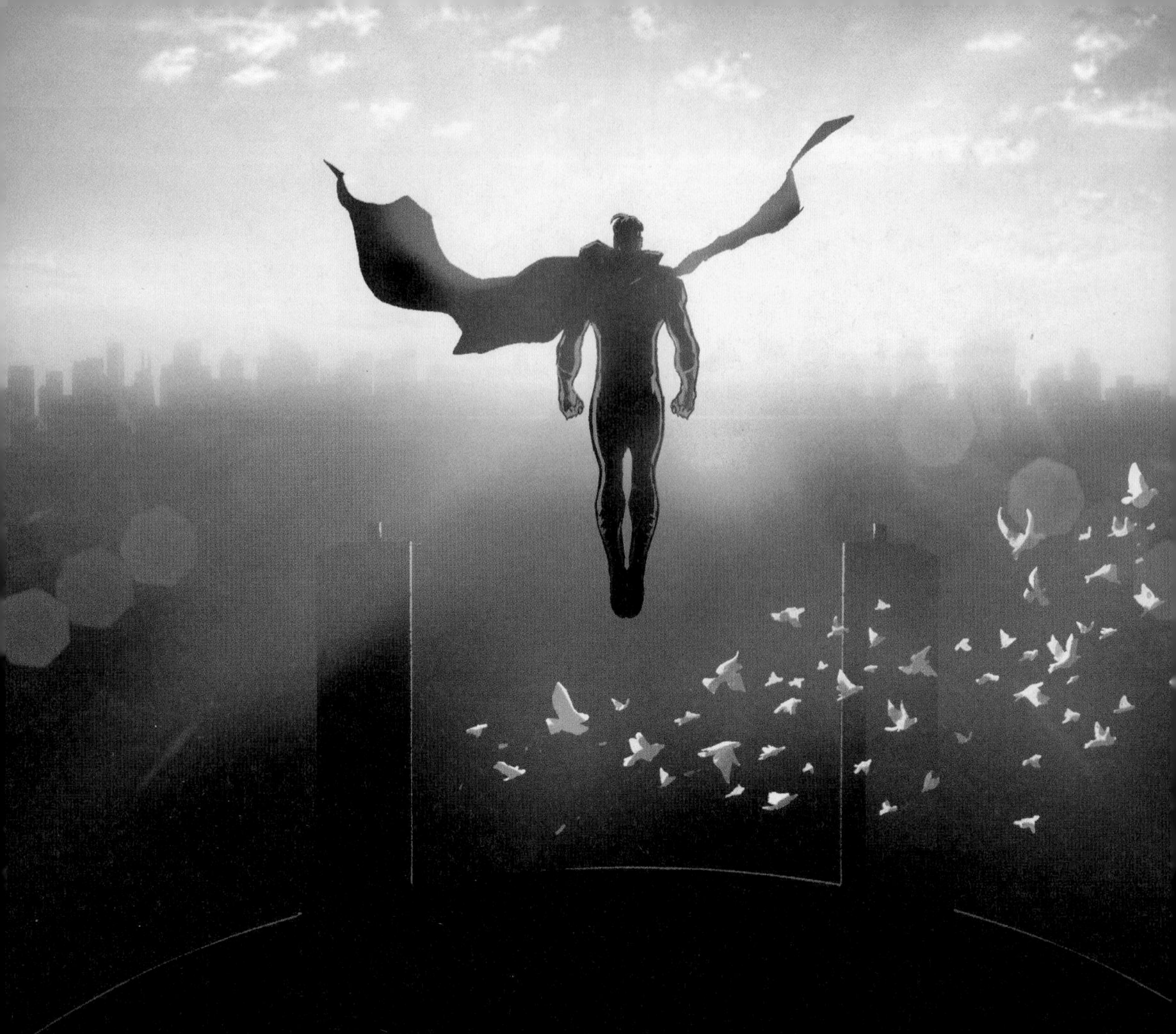

ALEX R. CARR
Editor – Original Series
ANDREA SHEA
Associate Editor – Original Series
BIXIE MATHIEU
Assistant Editor – Original Series
STEVE BUCCELLATO
PAUL KAMINSKI
Editors – Collected Edition
STEVE COOK
Design Director – Books
CURTIS KING JR.
Publication Design
CHRISTY SAWYER
Publication Production

MARIE JAVINS
Editor-in-Chief, DC Comics

ANNE DePIES
Senior VP – General Manager
JIM LEE
Publisher & Chief Creative Officer
DON FALLETTI
VP – Manufacturing Operations & Workflow Management
LAWRENCE GANEM
VP – Talent Services
ALISON GILL
Senior VP – Manufacturing & Operations
JEFFREY KAUFMAN
VP – Editorial Strategy & Programming
NICK J. NAPOLITANO
VP – Manufacturing Administration & Design
NANCY SPEARS
VP – Revenue

JUSTICE LEAGUE
VOL. 1: PRISMS

DC Comics, 2900 West Alameda Ave., Burbank, CA 91505
Printed by Transcontinental Interglobe, Beauceville, QC, Canada.
4/1/22. First Printing.
ISBN: 978-1-77951-437-0

Library of Congress Cataloging-in-Publication Data is available.

PEFC Certified
This product is from sustainably managed forests and controlled sources
PEFC/01-31-106
www.pefc.org

Justice League #59 cover by **David Marquez & Tamra Bonvillain**

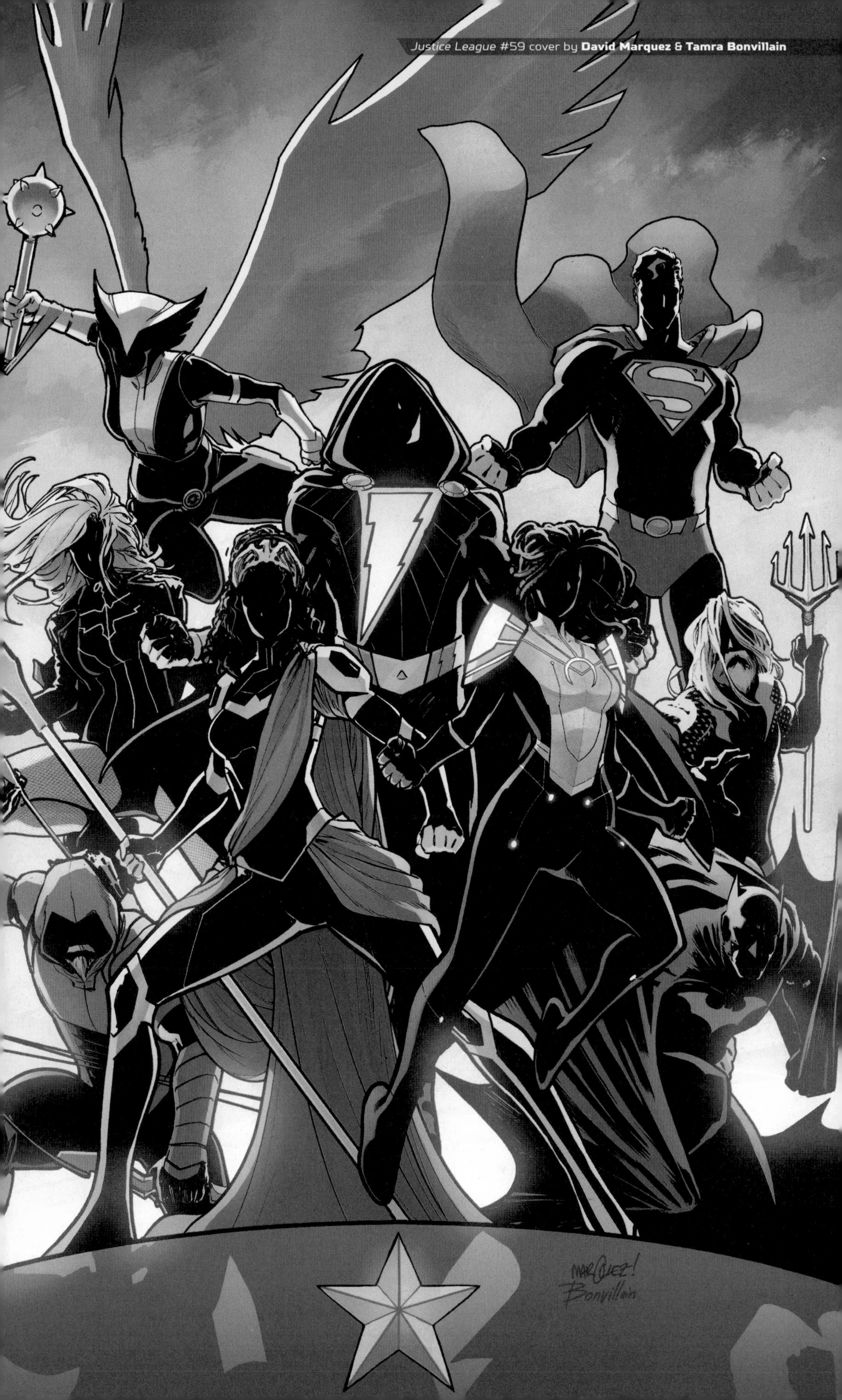
MARQUEZ!
Bonvillain

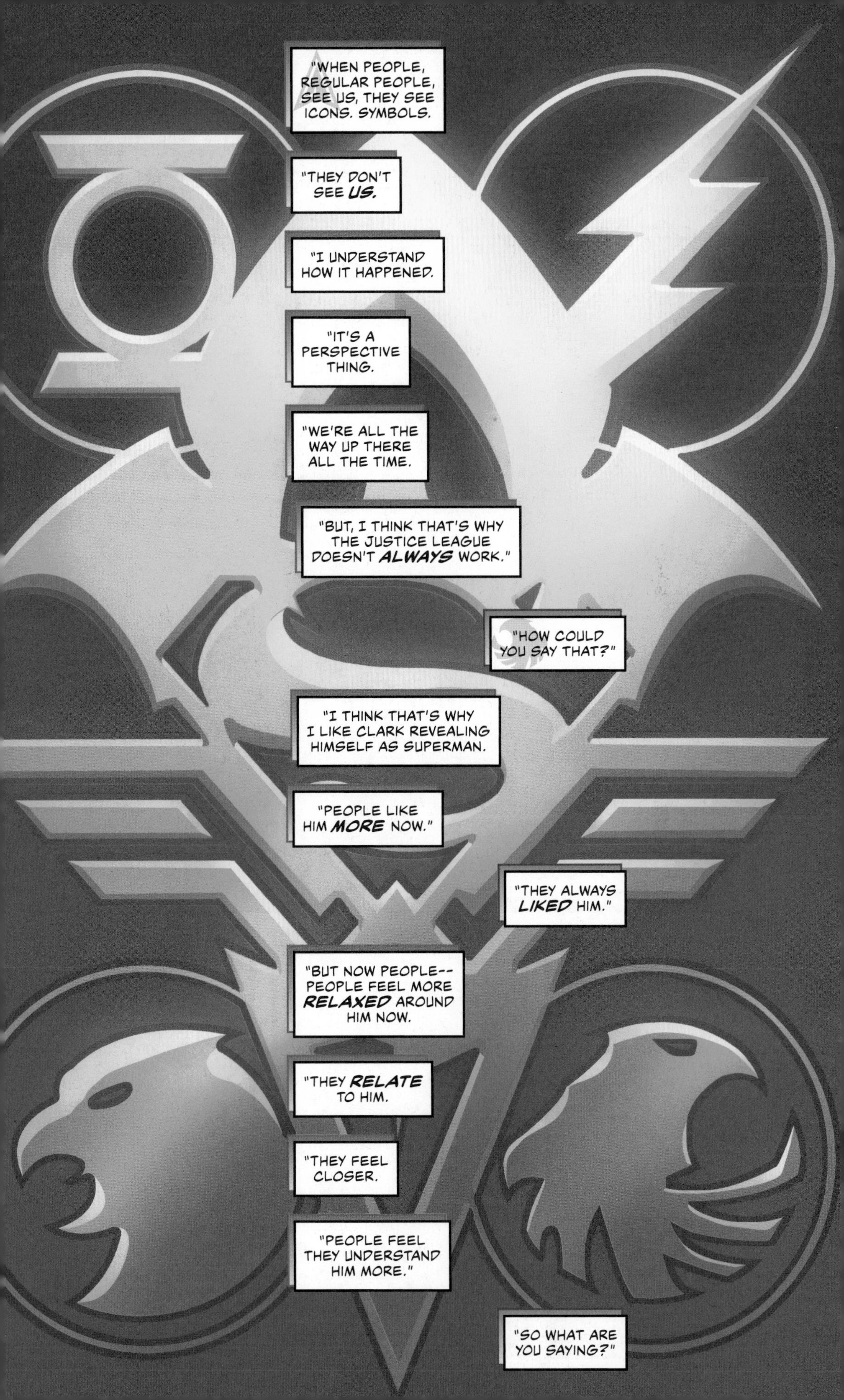

"WHEN PEOPLE, REGULAR PEOPLE, SEE US, THEY SEE ICONS. SYMBOLS.
"THEY DON'T SEE ***US.***
"I UNDERSTAND HOW IT HAPPENED.
"IT'S A PERSPECTIVE THING.
"WE'RE ALL THE WAY UP THERE ALL THE TIME.
"BUT, I THINK THAT'S WHY THE JUSTICE LEAGUE DOESN'T ***ALWAYS*** WORK."
"HOW COULD YOU SAY THAT?"
"I THINK THAT'S WHY I LIKE CLARK REVEALING HIMSELF AS SUPERMAN.
"PEOPLE LIKE HIM ***MORE*** NOW."
"THEY ALWAYS ***LIKED*** HIM."
"BUT NOW PEOPLE-- PEOPLE FEEL MORE ***RELAXED*** AROUND HIM NOW.
"THEY ***RELATE*** TO HIM.
"THEY FEEL CLOSER.
"PEOPLE FEEL THEY UNDERSTAND HIM MORE."
"SO WHAT ARE YOU SAYING?"

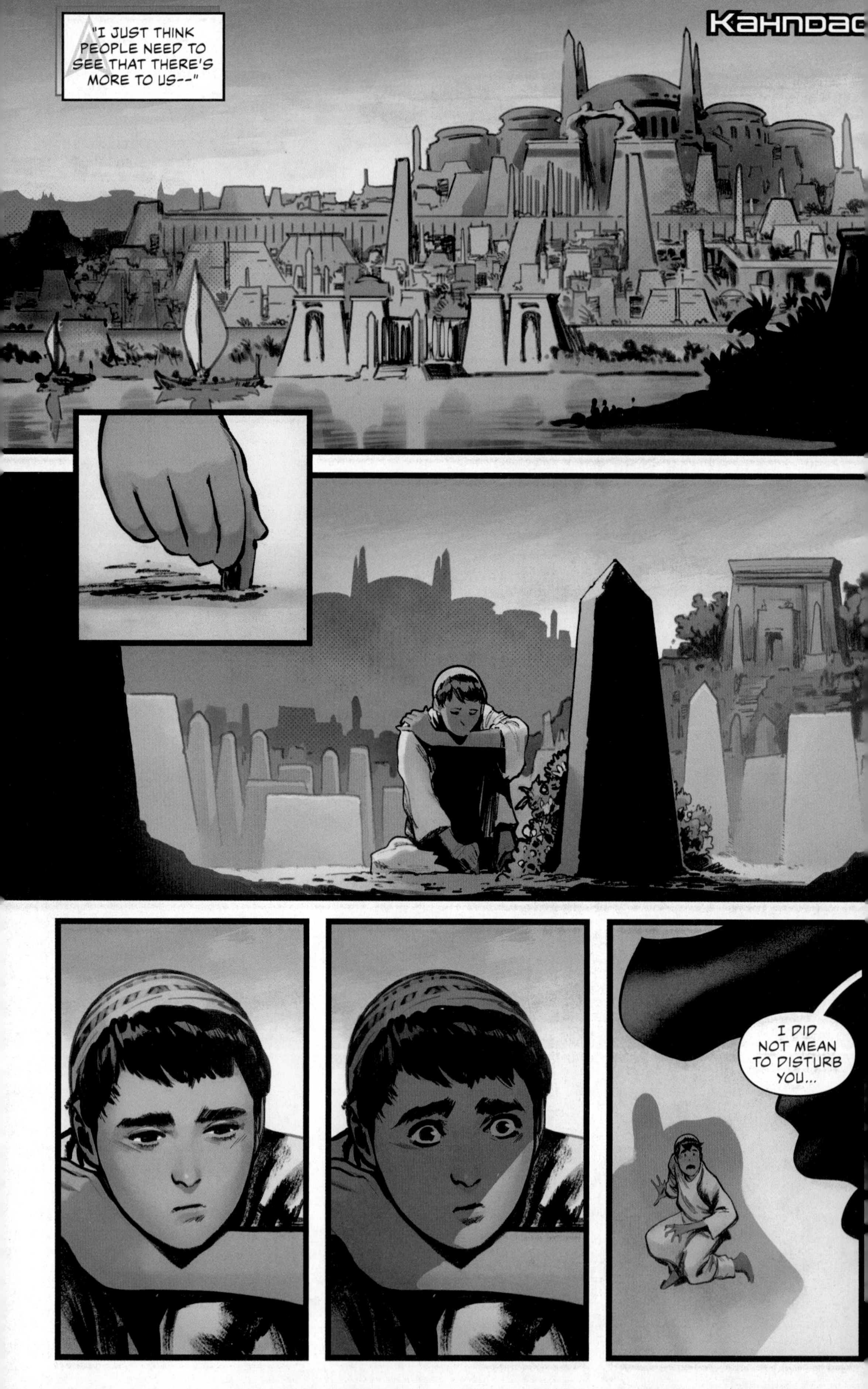
"I JUST THINK PEOPLE NEED TO SEE THAT THERE'S MORE TO US--"
KAHNDAQ
I DID NOT MEAN TO DISTURB YOU...

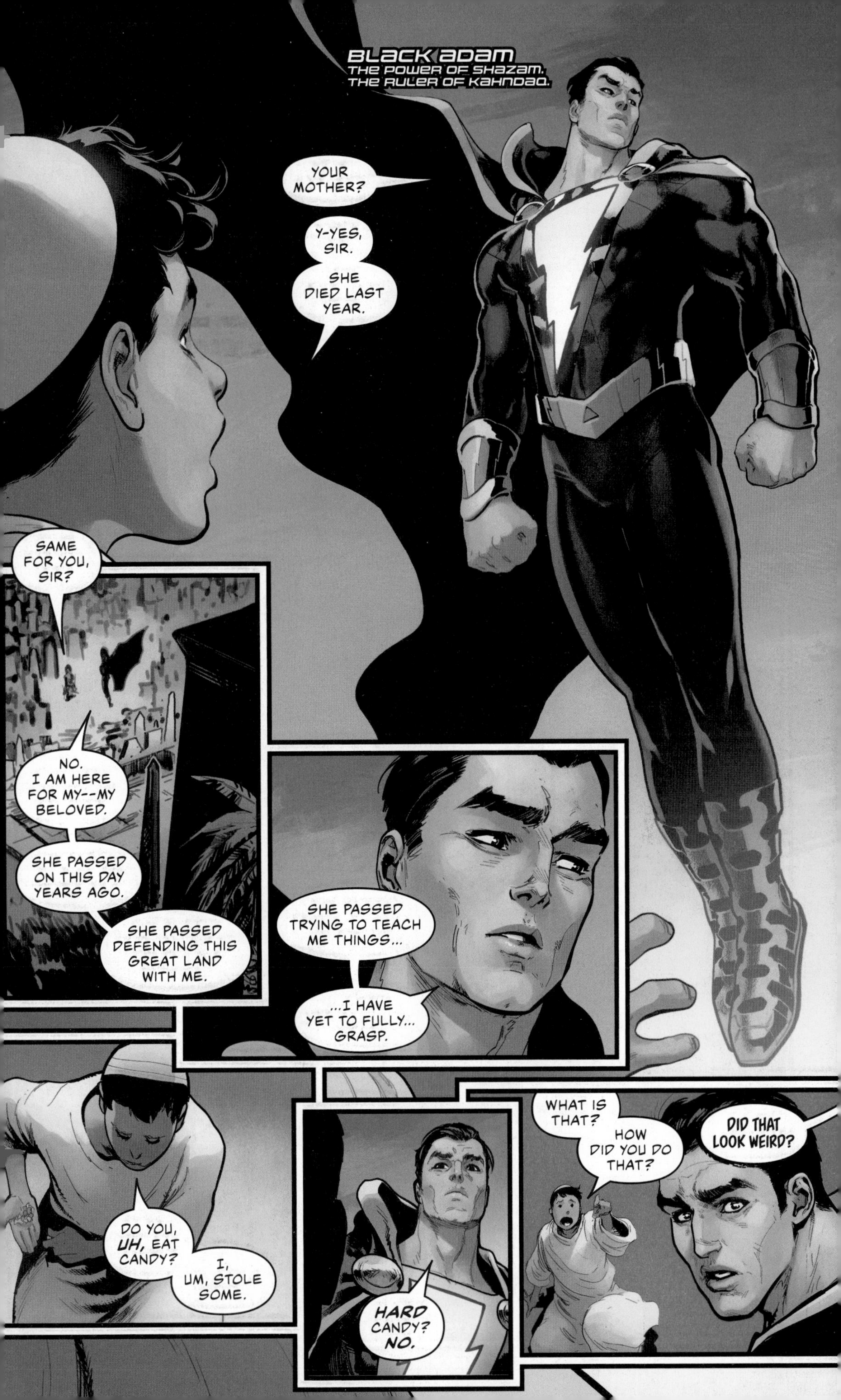
BLACK ADAM
THE POWER OF SHAZAM.
THE RULER OF KAHNDAQ.
YOUR MOTHER?
Y-YES, SIR.
SHE DIED LAST YEAR.
SAME FOR YOU, SIR?
NO. I AM HERE FOR MY--MY BELOVED.
SHE PASSED ON THIS DAY YEARS AGO.
SHE PASSED DEFENDING THIS GREAT LAND WITH ME.
SHE PASSED TRYING TO TEACH ME THINGS...
...I HAVE YET TO FULLY... GRASP.
DO YOU, UH, EAT CANDY?
I, UM, STOLE SOME.
HARD CANDY? NO.
WHAT IS THAT?
HOW DID YOU DO THAT?
DID THAT LOOK WEIRD?

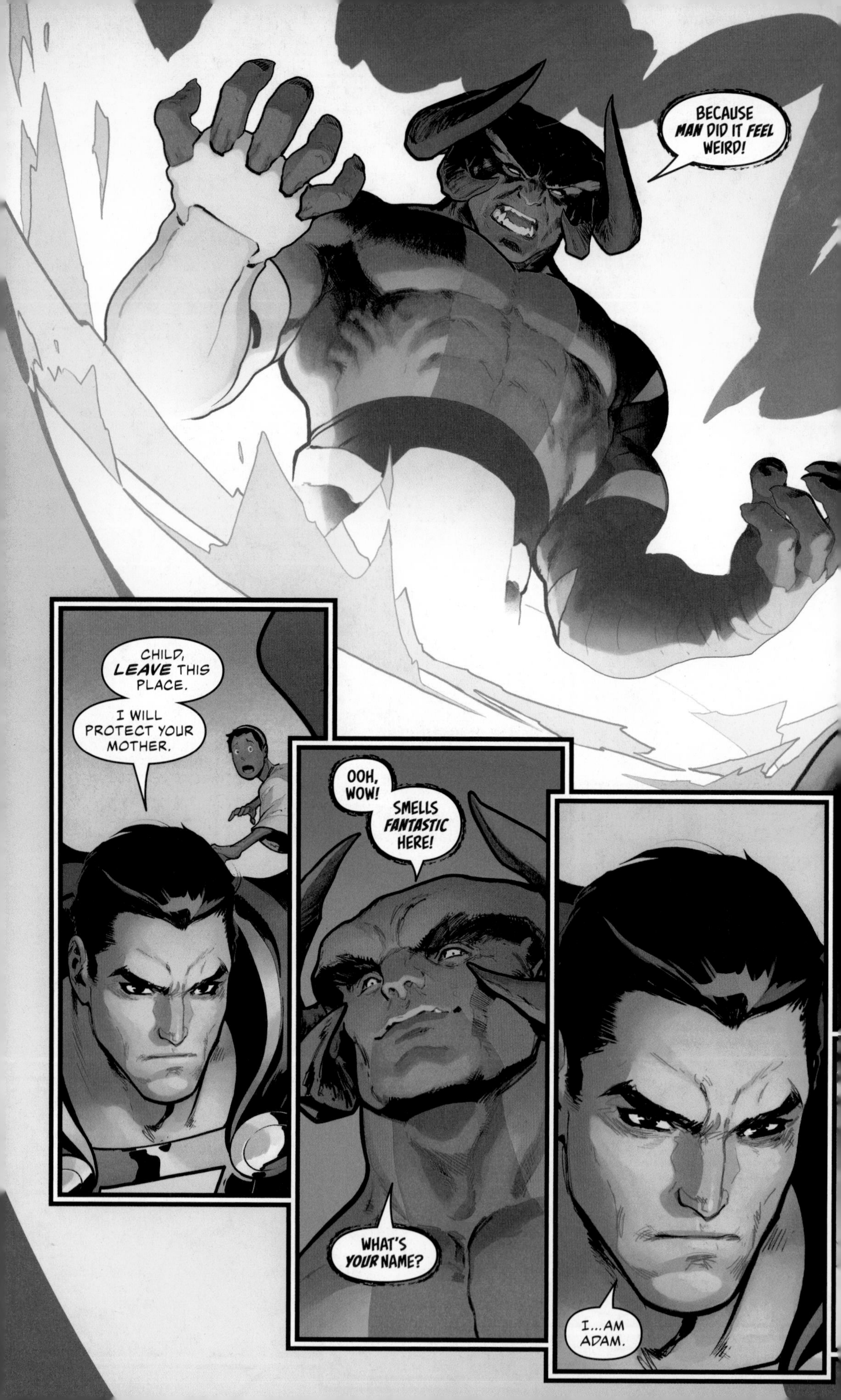
BECAUSE MAN DID IT FEEL WEIRD!
CHILD, LEAVE THIS PLACE.
I WILL PROTECT YOUR MOTHER.
OOH, WOW!
SMELLS FANTASTIC HERE!
WHAT'S YOUR NAME?
I...AM ADAM.

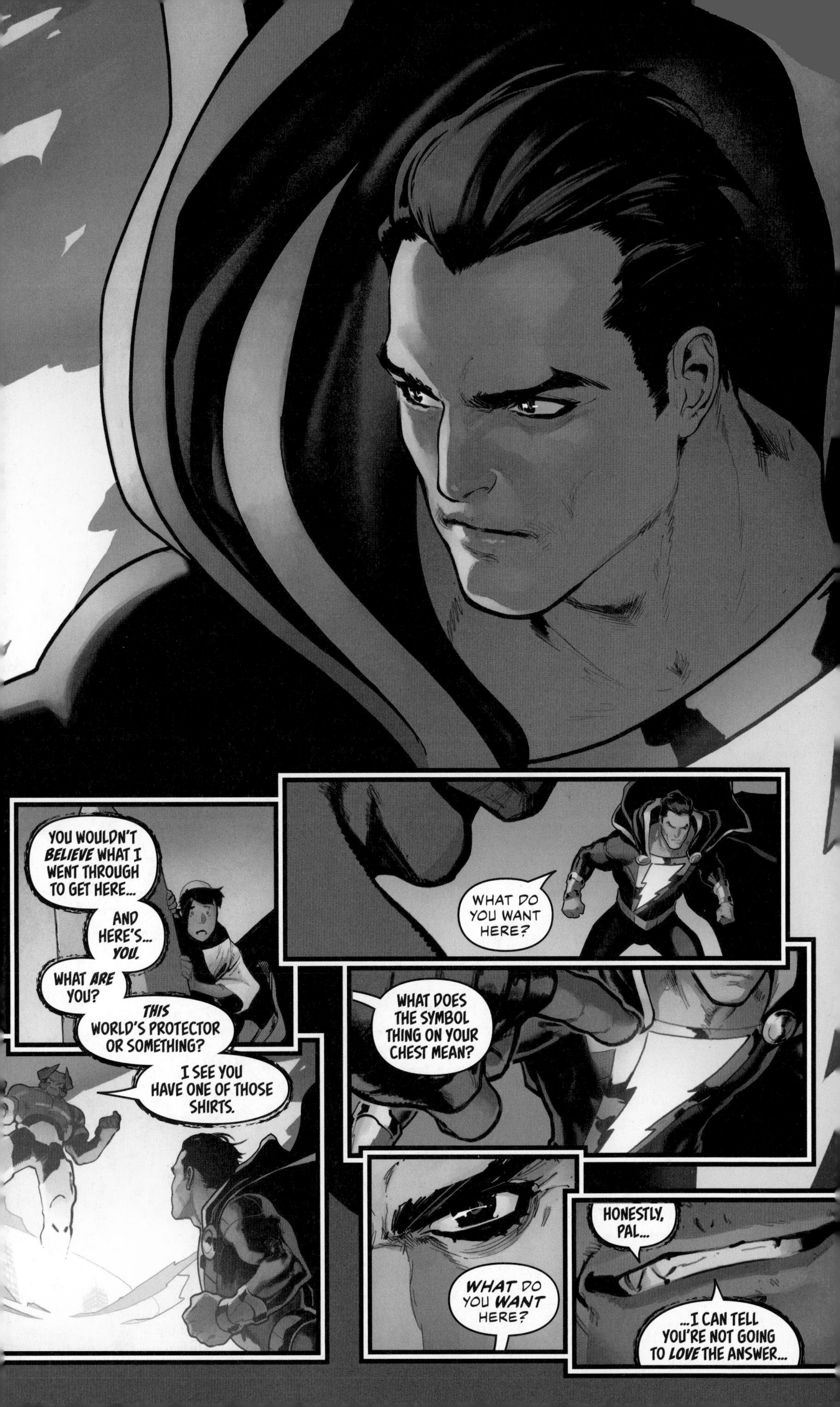

YOU WOULDN'T BELIEVE WHAT I WENT THROUGH TO GET HERE...
AND HERE'S... YOU.
WHAT ARE YOU?
THIS WORLD'S PROTECTOR OR SOMETHING?
I SEE YOU HAVE ONE OF THOSE SHIRTS.
WHAT DO YOU WANT HERE?
WHAT DOES THE SYMBOL THING ON YOUR CHEST MEAN?
WHAT DO YOU WANT HERE?
HONESTLY, PAL...
...I CAN TELL YOU'RE NOT GOING TO LOVE THE ANSWER...

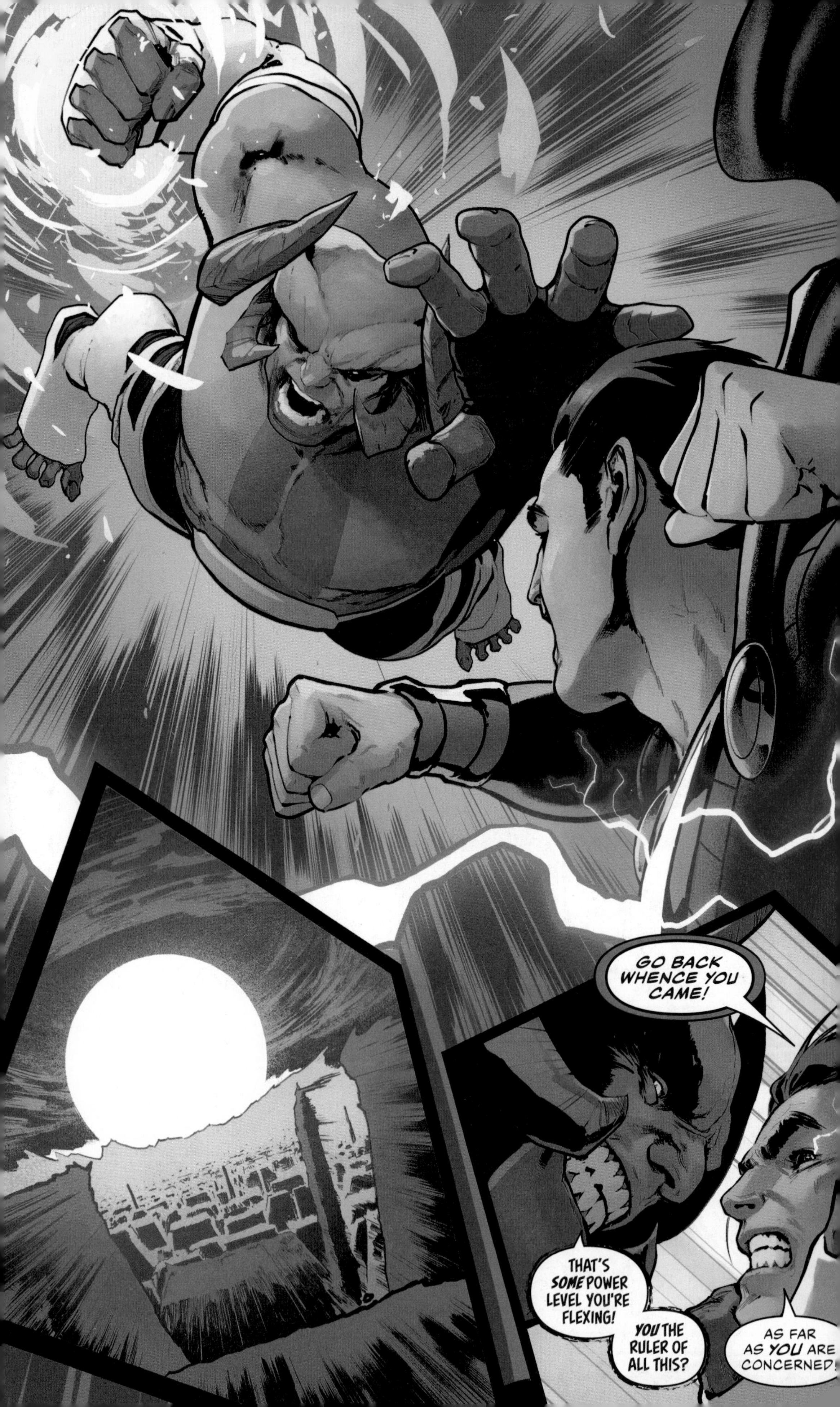
GO BACK WHENCE YOU CAME!
THAT'S SOME POWER LEVEL YOU'RE FLEXING!
YOU THE RULER OF ALL THIS?
AS FAR AS YOU ARE CONCERNED!

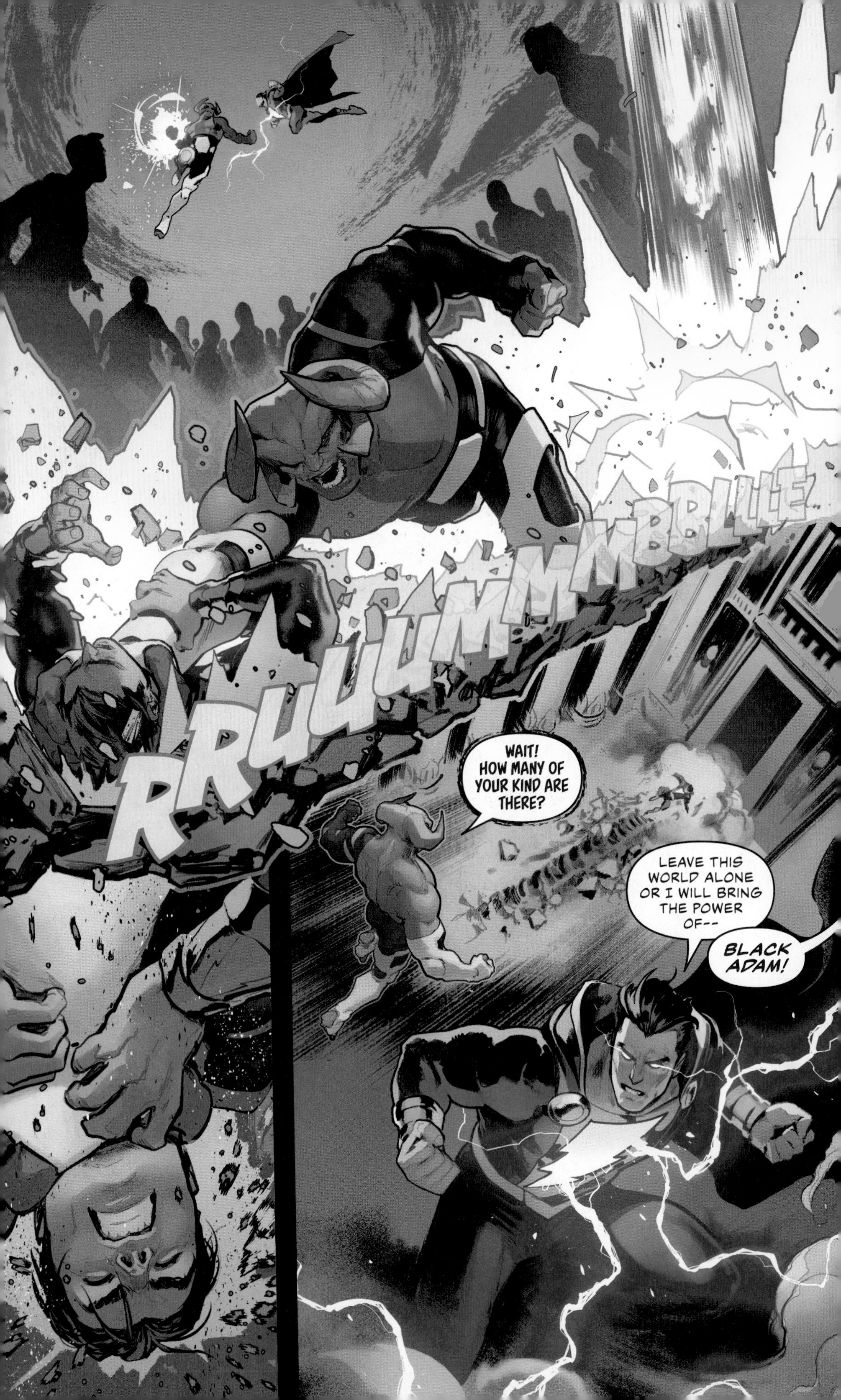
RRUUUMMMMBBLLLE
WAIT! HOW MANY OF YOUR KIND ARE THERE?
LEAVE THIS WORLD ALONE OR I WILL BRING THE POWER OF--
BLACK ADAM!

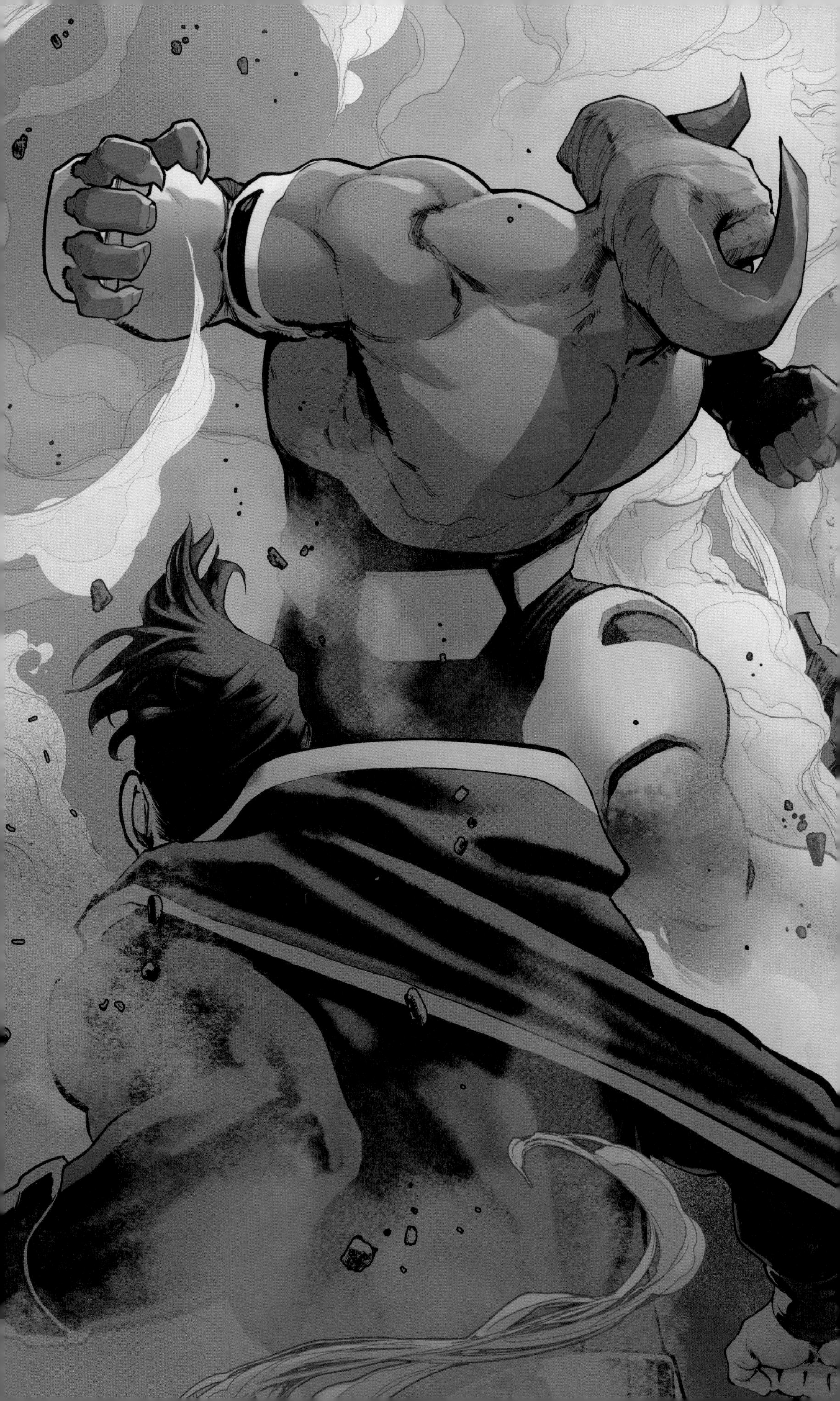

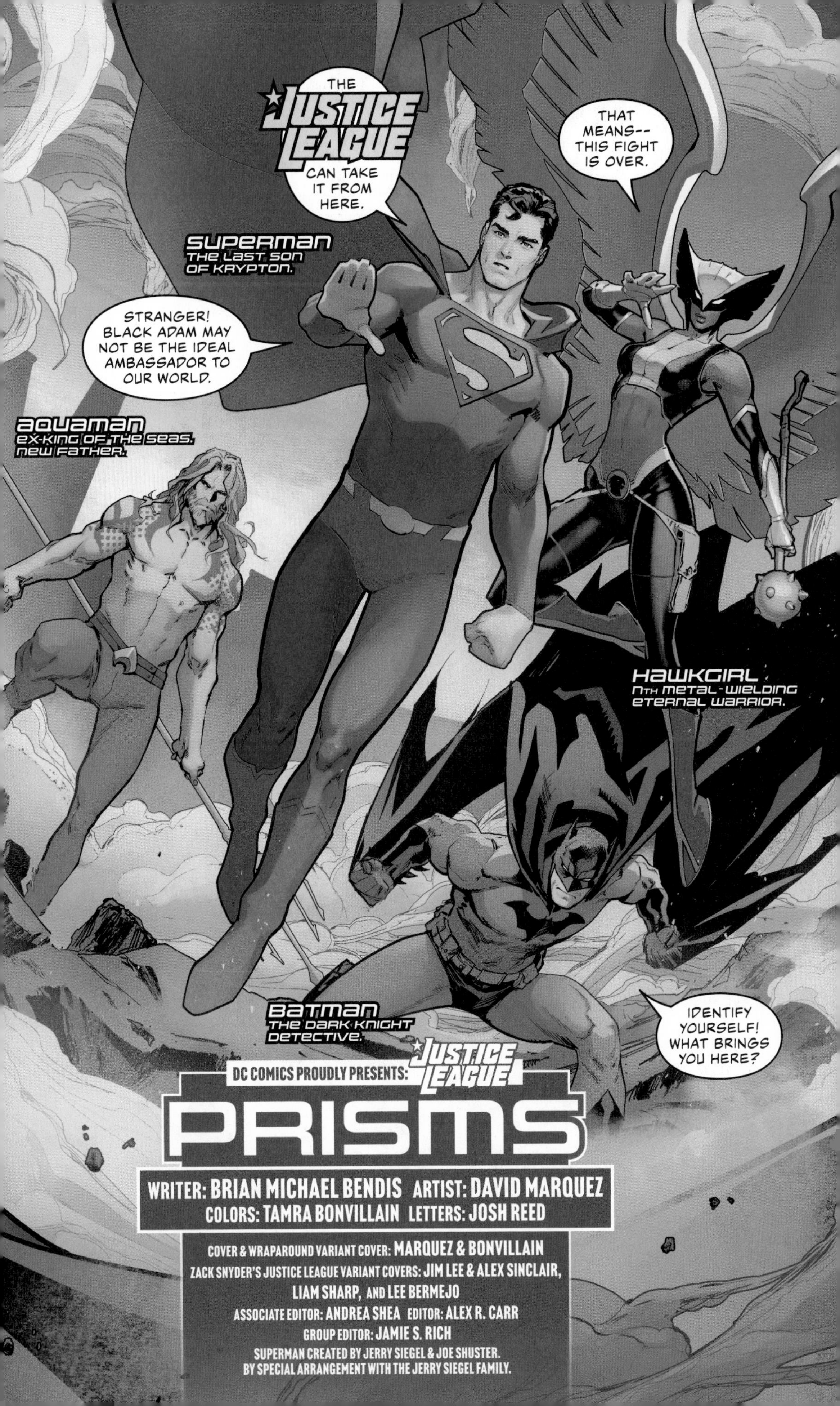
THE JUSTICE LEAGUE CAN TAKE IT FROM HERE.
THAT MEANS-- THIS FIGHT IS OVER.
SUPERMAN THE LAST SON OF KRYPTON.
STRANGER! BLACK ADAM MAY NOT BE THE IDEAL AMBASSADOR TO OUR WORLD.
AQUAMAN EX-KING OF THE SEAS. NEW FATHER.
HAWKGIRL NTH METAL-WIELDING ETERNAL WARRIOR.
BATMAN THE DARK KNIGHT DETECTIVE.
IDENTIFY YOURSELF! WHAT BRINGS YOU HERE?
DC COMICS PROUDLY PRESENTS: JUSTICE LEAGUE
PRISMS
WRITER: BRIAN MICHAEL BENDIS ARTIST: DAVID MARQUEZ
COLORS: TAMRA BONVILLAIN LETTERS: JOSH REED
COVER & WRAPAROUND VARIANT COVER: MARQUEZ & BONVILLAIN
ZACK SNYDER'S JUSTICE LEAGUE VARIANT COVERS: JIM LEE & ALEX SINCLAIR, LIAM SHARP, AND LEE BERMEJO
ASSOCIATE EDITOR: ANDREA SHEA EDITOR: ALEX R. CARR
GROUP EDITOR: JAMIE S. RICH
SUPERMAN CREATED BY JERRY SIEGEL & JOE SHUSTER.
BY SPECIAL ARRANGEMENT WITH THE JERRY SIEGEL FAMILY.

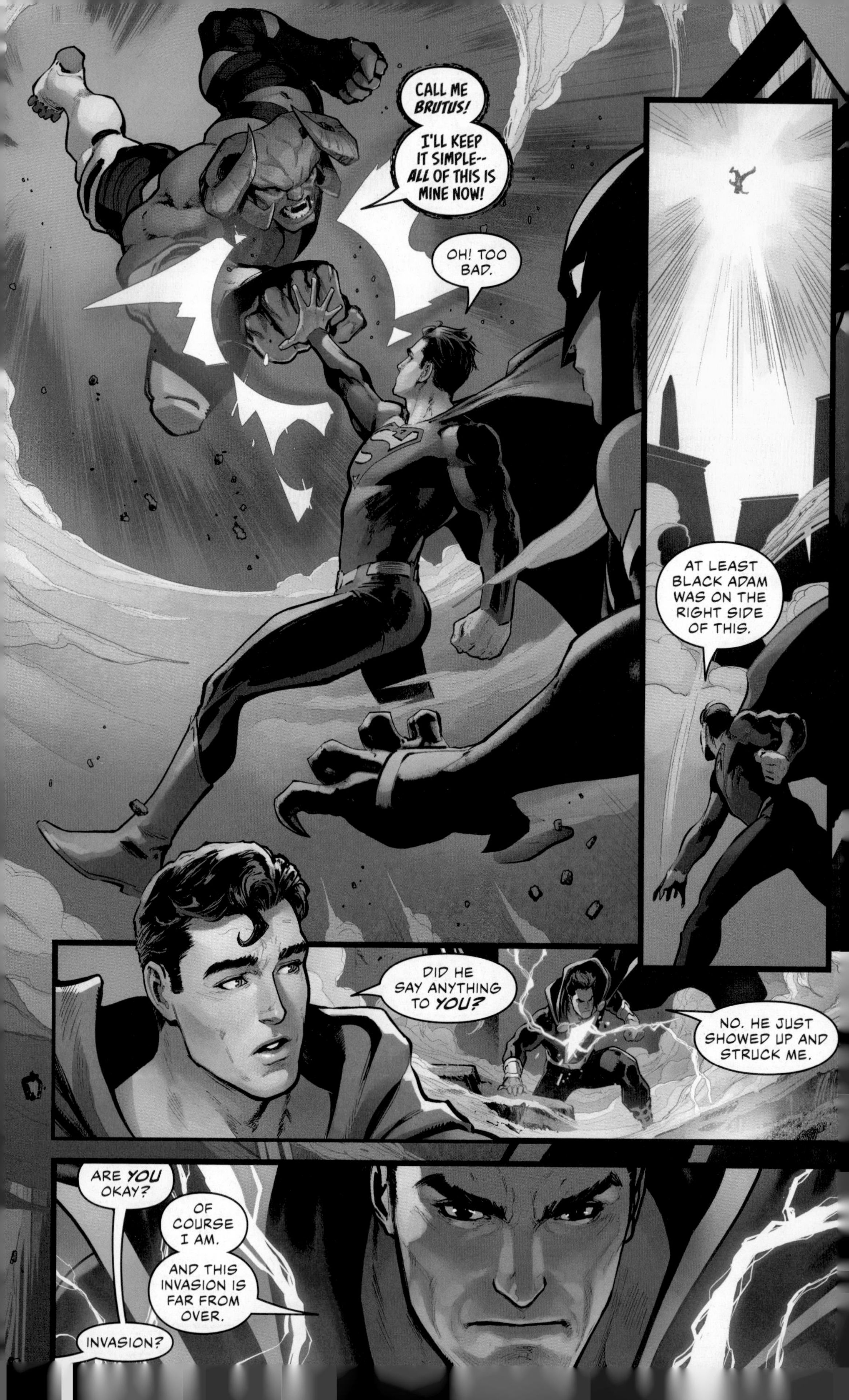
CALL ME BRUTUS!
I'LL KEEP IT SIMPLE-- ALL OF THIS IS MINE NOW!
OH! TOO BAD.
AT LEAST BLACK ADAM WAS ON THE RIGHT SIDE OF THIS.
DID HE SAY ANYTHING TO YOU?
NO. HE JUST SHOWED UP AND STRUCK ME.
ARE YOU OKAY?
OF COURSE I AM.
AND THIS INVASION IS FAR FROM OVER.
INVASION?

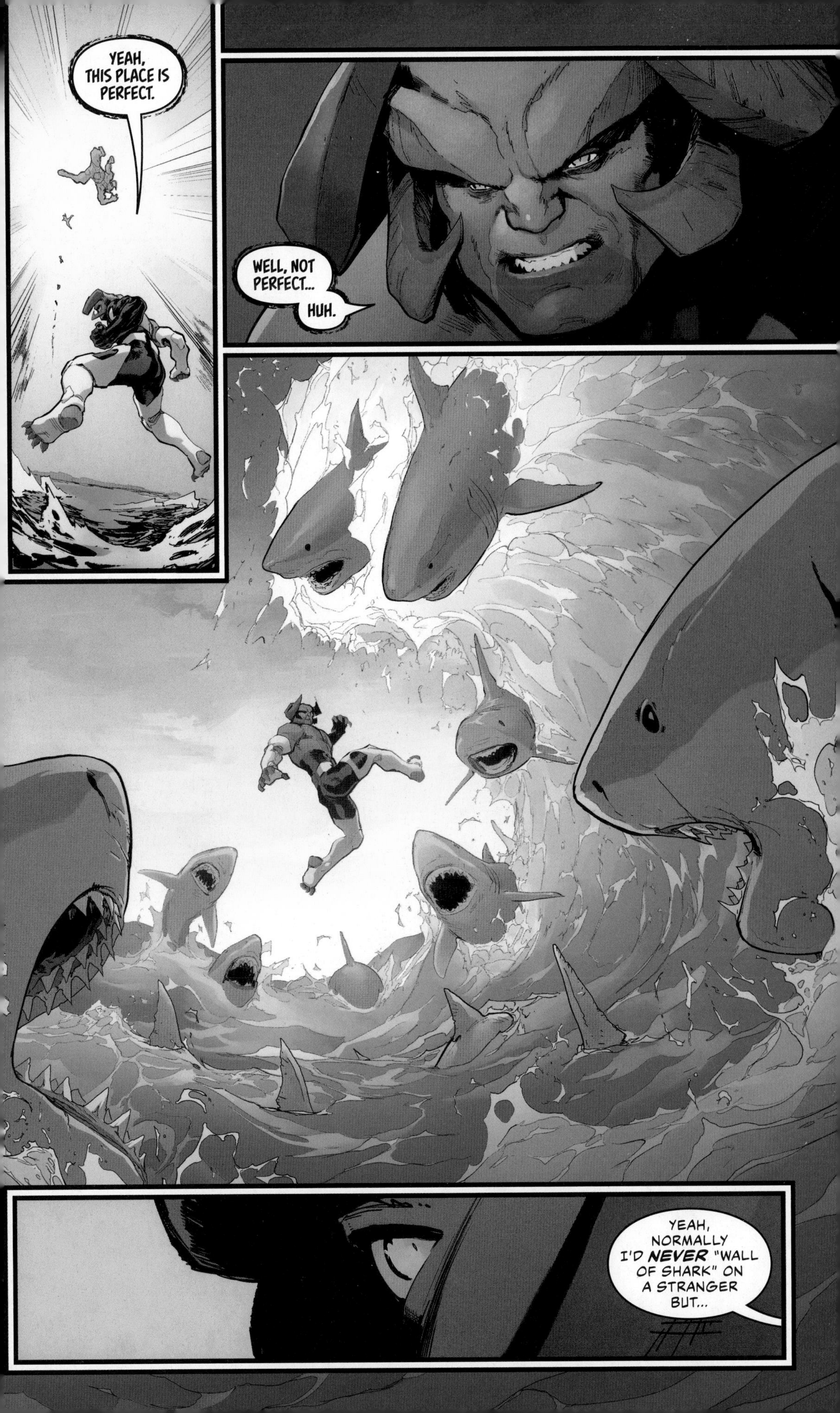
YEAH, THIS PLACE IS PERFECT.
WELL, NOT PERFECT...
HUH.
YEAH, NORMALLY I'D NEVER "WALL OF SHARK" ON A STRANGER BUT...

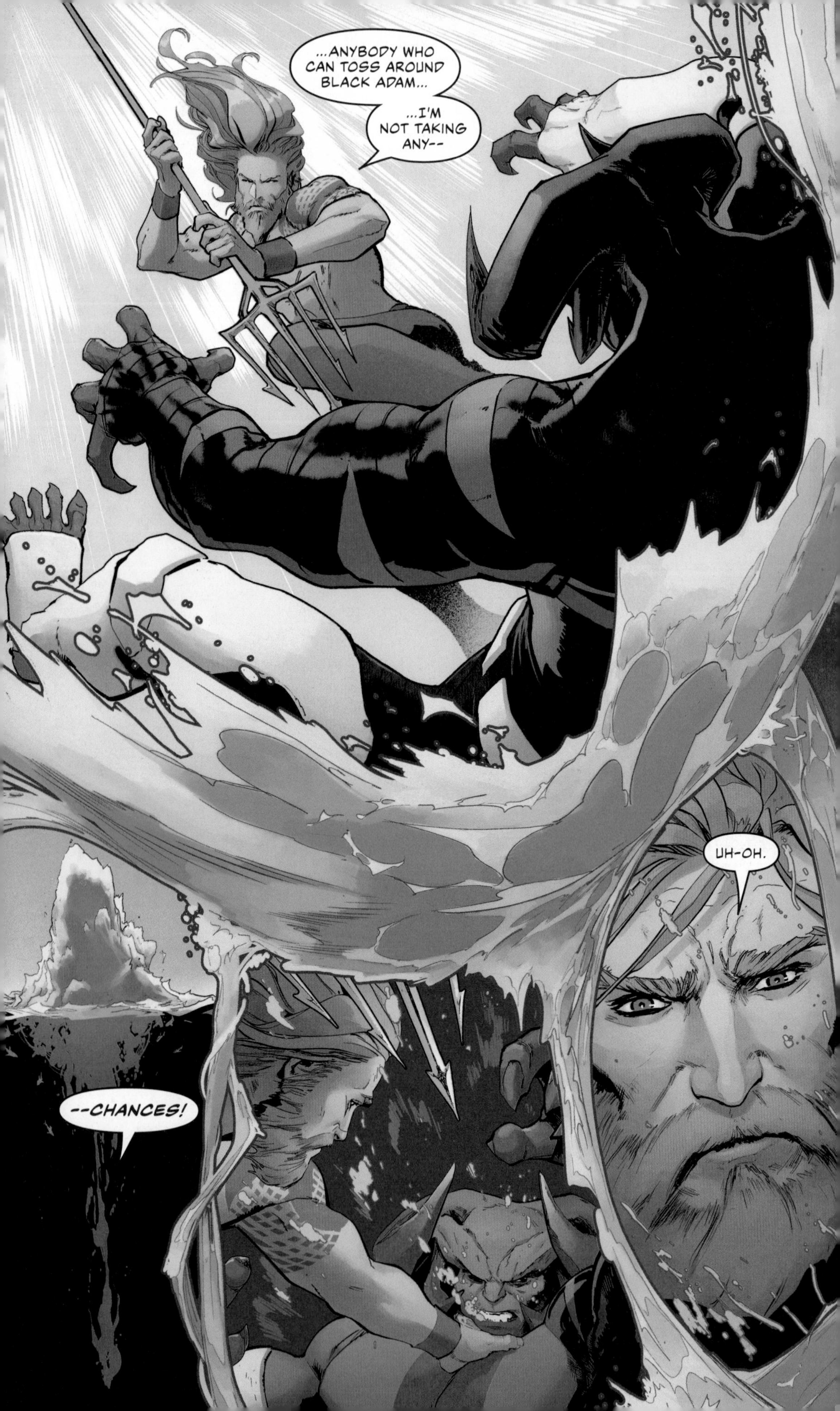
...ANYBODY WHO CAN TOSS AROUND BLACK ADAM...
...I'M NOT TAKING ANY--
UH-OH.
--CHANCES!

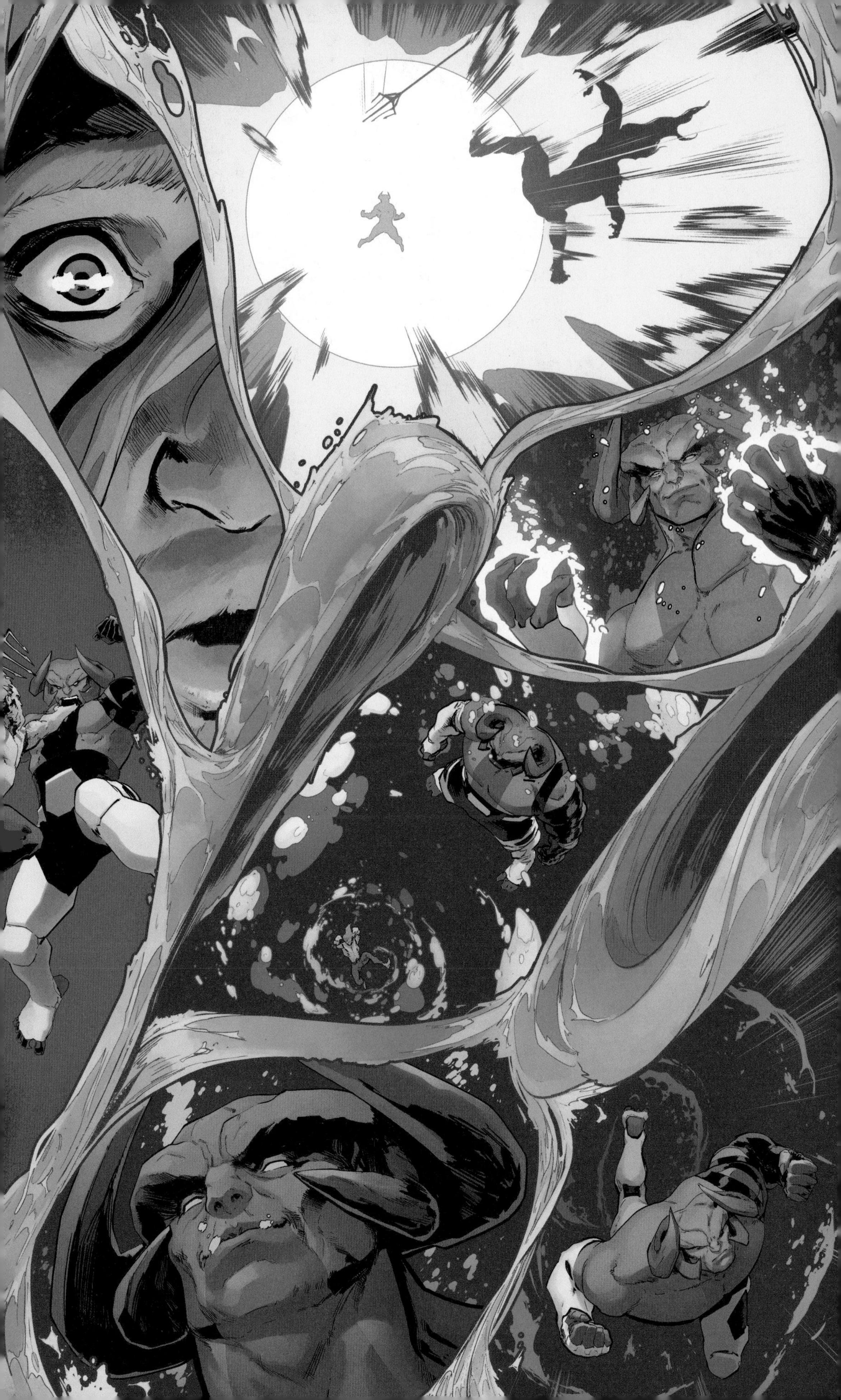

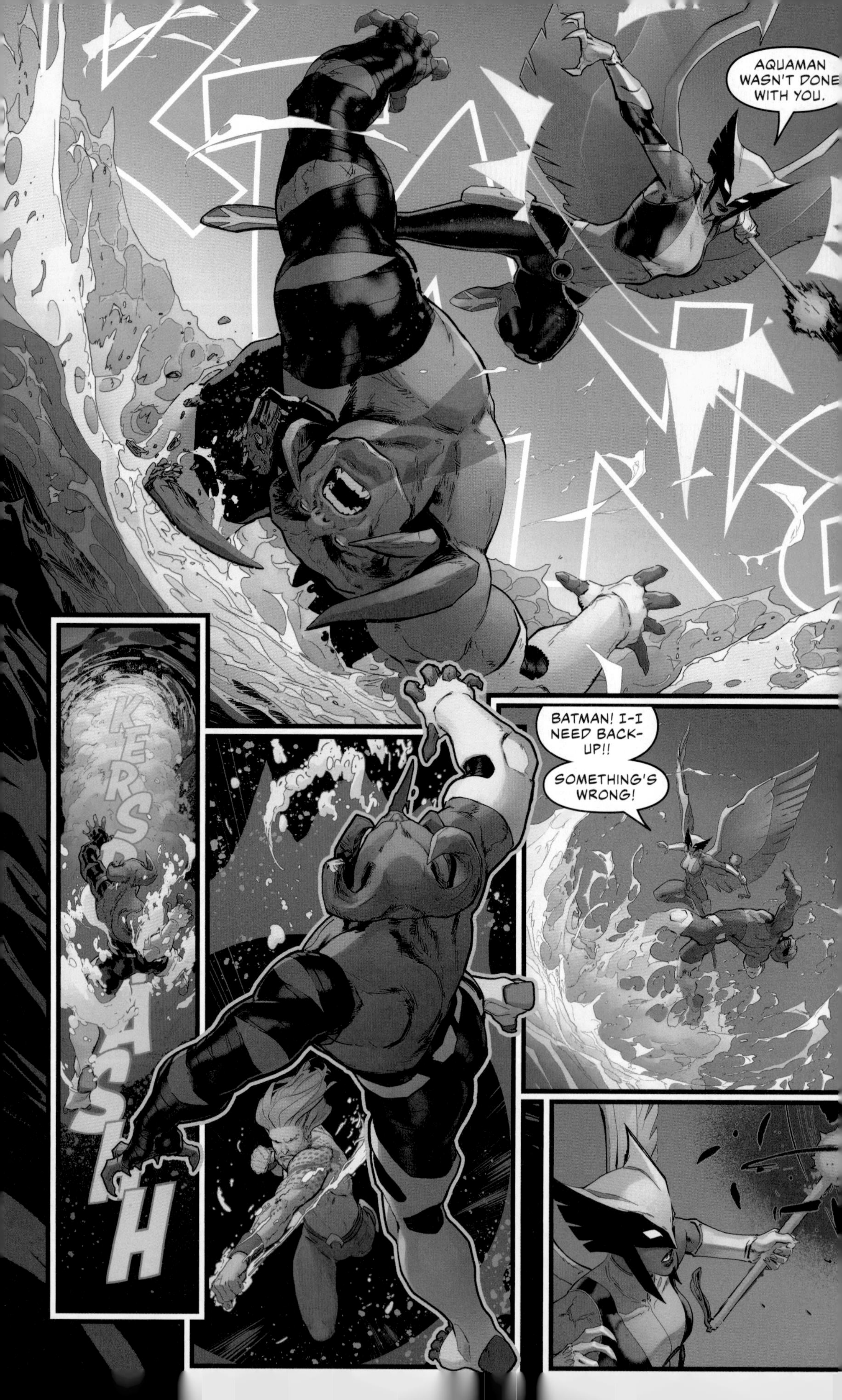

AQUAMAN WASN'T DONE WITH YOU.
KERSPLASH
BATMAN! I-I NEED BACK-UP!!
SOMETHING'S WRONG!

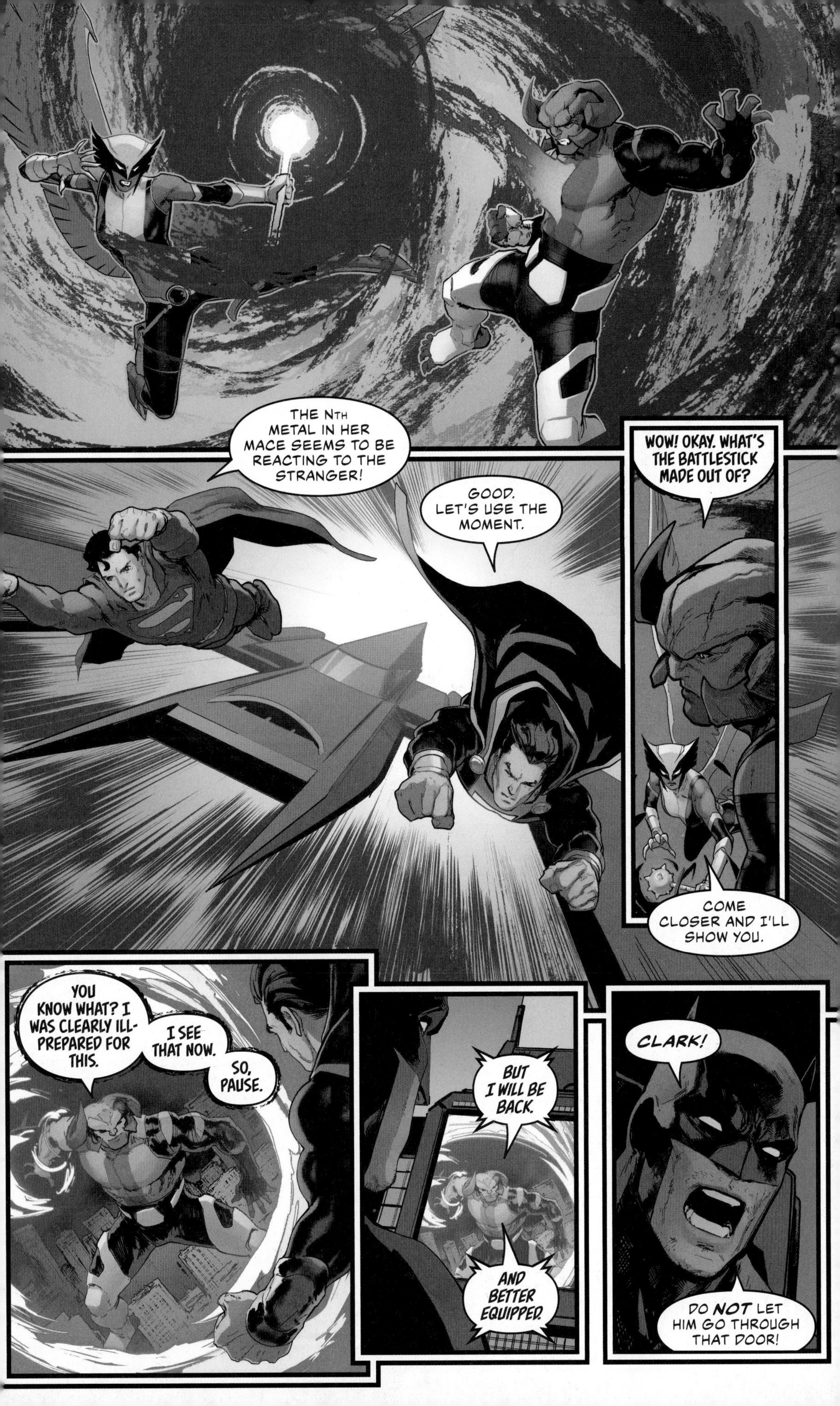
THE NTH METAL IN HER MACE SEEMS TO BE REACTING TO THE STRANGER!
GOOD. LET'S USE THE MOMENT.
WOW! OKAY. WHAT'S THE BATTLESTICK MADE OUT OF?
COME CLOSER AND I'LL SHOW YOU.
YOU KNOW WHAT? I WAS CLEARLY ILL-PREPARED FOR THIS.
I SEE THAT NOW.
SO, PAUSE.
BUT I WILL BE BACK.
AND BETTER EQUIPPED.
CLARK!
DO NOT LET HIM GO THROUGH THAT DOOR!

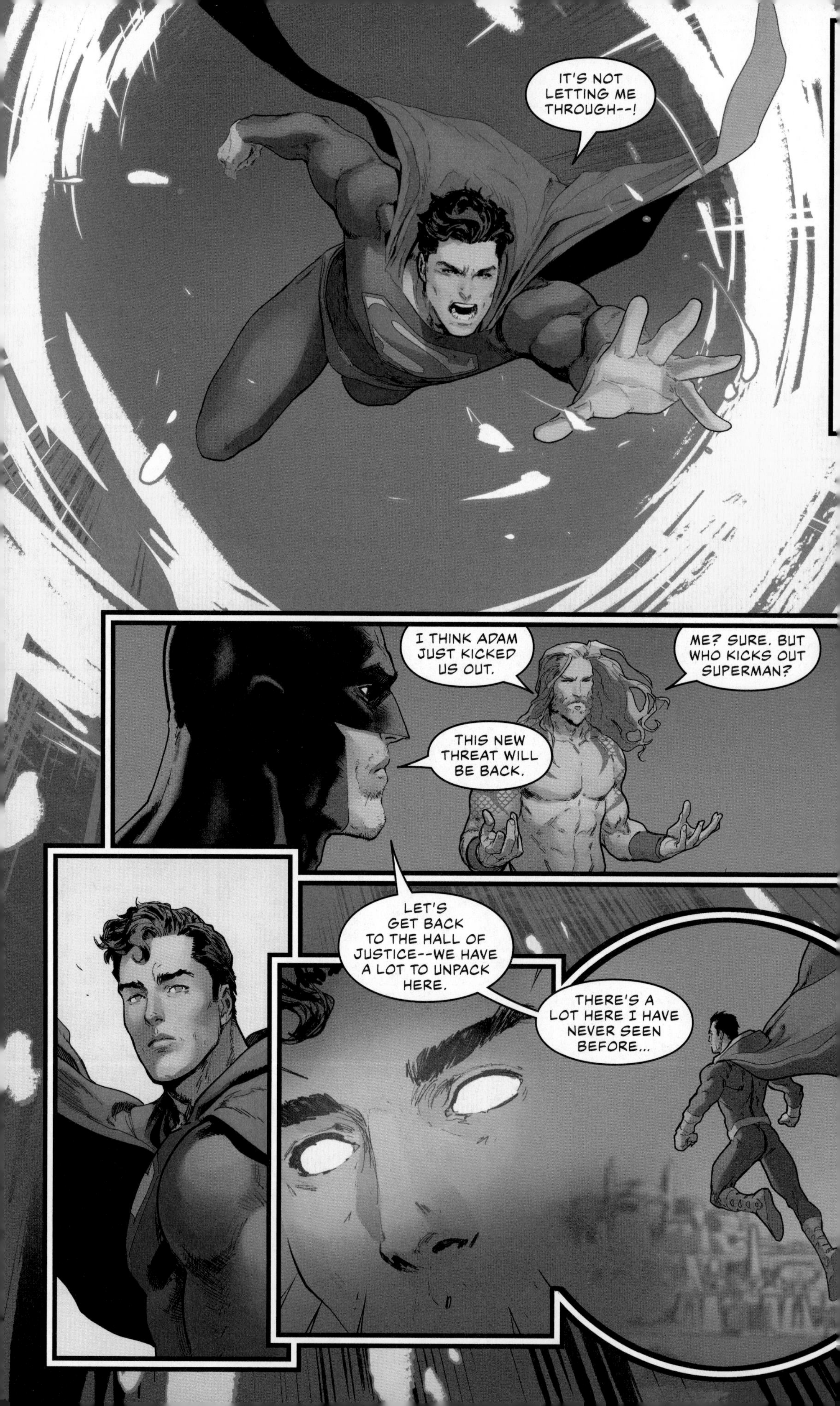
IT'S NOT LETTING ME THROUGH--!
I THINK ADAM JUST KICKED US OUT.
ME? SURE. BUT WHO KICKS OUT SUPERMAN?
THIS NEW THREAT WILL BE BACK.
LET'S GET BACK TO THE HALL OF JUSTICE--WE HAVE A LOT TO UNPACK HERE.
THERE'S A LOT HERE I HAVE NEVER SEEN BEFORE...

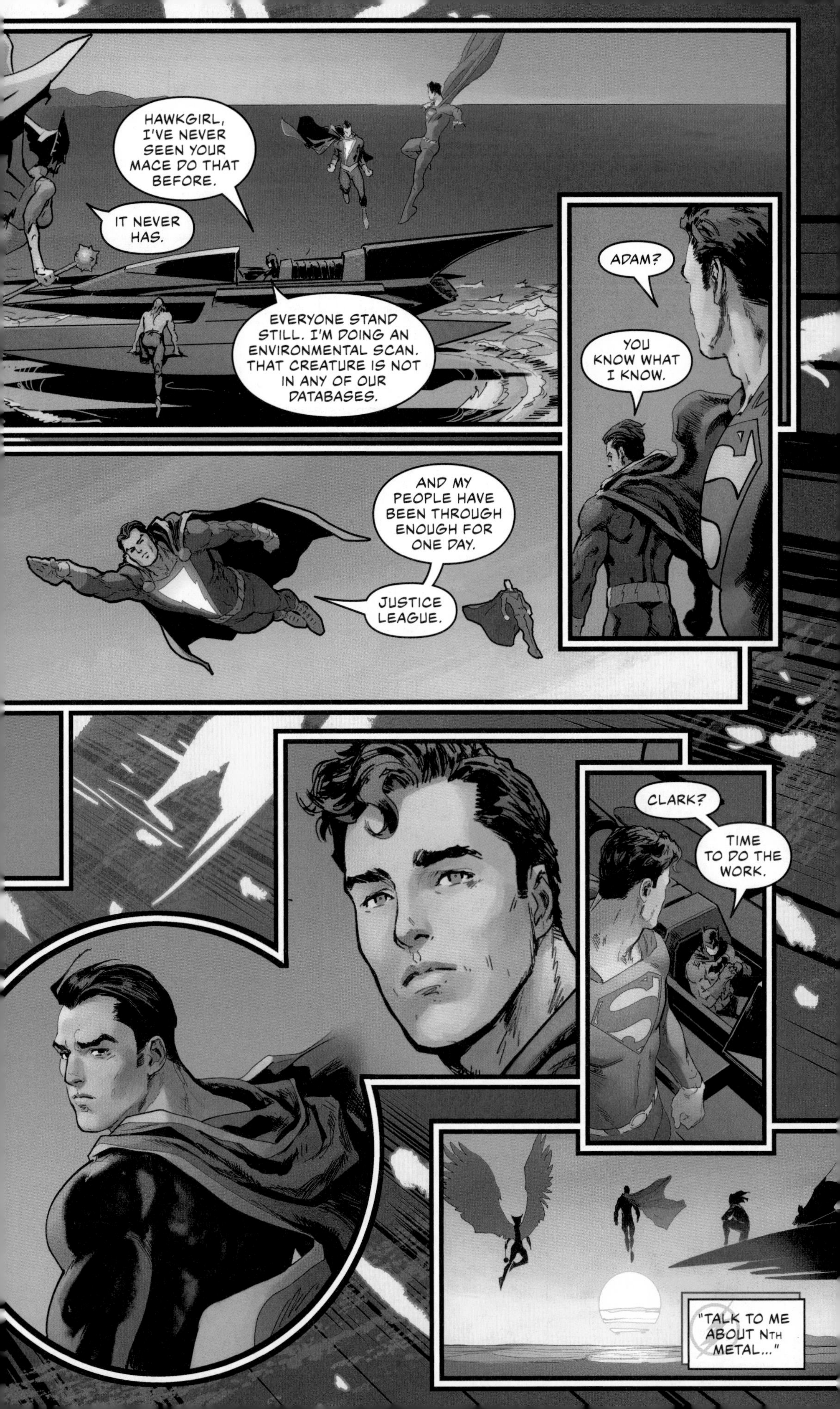
HAWKGIRL, I'VE NEVER SEEN YOUR MACE DO THAT BEFORE.
IT NEVER HAS.
EVERYONE STAND STILL. I'M DOING AN ENVIRONMENTAL SCAN. THAT CREATURE IS NOT IN ANY OF OUR DATABASES.
ADAM?
YOU KNOW WHAT I KNOW.
AND MY PEOPLE HAVE BEEN THROUGH ENOUGH FOR ONE DAY.
JUSTICE LEAGUE.
CLARK?
TIME TO DO THE WORK.
"TALK TO ME ABOUT NTH METAL..."

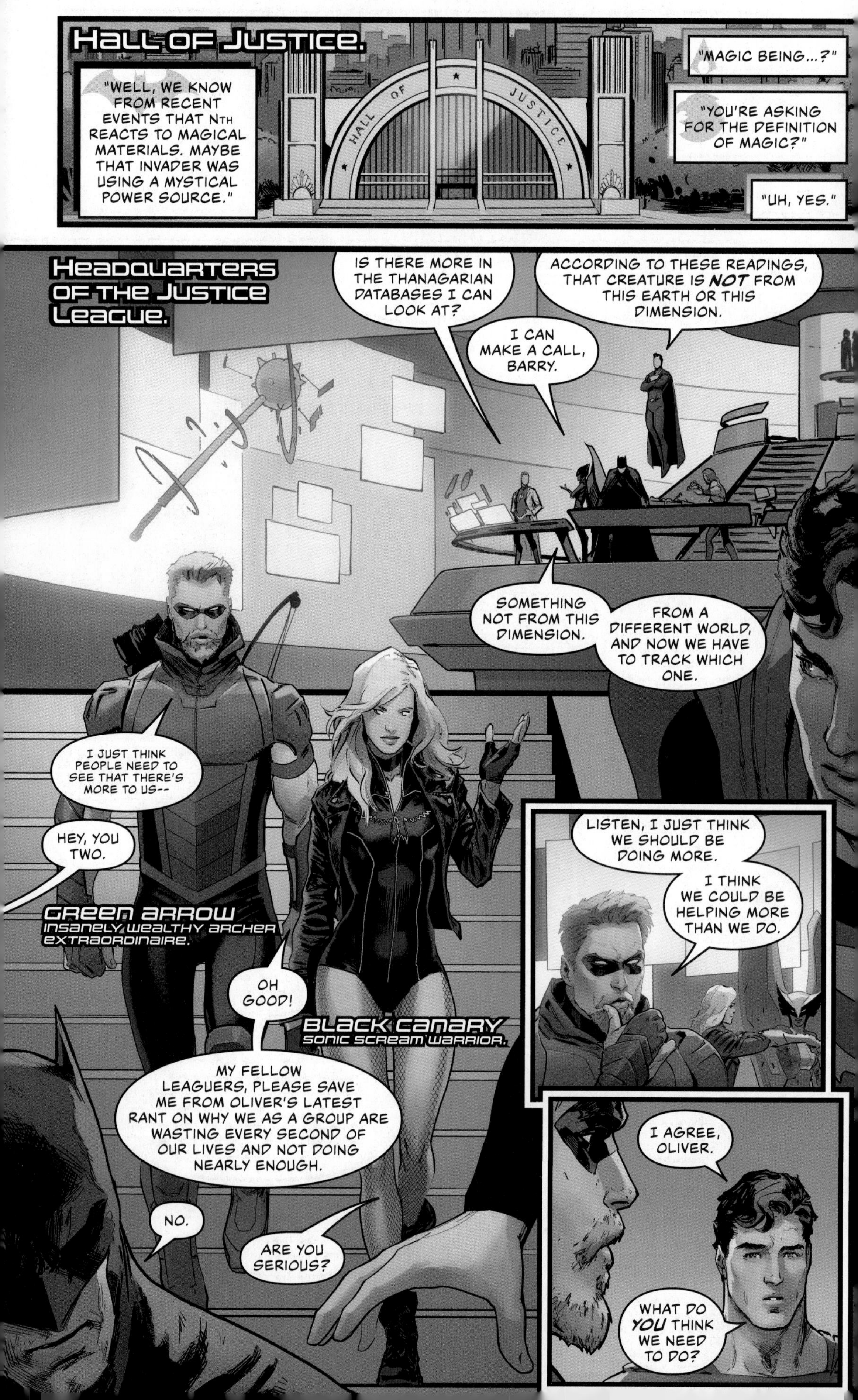

Hall of Justice.
"WELL, WE KNOW FROM RECENT EVENTS THAT Nth REACTS TO MAGICAL MATERIALS. MAYBE THAT INVADER WAS USING A MYSTICAL POWER SOURCE."
HALL OF JUSTICE
"MAGIC BEING...?"
"YOU'RE ASKING FOR THE DEFINITION OF MAGIC?"
"UH, YES."
Headquarters of the Justice League.
IS THERE MORE IN THE THANAGARIAN DATABASES I CAN LOOK AT?
ACCORDING TO THESE READINGS, THAT CREATURE IS NOT FROM THIS EARTH OR THIS DIMENSION.
I CAN MAKE A CALL, BARRY.
SOMETHING NOT FROM THIS DIMENSION.
FROM A DIFFERENT WORLD, AND NOW WE HAVE TO TRACK WHICH ONE.
I JUST THINK PEOPLE NEED TO SEE THAT THERE'S MORE TO US--
HEY, YOU TWO.
GREEN ARROW
Insanely wealthy archer extraordinaire.
OH GOOD!
BLACK CANARY
Sonic scream warrior.
MY FELLOW LEAGUERS, PLEASE SAVE ME FROM OLIVER'S LATEST RANT ON WHY WE AS A GROUP ARE WASTING EVERY SECOND OF OUR LIVES AND NOT DOING NEARLY ENOUGH.
NO.
ARE YOU SERIOUS?
LISTEN, I JUST THINK WE SHOULD BE DOING MORE.
I THINK WE COULD BE HELPING MORE THAN WE DO.
I AGREE, OLIVER.
WHAT DO YOU THINK WE NEED TO DO?

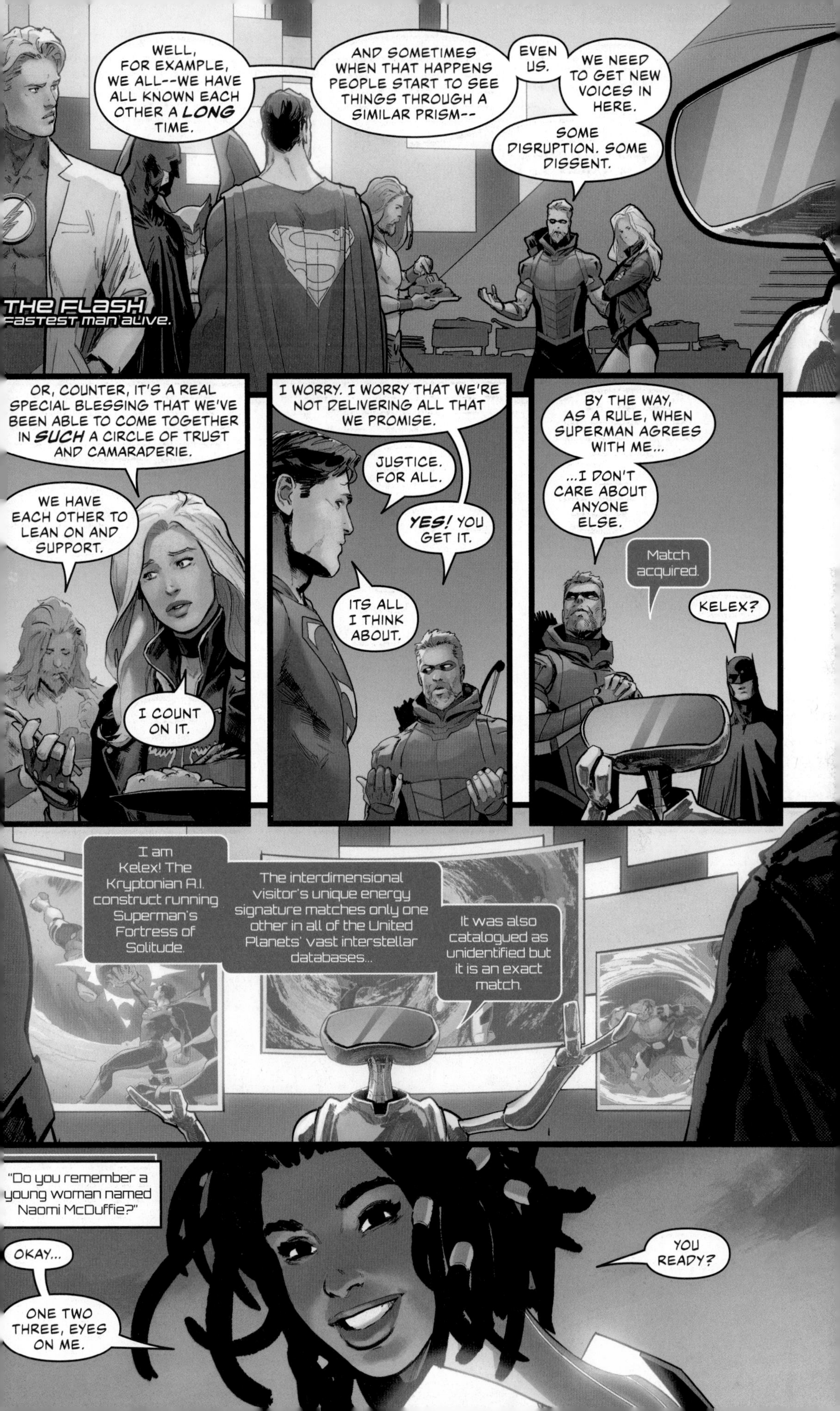
WELL, FOR EXAMPLE, WE ALL--WE HAVE ALL KNOWN EACH OTHER A LONG TIME.
AND SOMETIMES WHEN THAT HAPPENS PEOPLE START TO SEE THINGS THROUGH A SIMILAR PRISM--
EVEN US.
WE NEED TO GET NEW VOICES IN HERE.
SOME DISRUPTION. SOME DISSENT.
THE FLASH
FASTEST MAN ALIVE.
OR, COUNTER, IT'S A REAL SPECIAL BLESSING THAT WE'VE BEEN ABLE TO COME TOGETHER IN SUCH A CIRCLE OF TRUST AND CAMARADERIE.
WE HAVE EACH OTHER TO LEAN ON AND SUPPORT.
I COUNT ON IT.
I WORRY. I WORRY THAT WE'RE NOT DELIVERING ALL THAT WE PROMISE.
JUSTICE. FOR ALL.
YES! YOU GET IT.
ITS ALL I THINK ABOUT.
BY THE WAY, AS A RULE, WHEN SUPERMAN AGREES WITH ME...
...I DON'T CARE ABOUT ANYONE ELSE.
Match acquired.
KELEX?
I am Kelex! The Kryptonian A.I. construct running Superman's Fortress of Solitude.
The interdimensional visitor's unique energy signature matches only one other in all of the United Planets' vast interstellar databases...
It was also catalogued as unidentified but it is an exact match.
"Do you remember a young woman named Naomi McDuffie?"
OKAY...
ONE TWO THREE, EYES ON ME.
YOU READY?

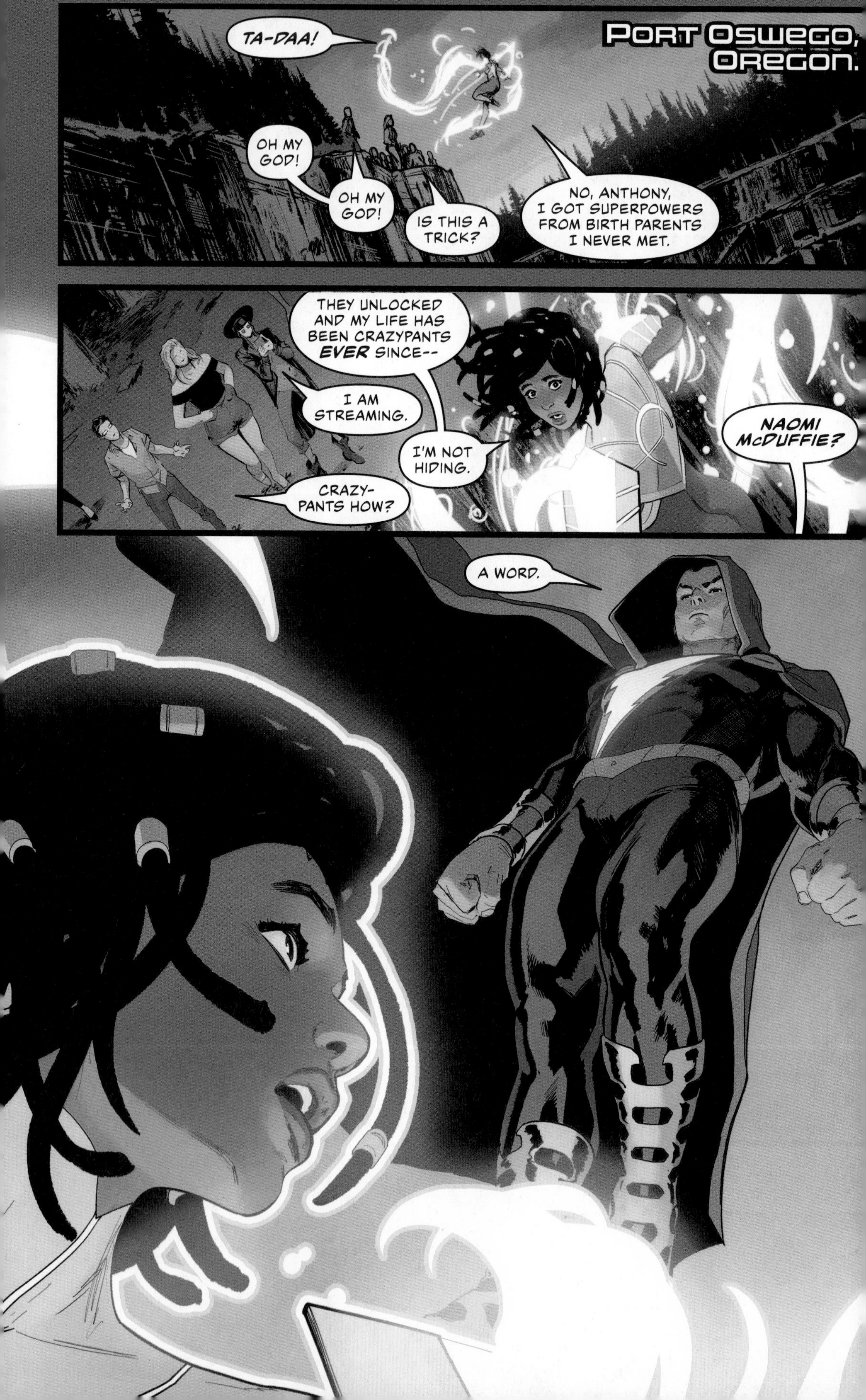
PORT OSWEGO, OREGON.
TA-DAA!
OH MY GOD!
OH MY GOD!
IS THIS A TRICK?
NO, ANTHONY, I GOT SUPERPOWERS FROM BIRTH PARENTS I NEVER MET.
THEY UNLOCKED AND MY LIFE HAS BEEN CRAZYPANTS EVER SINCE--
I AM STREAMING.
I'M NOT HIDING.
CRAZY-PANTS HOW?
NAOMI McDUFFIE?
A WORD.

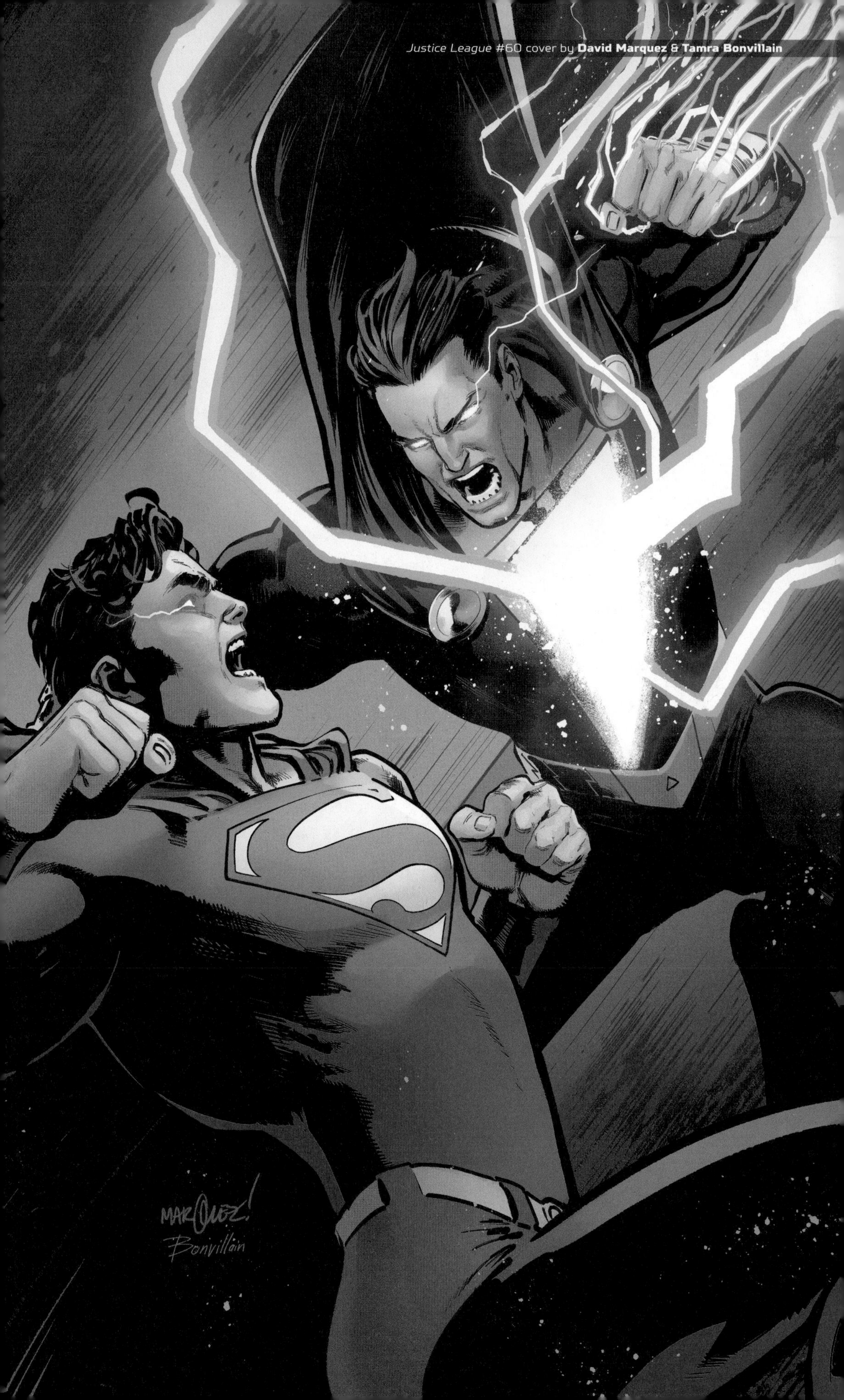
MARQUEZ!
Bonvillain

Justice League #60 cover by **David Marquez & Tamra Bonvillain**

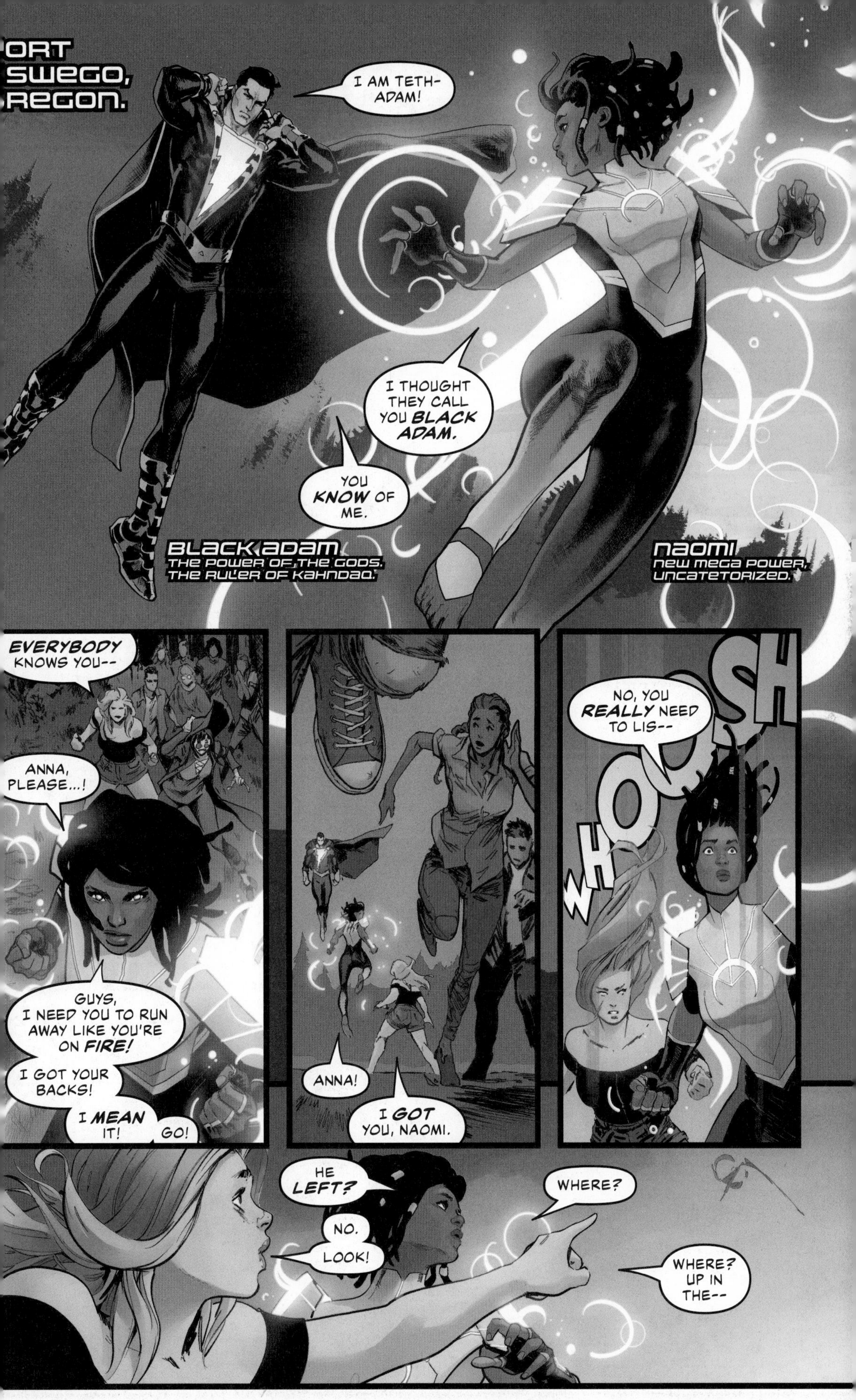
ORT
SWEGO,
REGON.
I AM TETH-ADAM!
I THOUGHT THEY CALL YOU BLACK ADAM.
YOU KNOW OF ME.
BLACK ADAM
THE POWER OF THE GODS.
THE RULER OF KAHNDAQ.
NAOMI
NEW MEGA POWER, UNCATETORIZED.
EVERYBODY KNOWS YOU--
ANNA, PLEASE...!
GUYS, I NEED YOU TO RUN AWAY LIKE YOU'RE ON FIRE!
I GOT YOUR BACKS!
I MEAN IT!
GO!
ANNA!
I GOT YOU, NAOMI.
NO, YOU REALLY NEED TO LIS--
WHOOSH
HE LEFT?
NO.
LOOK!
WHERE?
WHERE? UP IN THE--

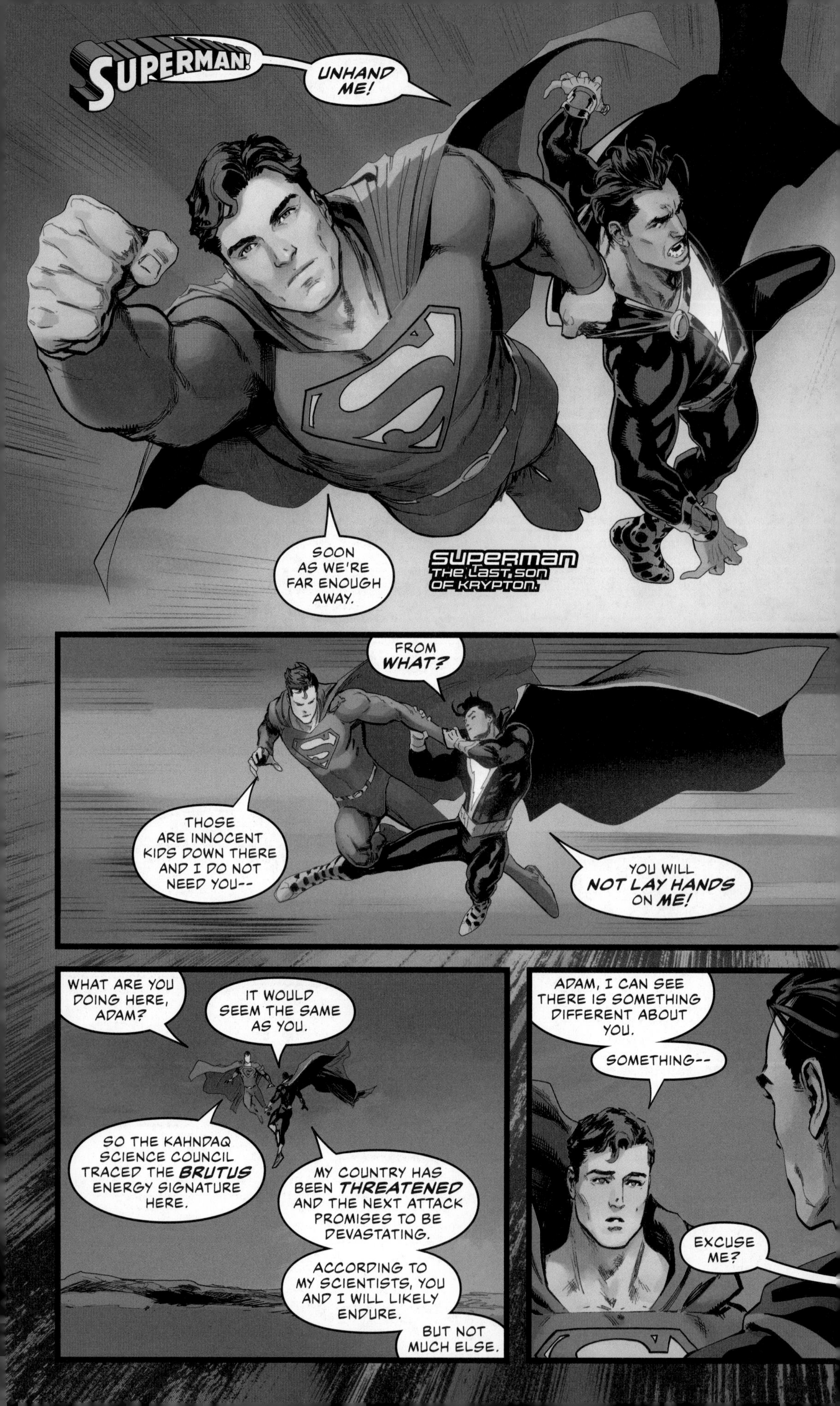
SUPERMAN!
UNHAND ME!
SOON AS WE'RE FAR ENOUGH AWAY.
SUPERMAN THE LAST SON OF KRYPTON.
FROM WHAT?
THOSE ARE INNOCENT KIDS DOWN THERE AND I DO NOT NEED YOU--
YOU WILL NOT LAY HANDS ON ME!
WHAT ARE YOU DOING HERE, ADAM?
IT WOULD SEEM THE SAME AS YOU.
SO THE KAHNDAQ SCIENCE COUNCIL TRACED THE BRUTUS ENERGY SIGNATURE HERE.
MY COUNTRY HAS BEEN THREATENED AND THE NEXT ATTACK PROMISES TO BE DEVASTATING.
ACCORDING TO MY SCIENTISTS, YOU AND I WILL LIKELY ENDURE.
BUT NOT MUCH ELSE.
ADAM, I CAN SEE THERE IS SOMETHING DIFFERENT ABOUT YOU.
SOMETHING--
EXCUSE ME?

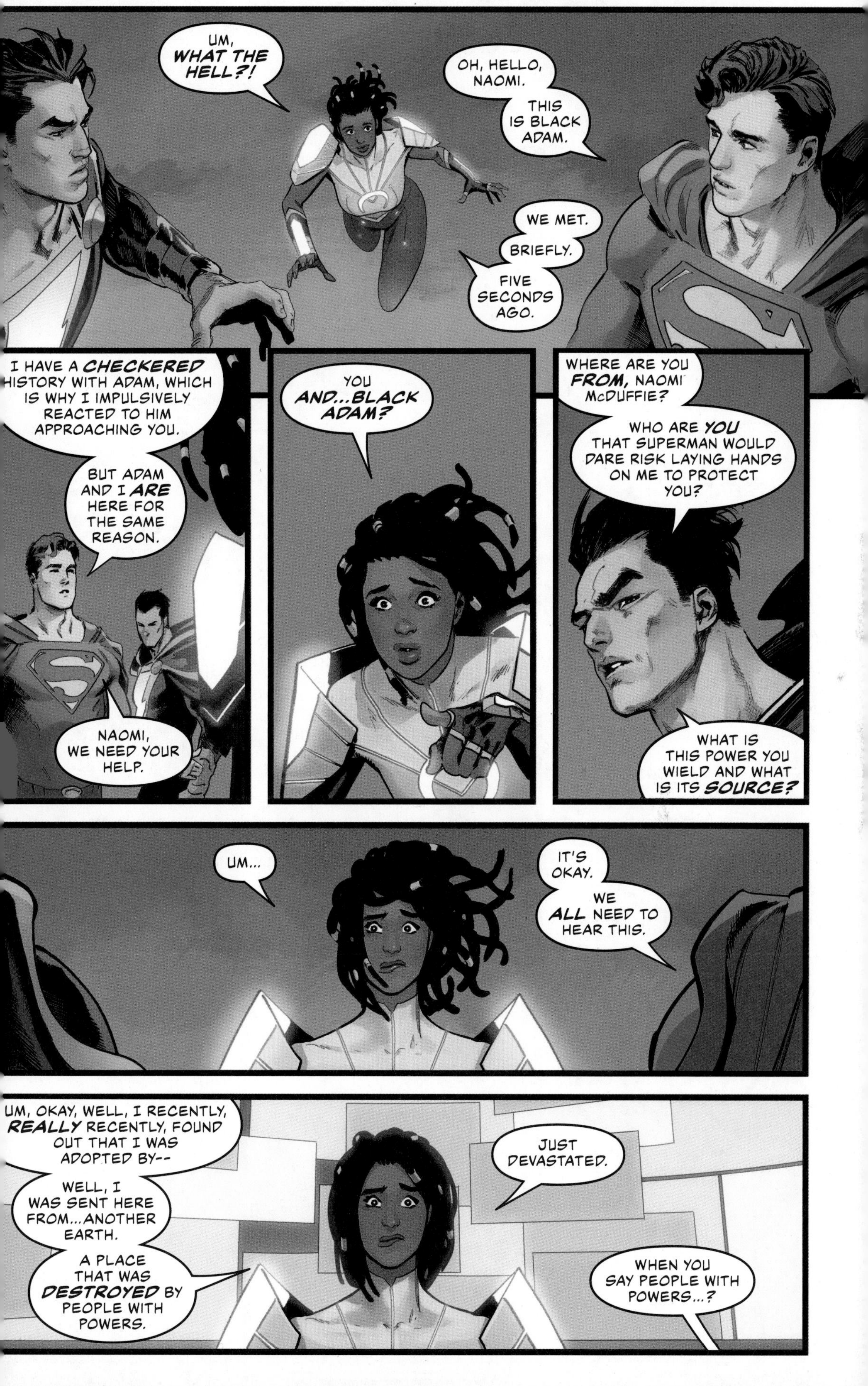
UM, WHAT THE HELL?!
OH, HELLO, NAOMI.
THIS IS BLACK ADAM.
WE MET.
BRIEFLY.
FIVE SECONDS AGO.
I HAVE A CHECKERED HISTORY WITH ADAM, WHICH IS WHY I IMPULSIVELY REACTED TO HIM APPROACHING YOU.
BUT ADAM AND I ARE HERE FOR THE SAME REASON.
NAOMI, WE NEED YOUR HELP.
YOU AND...BLACK ADAM?
WHERE ARE YOU FROM, NAOMI McDUFFIE?
WHO ARE YOU THAT SUPERMAN WOULD DARE RISK LAYING HANDS ON ME TO PROTECT YOU?
WHAT IS THIS POWER YOU WIELD AND WHAT IS ITS SOURCE?
UM...
IT'S OKAY.
WE ALL NEED TO HEAR THIS.
UM, OKAY, WELL, I RECENTLY, REALLY RECENTLY, FOUND OUT THAT I WAS ADOPTED BY--
WELL, I WAS SENT HERE FROM...ANOTHER EARTH.
A PLACE THAT WAS DESTROYED BY PEOPLE WITH POWERS.
JUST DEVASTATED.
WHEN YOU SAY PEOPLE WITH POWERS...?

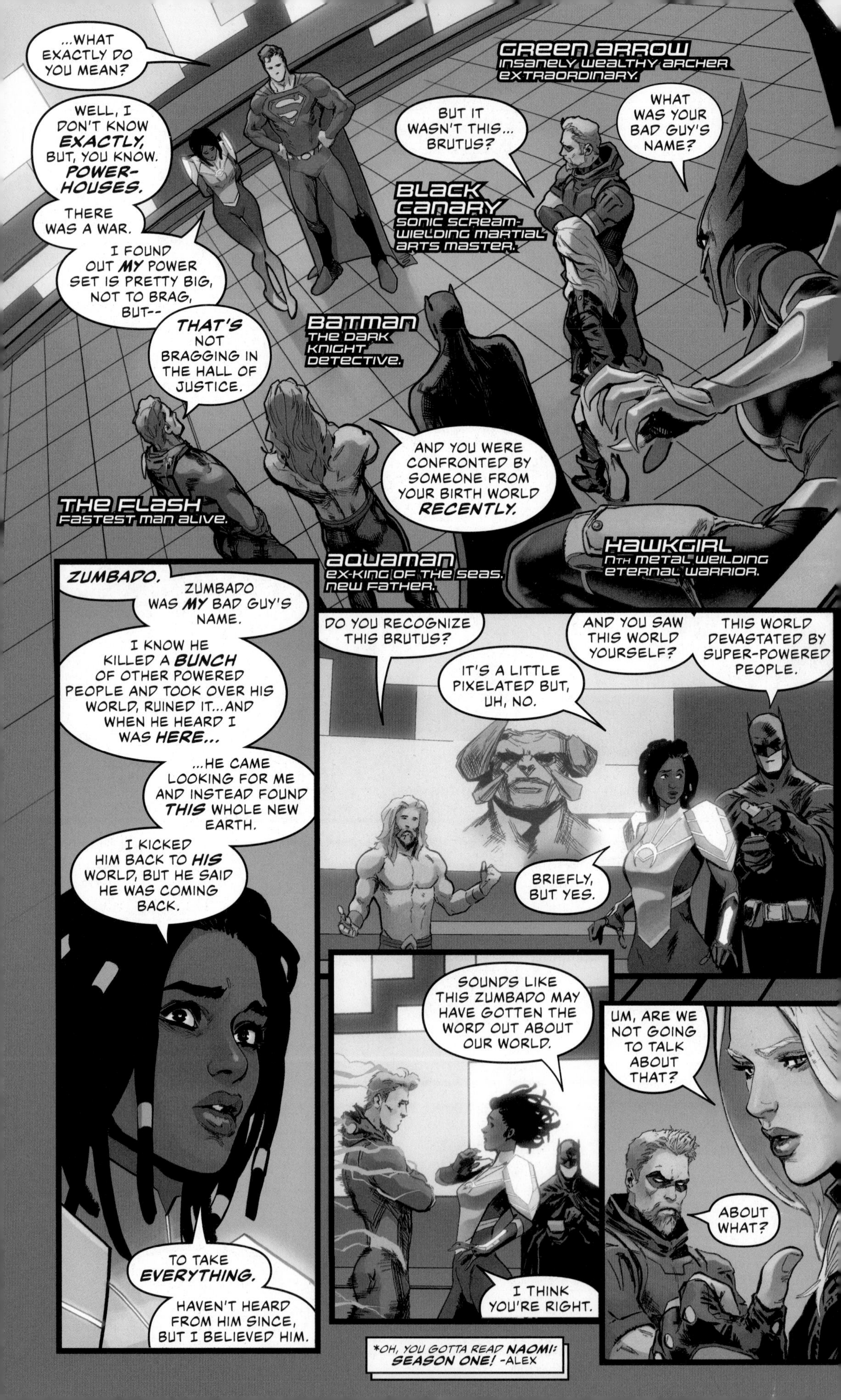
...WHAT EXACTLY DO YOU MEAN?
GREEN ARROW
INSANELY WEALTHY ARCHER EXTRAORDINARY.
WELL, I DON'T KNOW EXACTLY, BUT, YOU KNOW. POWER-HOUSES.
THERE WAS A WAR.
I FOUND OUT MY POWER SET IS PRETTY BIG, NOT TO BRAG, BUT--
BUT IT WASN'T THIS... BRUTUS?
WHAT WAS YOUR BAD GUY'S NAME?
BLACK CANARY
SONIC SCREAM-WIELDING MARTIAL ARTS MASTER.
THAT'S NOT BRAGGING IN THE HALL OF JUSTICE.
BATMAN
THE DARK KNIGHT DETECTIVE.
AND YOU WERE CONFRONTED BY SOMEONE FROM YOUR BIRTH WORLD RECENTLY.
THE FLASH
FASTEST MAN ALIVE.
AQUAMAN
EX-KING OF THE SEAS. NEW FATHER.
HAWKGIRL
NTH METAL WEILDING ETERNAL WARRIOR.
ZUMBADO.
ZUMBADO WAS MY BAD GUY'S NAME.
I KNOW HE KILLED A BUNCH OF OTHER POWERED PEOPLE AND TOOK OVER HIS WORLD, RUINED IT...AND WHEN HE HEARD I WAS HERE...
...HE CAME LOOKING FOR ME AND INSTEAD FOUND THIS WHOLE NEW EARTH.
I KICKED HIM BACK TO HIS WORLD, BUT HE SAID HE WAS COMING BACK.
TO TAKE EVERYTHING.
HAVEN'T HEARD FROM HIM SINCE, BUT I BELIEVED HIM.
DO YOU RECOGNIZE THIS BRUTUS?
IT'S A LITTLE PIXELATED BUT, UH, NO.
AND YOU SAW THIS WORLD YOURSELF?
THIS WORLD DEVASTATED BY SUPER-POWERED PEOPLE.
BRIEFLY, BUT YES.
SOUNDS LIKE THIS ZUMBADO MAY HAVE GOTTEN THE WORD OUT ABOUT OUR WORLD.
I THINK YOU'RE RIGHT.
UM, ARE WE NOT GOING TO TALK ABOUT THAT?
ABOUT WHAT?
*OH, YOU GOTTA READ NAOMI: SEASON ONE! -ALEX

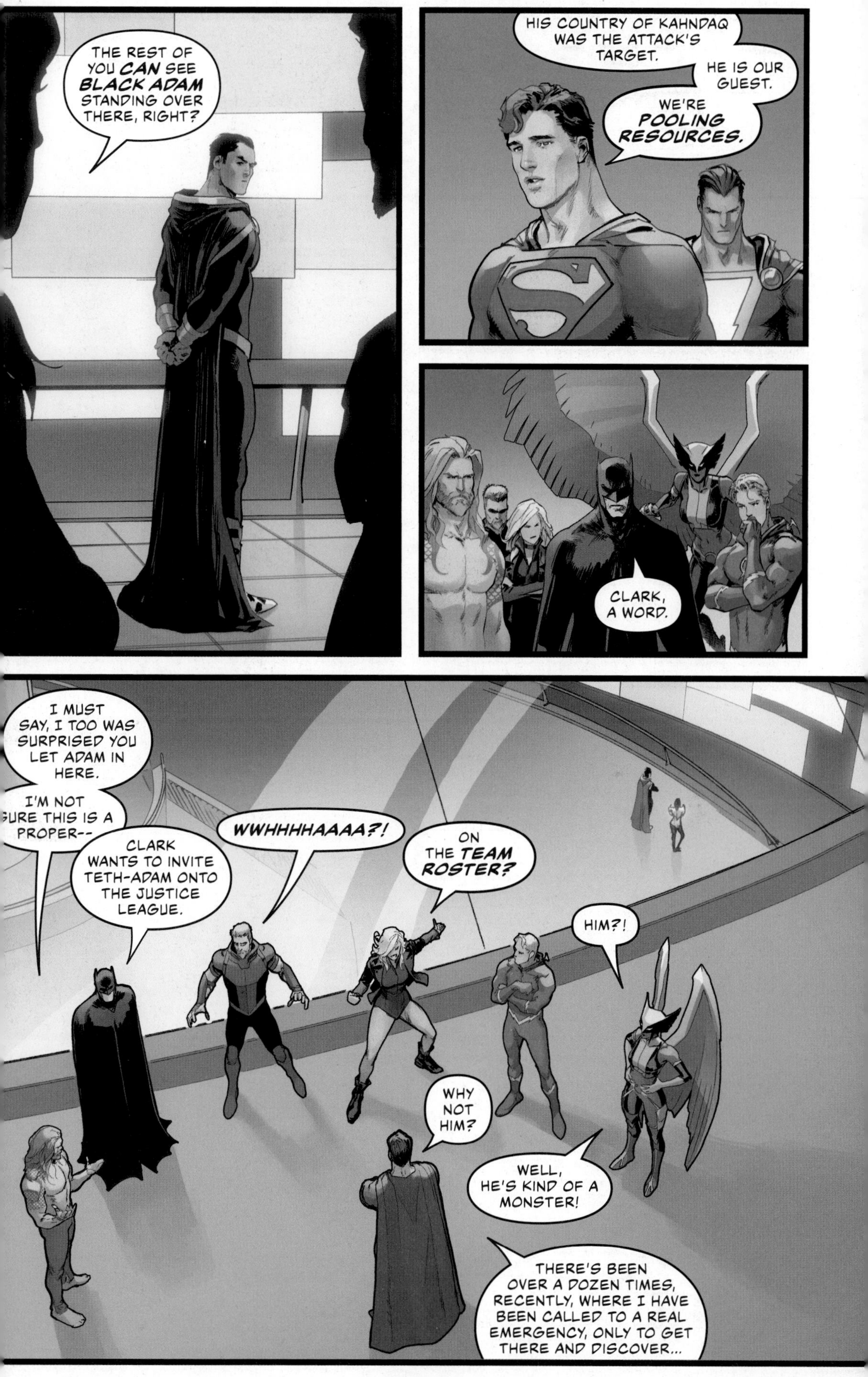
THE REST OF YOU CAN SEE BLACK ADAM STANDING OVER THERE, RIGHT?
HIS COUNTRY OF KAHNDAQ WAS THE ATTACK'S TARGET.
HE IS OUR GUEST.
WE'RE POOLING RESOURCES.
CLARK, A WORD.
I MUST SAY, I TOO WAS SURPRISED YOU LET ADAM IN HERE.
I'M NOT SURE THIS IS A PROPER--
CLARK WANTS TO INVITE TETH-ADAM ONTO THE JUSTICE LEAGUE.
WWHHHHAAAA?!
ON THE TEAM ROSTER?
HIM?!
WHY NOT HIM?
WELL, HE'S KIND OF A MONSTER!
THERE'S BEEN OVER A DOZEN TIMES, RECENTLY, WHERE I HAVE BEEN CALLED TO A REAL EMERGENCY, ONLY TO GET THERE AND DISCOVER...

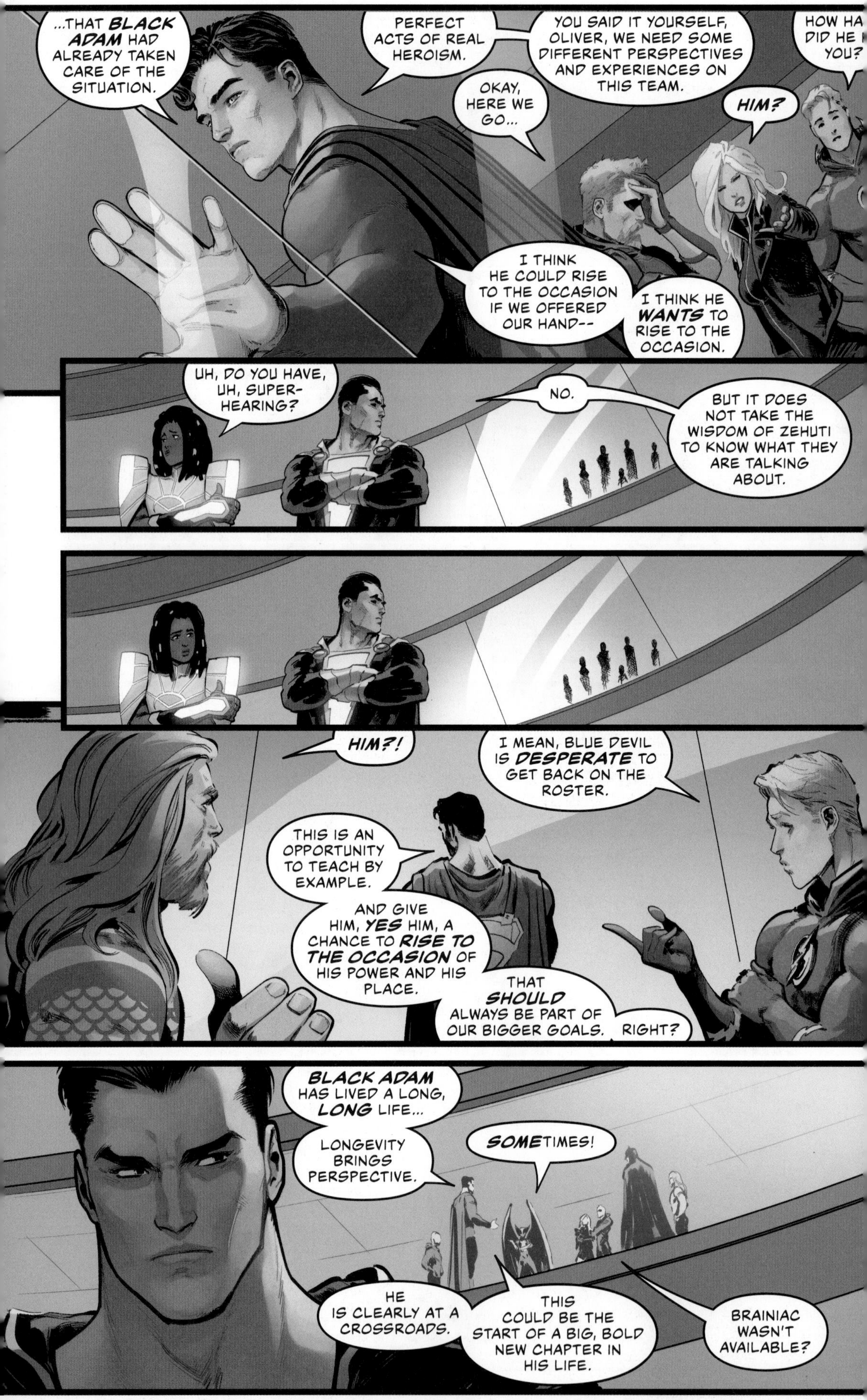
...THAT BLACK ADAM HAD ALREADY TAKEN CARE OF THE SITUATION.
PERFECT ACTS OF REAL HEROISM.
OKAY, HERE WE GO...
YOU SAID IT YOURSELF, OLIVER, WE NEED SOME DIFFERENT PERSPECTIVES AND EXPERIENCES ON THIS TEAM.
HIM?
HOW HA DID HE YOU?
I THINK HE COULD RISE TO THE OCCASION IF WE OFFERED OUR HAND--
I THINK HE WANTS TO RISE TO THE OCCASION.
UH, DO YOU HAVE, UH, SUPER-HEARING?
NO.
BUT IT DOES NOT TAKE THE WISDOM OF ZEHUTI TO KNOW WHAT THEY ARE TALKING ABOUT.
HIM?!
I MEAN, BLUE DEVIL IS DESPERATE TO GET BACK ON THE ROSTER.
THIS IS AN OPPORTUNITY TO TEACH BY EXAMPLE.
AND GIVE HIM, YES HIM, A CHANCE TO RISE TO THE OCCASION OF HIS POWER AND HIS PLACE.
THAT SHOULD ALWAYS BE PART OF OUR BIGGER GOALS.
RIGHT?
BLACK ADAM HAS LIVED A LONG, LONG LIFE...
LONGEVITY BRINGS PERSPECTIVE.
SOMETIMES!
HE IS CLEARLY AT A CROSSROADS.
THIS COULD BE THE START OF A BIG, BOLD NEW CHAPTER IN HIS LIFE.
BRAINIAC WASN'T AVAILABLE?

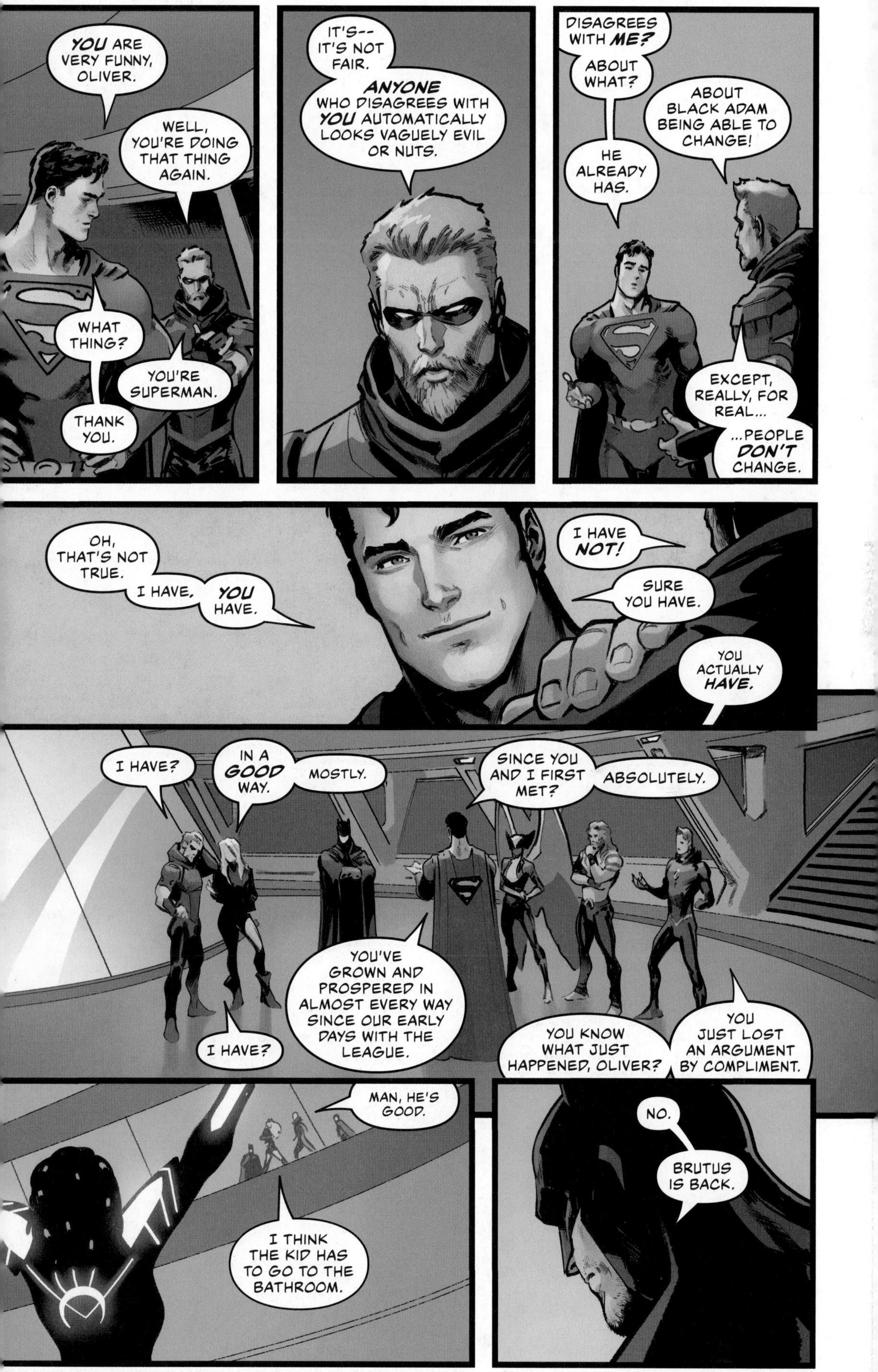

YOU ARE VERY FUNNY, OLIVER.
WELL, YOU'RE DOING THAT THING AGAIN.
WHAT THING?
YOU'RE SUPERMAN.
THANK YOU.
IT'S-- IT'S NOT FAIR.
ANYONE WHO DISAGREES WITH YOU AUTOMATICALLY LOOKS VAGUELY EVIL OR NUTS.
DISAGREES WITH ME?
ABOUT WHAT?
ABOUT BLACK ADAM BEING ABLE TO CHANGE!
HE ALREADY HAS.
EXCEPT, REALLY, FOR REAL...
...PEOPLE DON'T CHANGE.
OH, THAT'S NOT TRUE.
I HAVE.
YOU HAVE.
I HAVE NOT!
SURE YOU HAVE.
YOU ACTUALLY HAVE.
I HAVE?
IN A GOOD WAY.
MOSTLY.
SINCE YOU AND I FIRST MET?
ABSOLUTELY.
YOU'VE GROWN AND PROSPERED IN ALMOST EVERY WAY SINCE OUR EARLY DAYS WITH THE LEAGUE.
I HAVE?
YOU KNOW WHAT JUST HAPPENED, OLIVER?
YOU JUST LOST AN ARGUMENT BY COMPLIMENT.
MAN, HE'S GOOD.
I THINK THE KID HAS TO GO TO THE BATHROOM.
NO.
BRUTUS IS BACK.

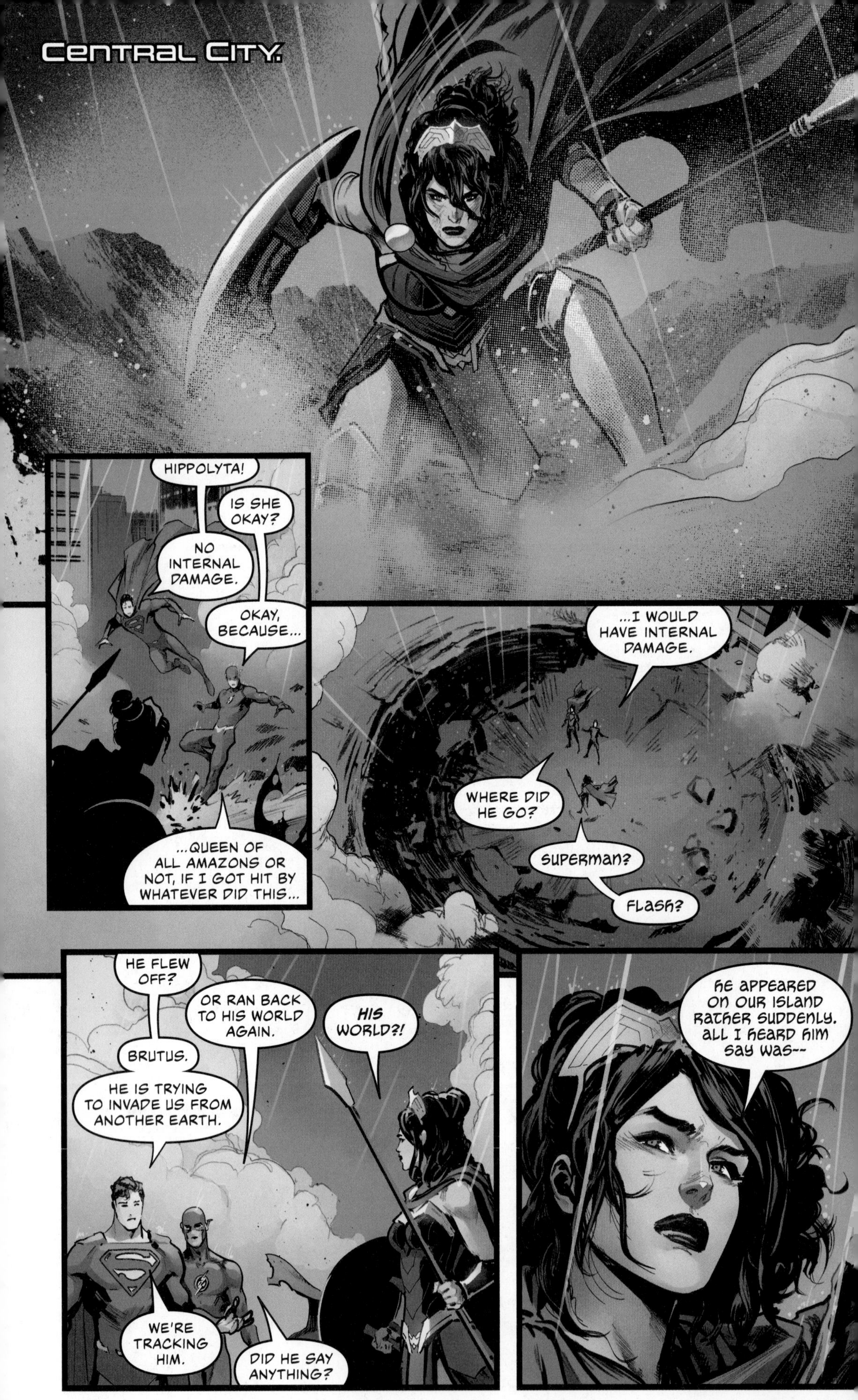
CENTRAL CITY.
HIPPOLYTA!
IS SHE OKAY?
NO INTERNAL DAMAGE.
OKAY, BECAUSE...
...QUEEN OF ALL AMAZONS OR NOT, IF I GOT HIT BY WHATEVER DID THIS...
...I WOULD HAVE INTERNAL DAMAGE.
WHERE DID HE GO?
SUPERMAN?
FLASH?
HE FLEW OFF?
OR RAN BACK TO HIS WORLD AGAIN.
HIS WORLD?!
BRUTUS.
HE IS TRYING TO INVADE US FROM ANOTHER EARTH.
WE'RE TRACKING HIM.
DID HE SAY ANYTHING?
HE APPEARED ON OUR ISLAND RATHER SUDDENLY. ALL I HEARD HIM SAY WAS--

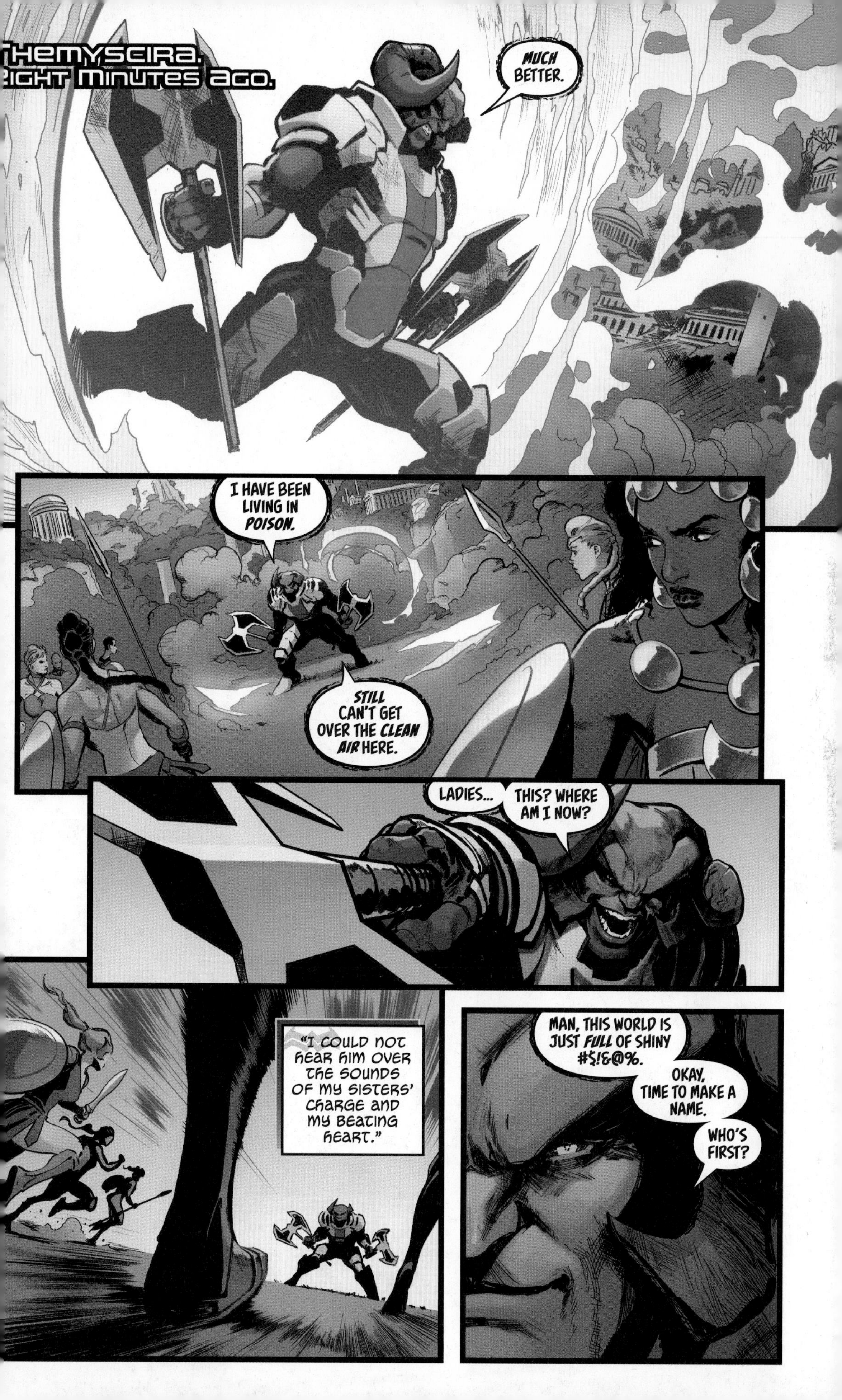

Themysceira.
Eight Minutes ago.
MUCH BETTER.
I HAVE BEEN LIVING IN POISON.
STILL CAN'T GET OVER THE CLEAN AIR HERE.
LADIES...
THIS? WHERE AM I NOW?
"I COULD NOT HEAR HIM OVER THE SOUNDS OF MY SISTERS' CHARGE AND MY BEATING HEART."
MAN, THIS WORLD IS JUST FULL OF SHINY #$!&@%.
OKAY, TIME TO MAKE A NAME.
WHO'S FIRST?

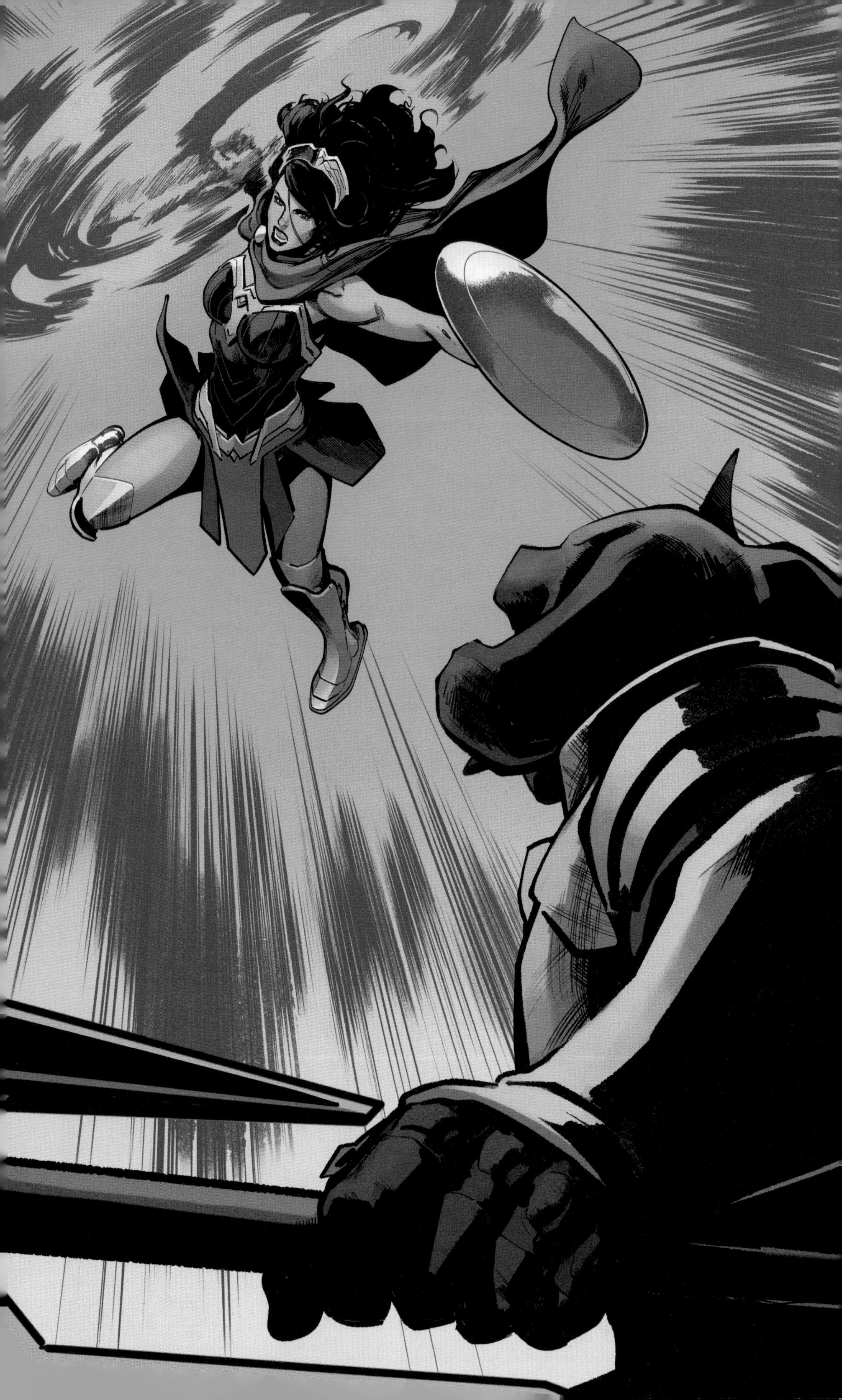

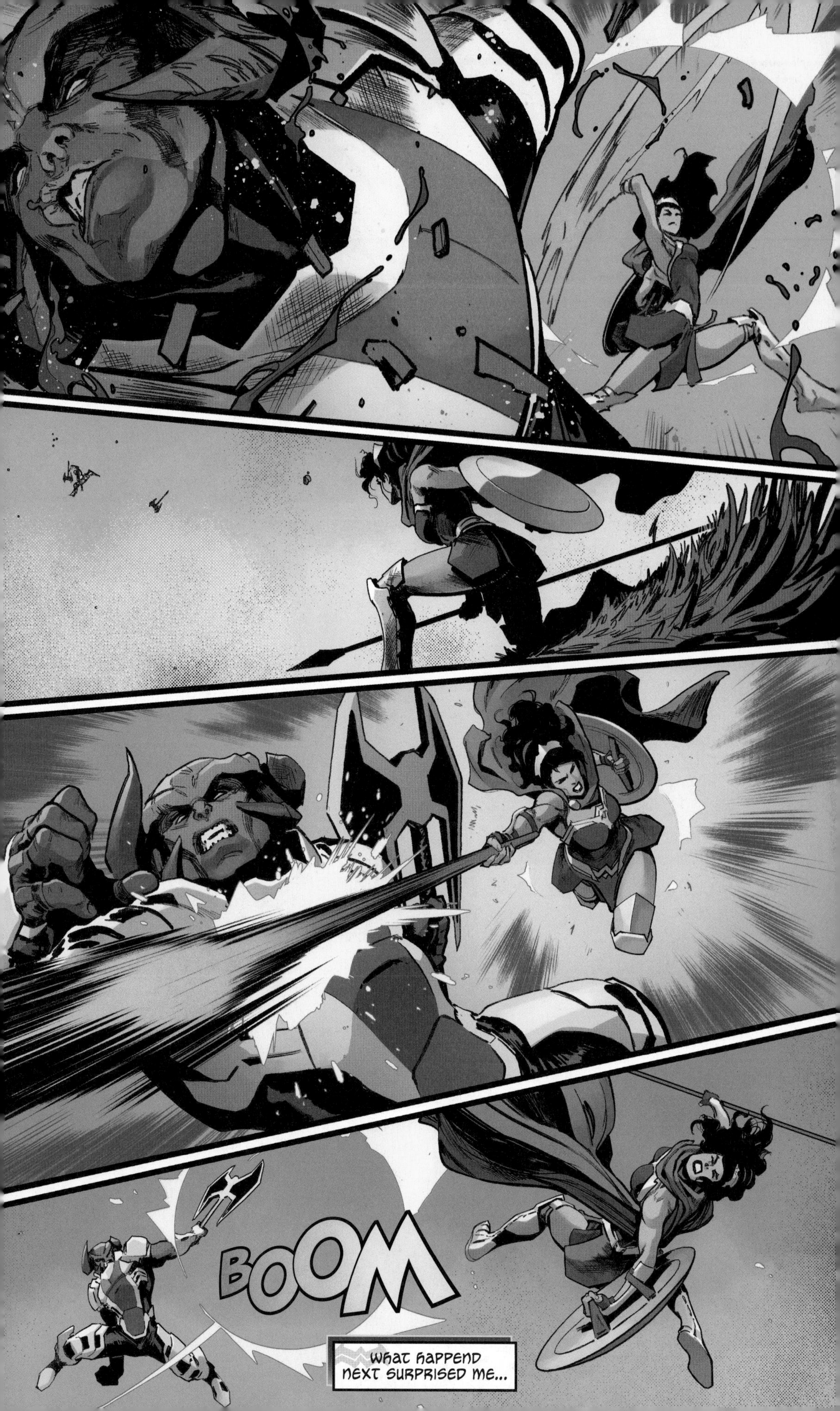
BOOM
WHAT HAPPEND NEXT SURPRISED ME...

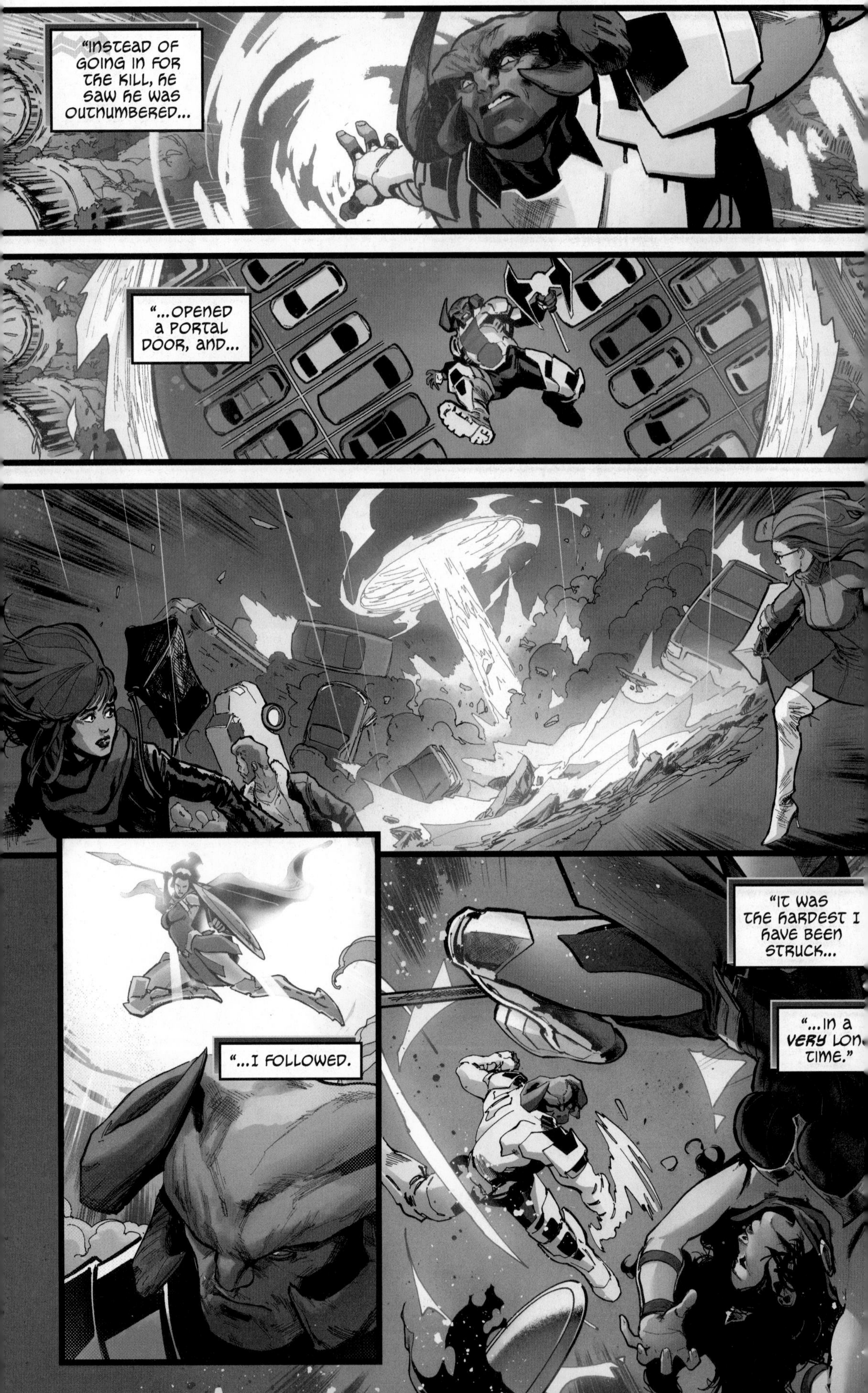
"INSTEAD OF GOING IN FOR THE KILL, HE SAW HE WAS OUTNUMBERED...
"...OPENED A PORTAL DOOR, AND...
"...I FOLLOWED.
"IT WAS THE HARDEST I HAVE BEEN STRUCK...
"...IN A VERY LON TIME."

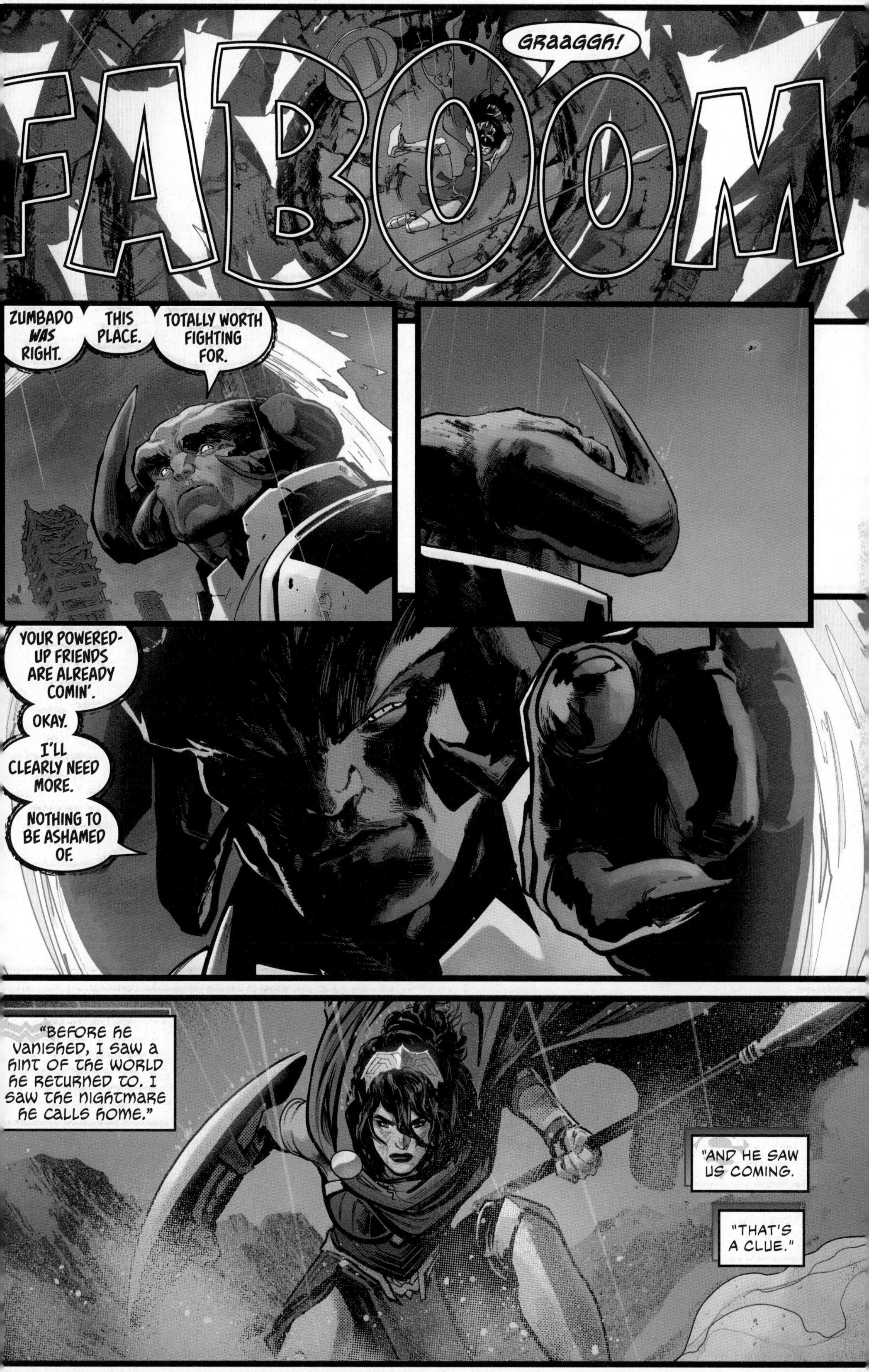
FABOOM
GRAAGGH!
ZUMBADO WAS RIGHT.
THIS PLACE.
TOTALLY WORTH FIGHTING FOR.
YOUR POWERED-UP FRIENDS ARE ALREADY COMIN'.
OKAY.
I'LL CLEARLY NEED MORE.
NOTHING TO BE ASHAMED OF.
"BEFORE HE VANISHED, I SAW A HINT OF THE WORLD HE RETURNED TO. I SAW THE NIGHTMARE HE CALLS HOME."
"AND HE SAW US COMING.
"THAT'S A CLUE."

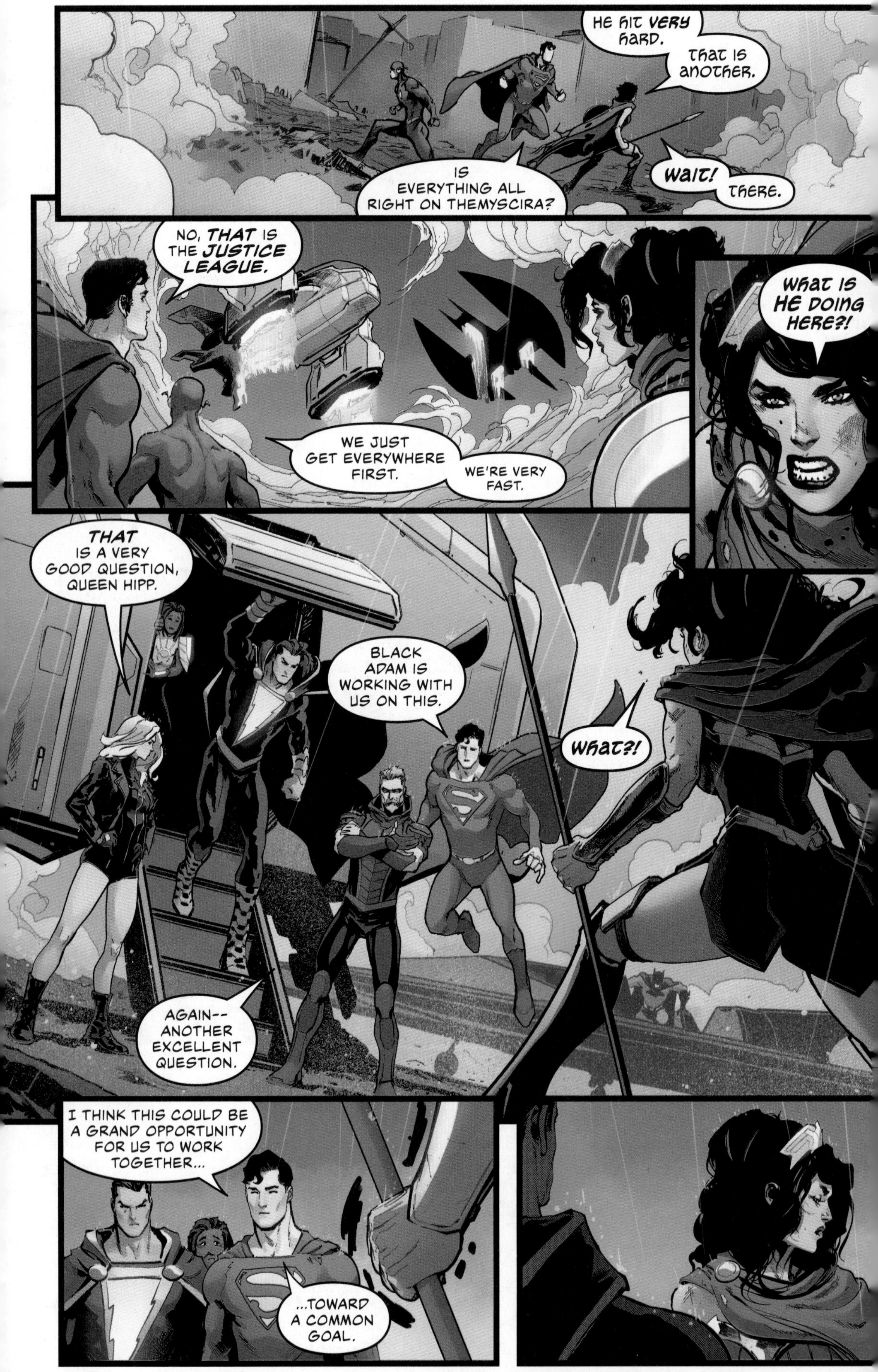

HE HIT VERY HARD.
THAT IS ANOTHER.
IS EVERYTHING ALL RIGHT ON THEMYSCIRA?
WAIT! THERE.
NO, THAT IS THE JUSTICE LEAGUE.
WE JUST GET EVERYWHERE FIRST.
WE'RE VERY FAST.
WHAT IS HE DOING HERE?!
THAT IS A VERY GOOD QUESTION, QUEEN HIPP.
BLACK ADAM IS WORKING WITH US ON THIS.
WHAT?!
AGAIN--ANOTHER EXCELLENT QUESTION.
I THINK THIS COULD BE A GRAND OPPORTUNITY FOR US TO WORK TOGETHER...
...TOWARD A COMMON GOAL.

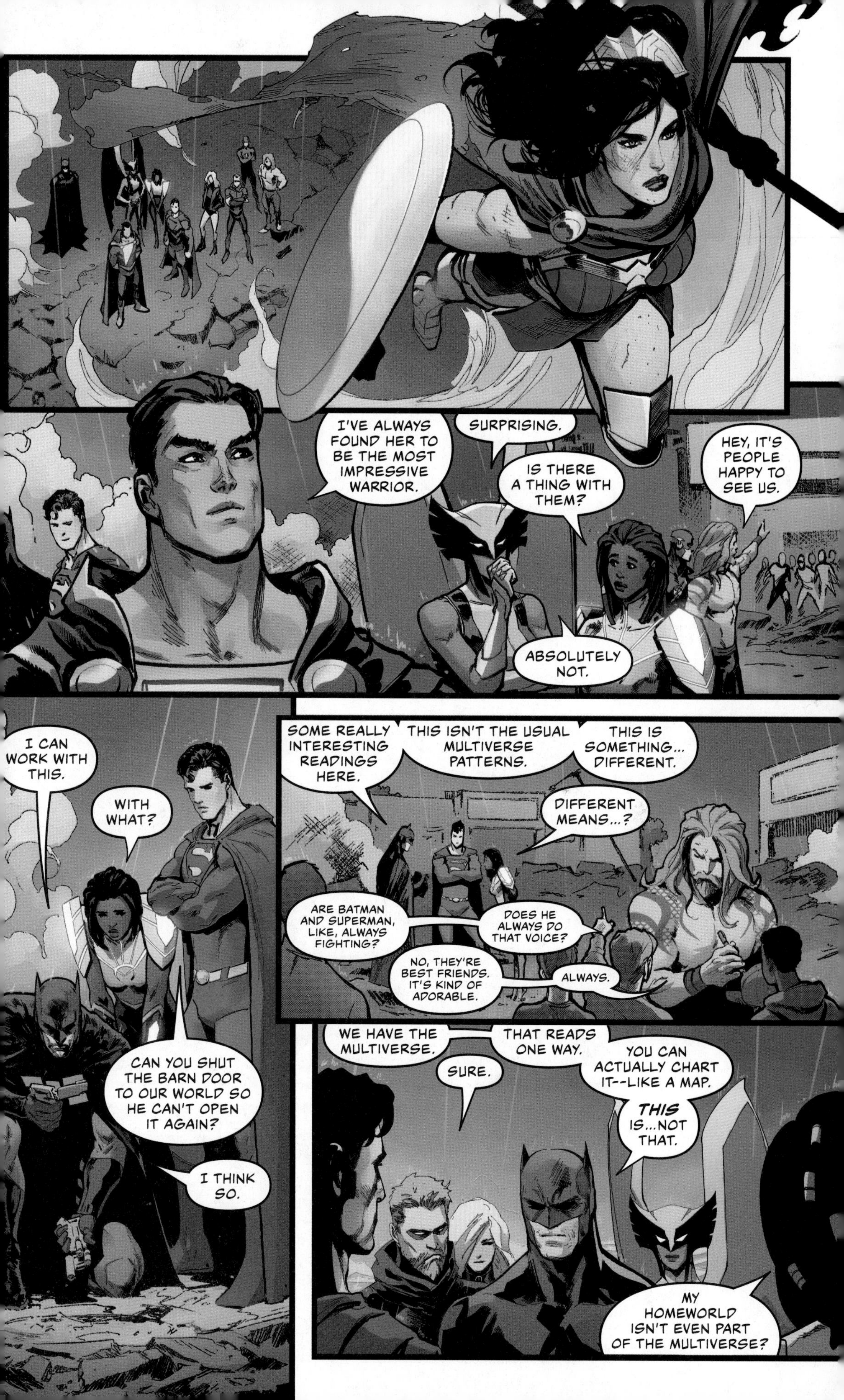
I'VE ALWAYS FOUND HER TO BE THE MOST IMPRESSIVE WARRIOR.
SURPRISING.
IS THERE A THING WITH THEM?
HEY, IT'S PEOPLE HAPPY TO SEE US.
ABSOLUTELY NOT.
I CAN WORK WITH THIS.
WITH WHAT?
CAN YOU SHUT THE BARN DOOR TO OUR WORLD SO HE CAN'T OPEN IT AGAIN?
I THINK SO.
SOME REALLY INTERESTING READINGS HERE.
THIS ISN'T THE USUAL MULTIVERSE PATTERNS.
THIS IS SOMETHING... DIFFERENT.
DIFFERENT MEANS...?
ARE BATMAN AND SUPERMAN, LIKE, ALWAYS FIGHTING?
DOES HE ALWAYS DO THAT VOICE?
NO, THEY'RE BEST FRIENDS. IT'S KIND OF ADORABLE.
ALWAYS.
WE HAVE THE MULTIVERSE.
THAT READS ONE WAY.
SURE.
YOU CAN ACTUALLY CHART IT--LIKE A MAP.
THIS IS...NOT THAT.
MY HOMEWORLD ISN'T EVEN PART OF THE MULTIVERSE?

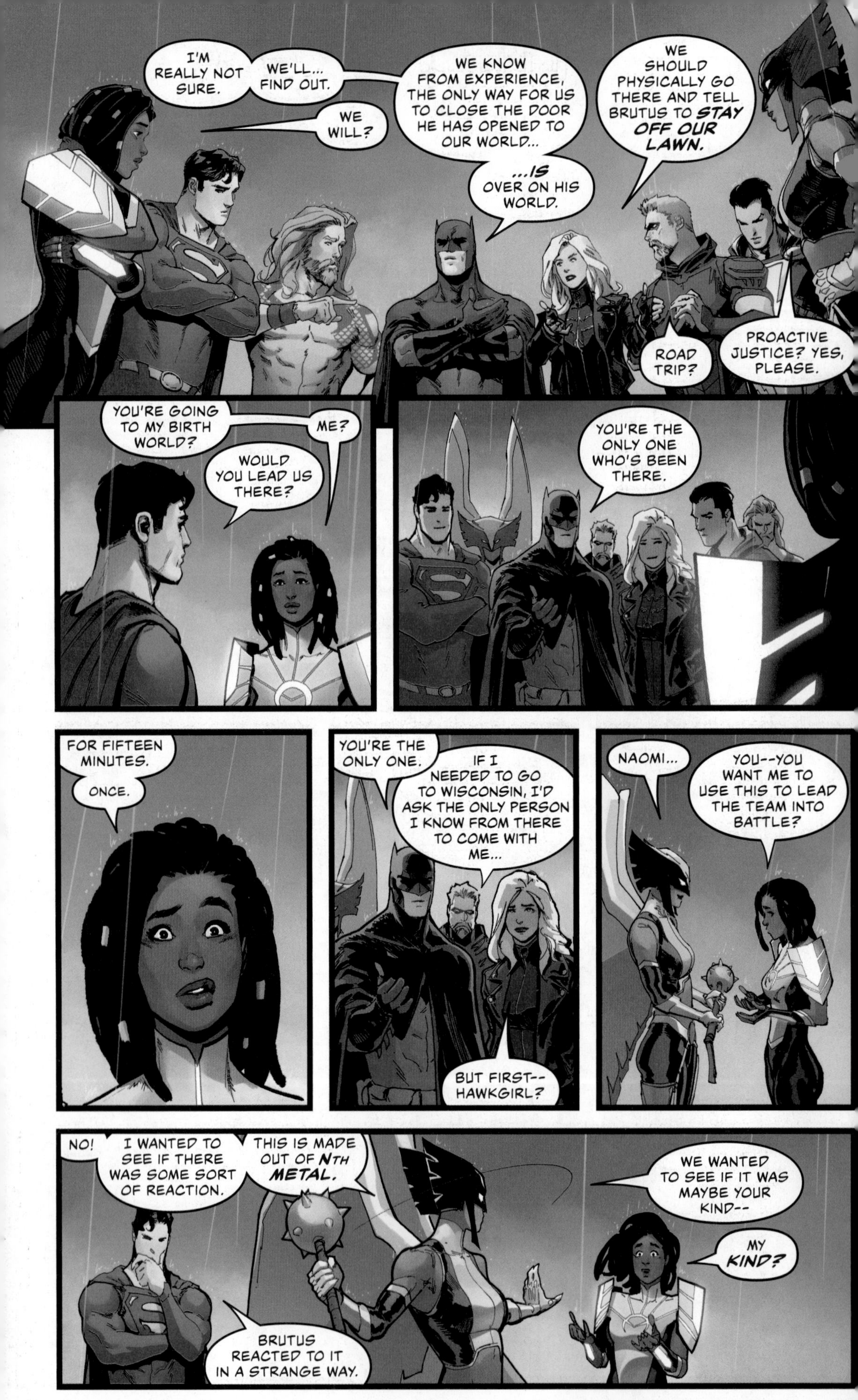

I'M REALLY NOT SURE.
WE'LL... FIND OUT.
WE WILL?
WE KNOW FROM EXPERIENCE, THE ONLY WAY FOR US TO CLOSE THE DOOR HE HAS OPENED TO OUR WORLD...
...IS OVER ON HIS WORLD.
WE SHOULD PHYSICALLY GO THERE AND TELL BRUTUS TO STAY OFF OUR LAWN.
ROAD TRIP?
PROACTIVE JUSTICE? YES, PLEASE.
YOU'RE GOING TO MY BIRTH WORLD?
ME?
WOULD YOU LEAD US THERE?
YOU'RE THE ONLY ONE WHO'S BEEN THERE.
FOR FIFTEEN MINUTES.
ONCE.
YOU'RE THE ONLY ONE.
IF I NEEDED TO GO TO WISCONSIN, I'D ASK THE ONLY PERSON I KNOW FROM THERE TO COME WITH ME...
BUT FIRST-- HAWKGIRL?
NAOMI...
YOU--YOU WANT ME TO USE THIS TO LEAD THE TEAM INTO BATTLE?
NO!
I WANTED TO SEE IF THERE WAS SOME SORT OF REACTION.
THIS IS MADE OUT OF NTH METAL.
WE WANTED TO SEE IF IT WAS MAYBE YOUR KIND--
MY KIND?
BRUTUS REACTED TO IT IN A STRANGE WAY.

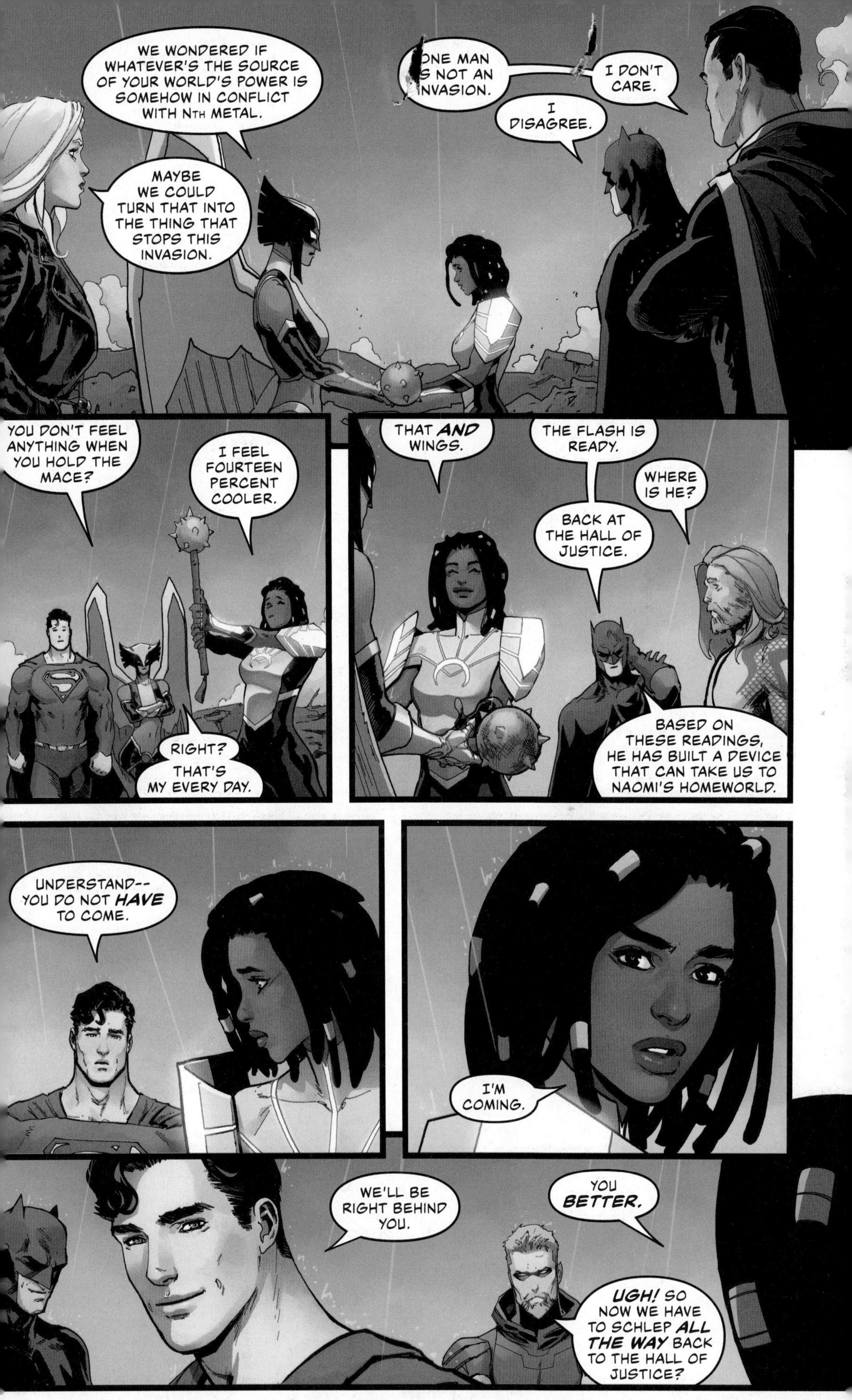
WE WONDERED IF WHATEVER'S THE SOURCE OF YOUR WORLD'S POWER IS SOMEHOW IN CONFLICT WITH NTH METAL.
MAYBE WE COULD TURN THAT INTO THE THING THAT STOPS THIS INVASION.
ONE MAN IS NOT AN INVASION.
I DON'T CARE.
I DISAGREE.
YOU DON'T FEEL ANYTHING WHEN YOU HOLD THE MACE?
I FEEL FOURTEEN PERCENT COOLER.
RIGHT? THAT'S MY EVERY DAY.
THAT AND WINGS.
THE FLASH IS READY.
WHERE IS HE?
BACK AT THE HALL OF JUSTICE.
BASED ON THESE READINGS, HE HAS BUILT A DEVICE THAT CAN TAKE US TO NAOMI'S HOMEWORLD.
UNDERSTAND-- YOU DO NOT HAVE TO COME.
I'M COMING.
WE'LL BE RIGHT BEHIND YOU.
YOU BETTER.
UGH! SO NOW WE HAVE TO SCHLEP ALL THE WAY BACK TO THE HALL OF JUSTICE?

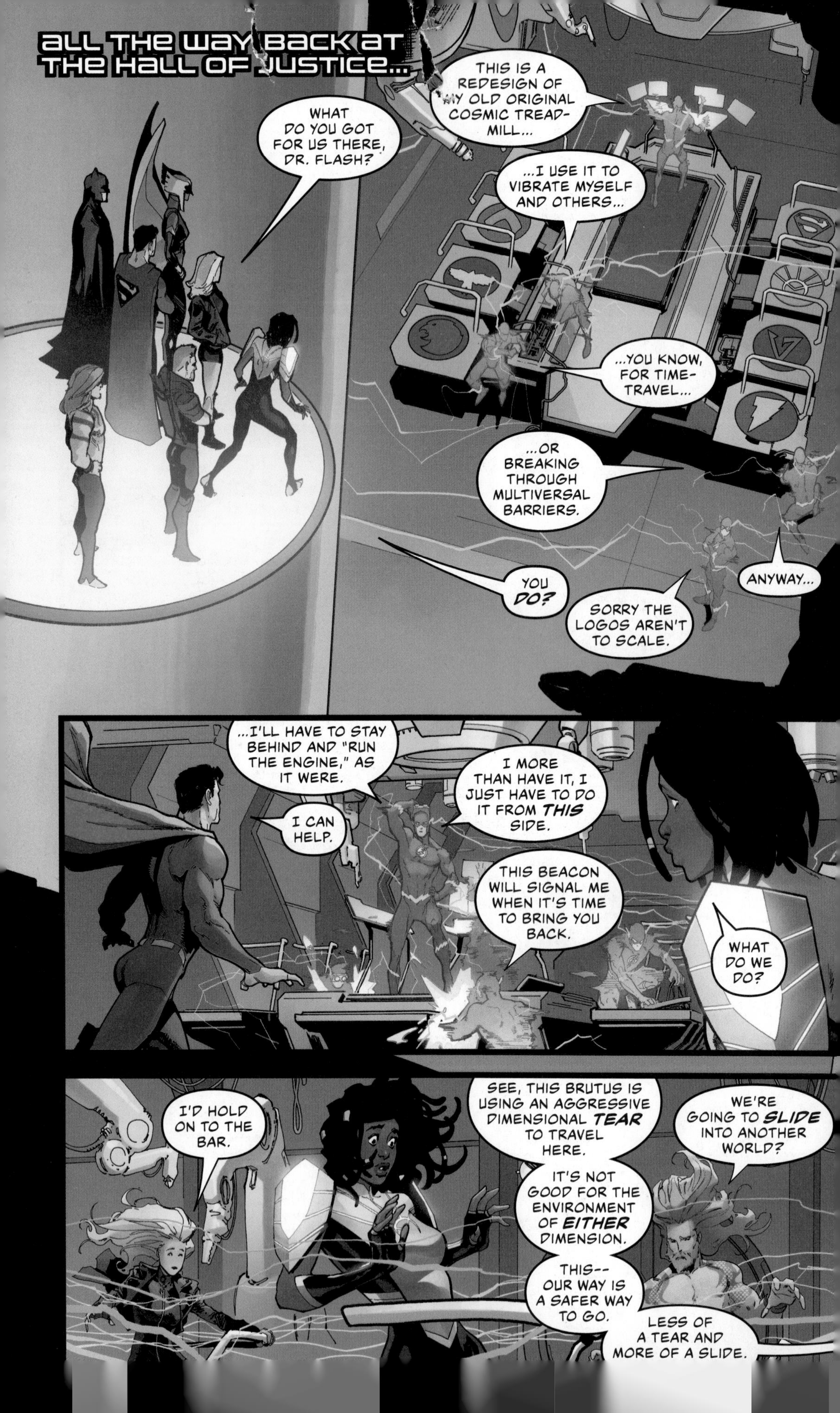
ALL THE WAY BACK AT THE HALL OF JUSTICE...
WHAT DO YOU GOT FOR US THERE, DR. FLASH?
THIS IS A REDESIGN OF MY OLD ORIGINAL COSMIC TREAD-MILL...
...I USE IT TO VIBRATE MYSELF AND OTHERS...
...YOU KNOW, FOR TIME-TRAVEL...
...OR BREAKING THROUGH MULTIVERSAL BARRIERS.
YOU *DO?*
SORRY THE LOGOS AREN'T TO SCALE.
ANYWAY...
...I'LL HAVE TO STAY BEHIND AND "RUN THE ENGINE," AS IT WERE.
I CAN HELP.
I MORE THAN HAVE IT, I JUST HAVE TO DO IT FROM *THIS* SIDE.
THIS BEACON WILL SIGNAL ME WHEN IT'S TIME TO BRING YOU BACK.
WHAT DO WE DO?
I'D HOLD ON TO THE BAR.
SEE, THIS BRUTUS IS USING AN AGGRESSIVE DIMENSIONAL *TEAR* TO TRAVEL HERE.
IT'S NOT GOOD FOR THE ENVIRONMENT OF *EITHER* DIMENSION.
THIS-- OUR WAY IS A SAFER WAY TO GO.
LESS OF A TEAR AND MORE OF A SLIDE.
WE'RE GOING TO *SLIDE* INTO ANOTHER WORLD?

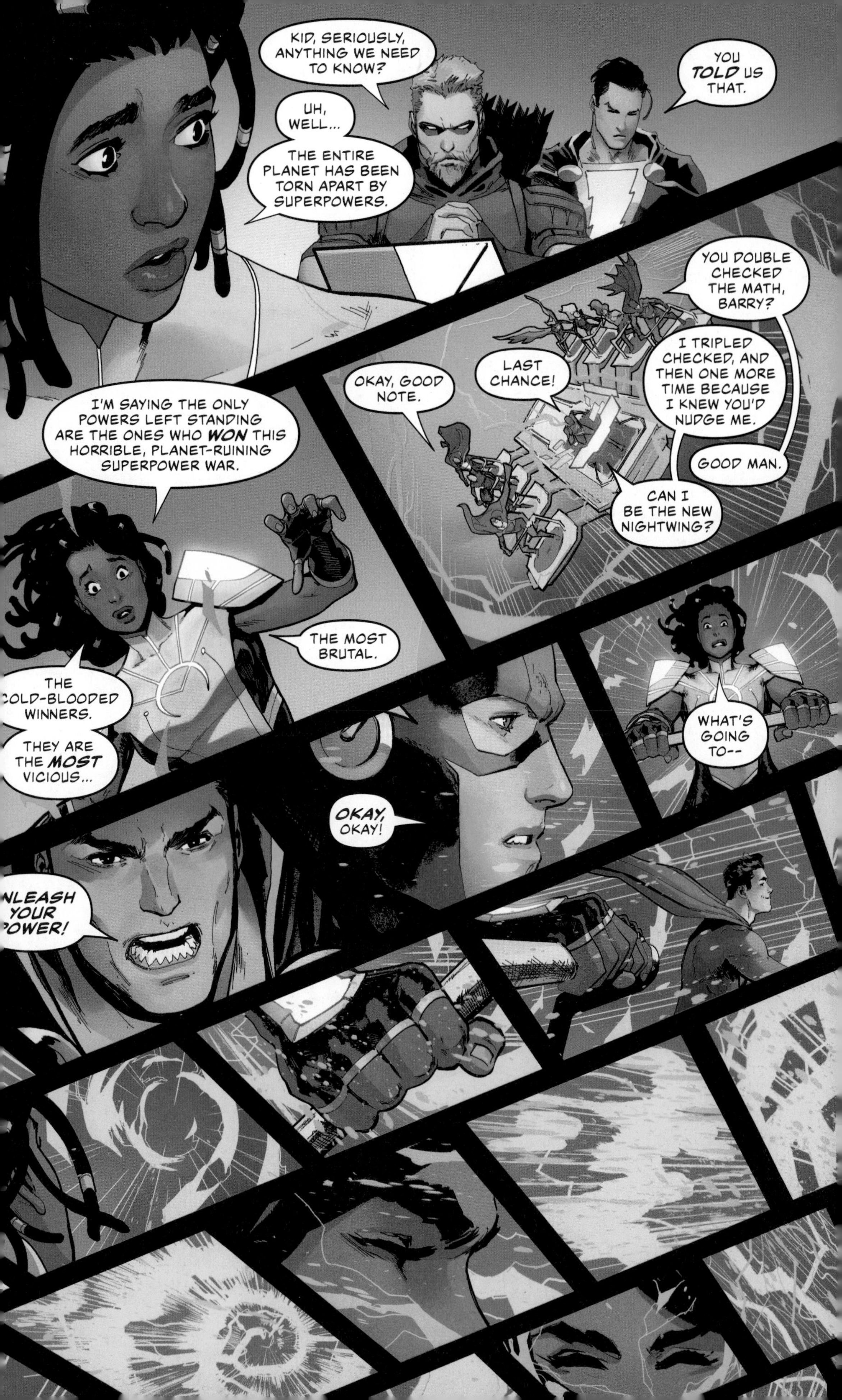
KID, SERIOUSLY, ANYTHING WE NEED TO KNOW?
UH, WELL...
THE ENTIRE PLANET HAS BEEN TORN APART BY SUPERPOWERS.
YOU TOLD US THAT.
I'M SAYING THE ONLY POWERS LEFT STANDING ARE THE ONES WHO WON THIS HORRIBLE, PLANET-RUINING SUPERPOWER WAR.
THE MOST BRUTAL.
THE COLD-BLOODED WINNERS.
THEY ARE THE MOST VICIOUS...
YOU DOUBLE CHECKED THE MATH, BARRY?
I TRIPLED CHECKED, AND THEN ONE MORE TIME BECAUSE I KNEW YOU'D NUDGE ME.
GOOD MAN.
LAST CHANCE!
OKAY, GOOD NOTE.
CAN I BE THE NEW NIGHTWING?
WHAT'S GOING TO--
OKAY, OKAY!
NLEASH YOUR POWER!

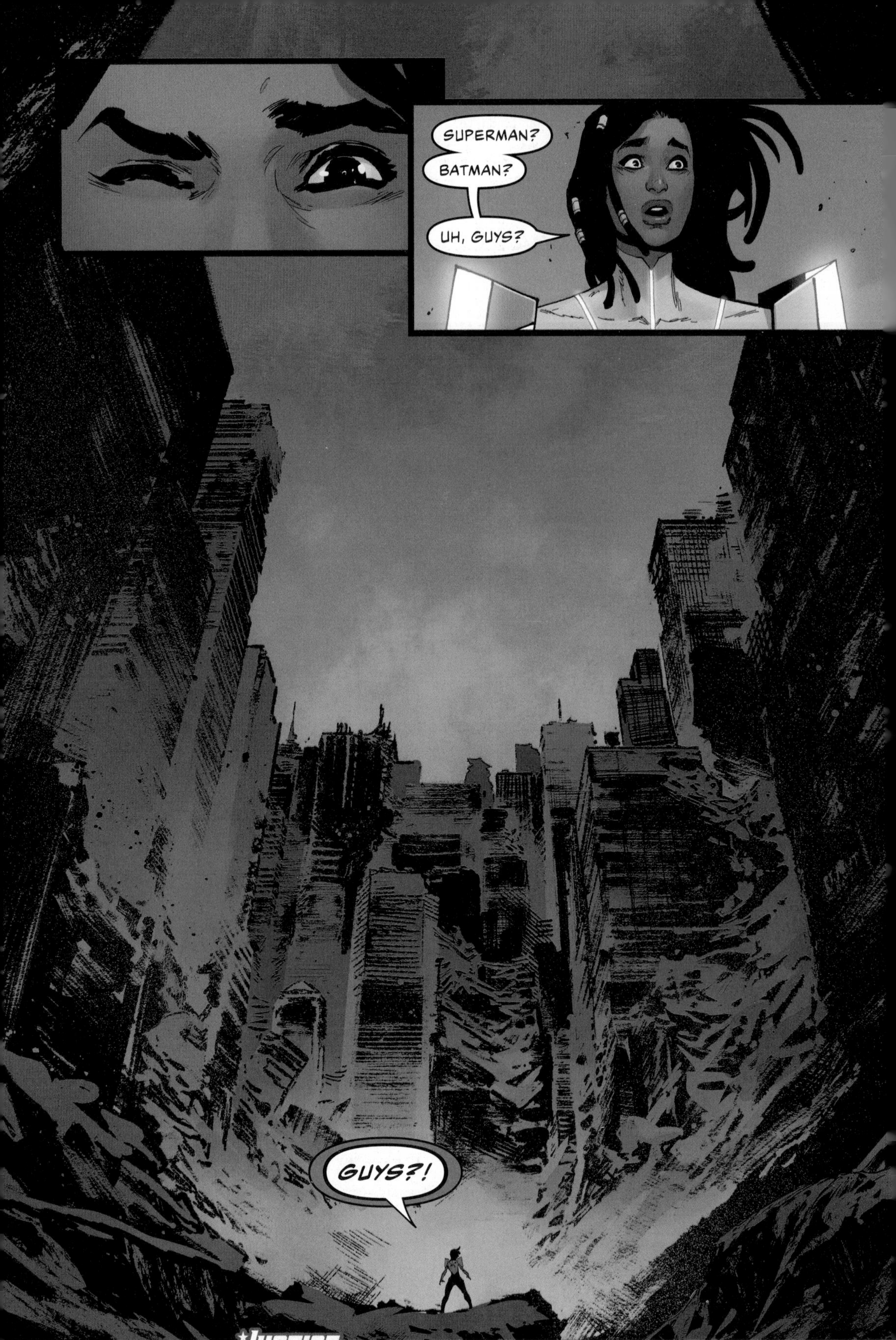

SUPERMAN?
BATMAN?
UH, GUYS?
GUYS?!

DC COMICS PROUDLY PRESENTS: JUSTICE LEAGUE

PRISMS
PART TWO

WRITER: BRIAN MICHAEL BENDIS ARTIST: DAVID MARQUEZ
COLORS: TAMRA BONVILLAIN LETTERS: JOSH REED
COVER: MARQUEZ & BONVILLAIN VARIANT COVER: KAEL NGU
ASSOCIATE EDITOR: ANDREA SHEA EDITOR: ALEX R. CARR GROUP EDITOR: JAMIE S. RICH

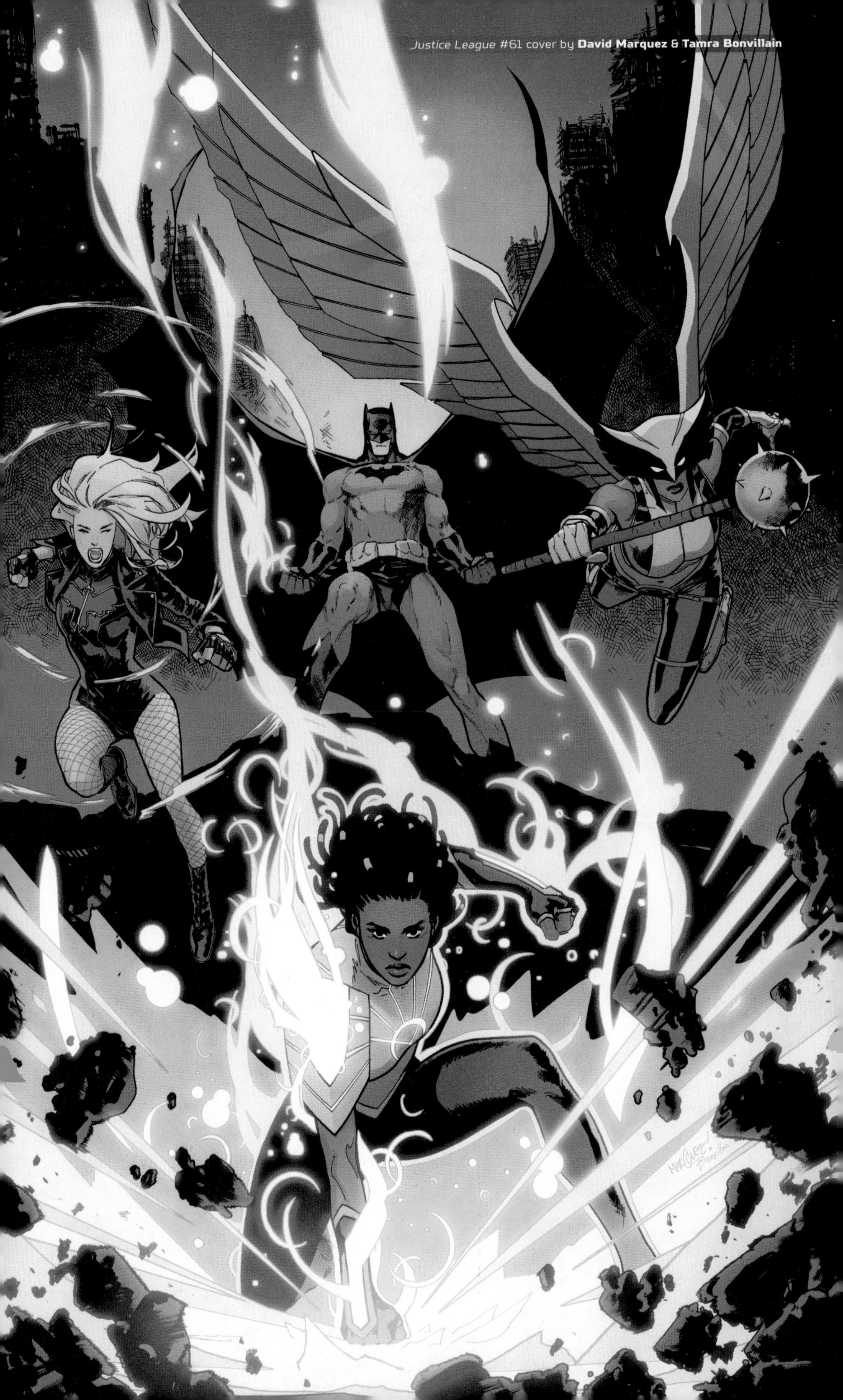

Justice League #61 cover by **David Marquez & Tamra Bonvillain**

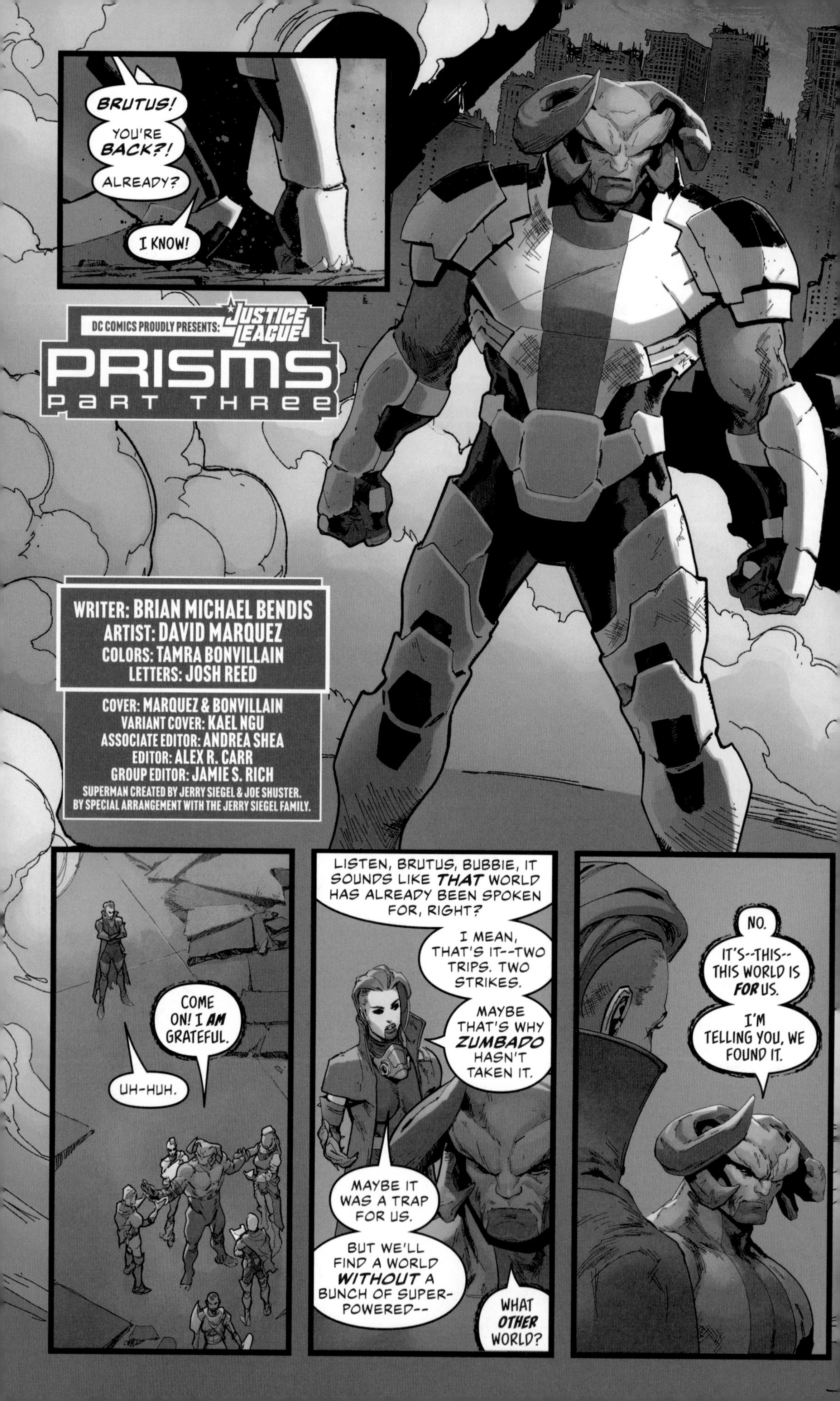
BRUTUS!
YOU'RE BACK?!
ALREADY?
I KNOW!
DC COMICS PROUDLY PRESENTS: JUSTICE LEAGUE
PRISMS
PART THREE
WRITER: BRIAN MICHAEL BENDIS
ARTIST: DAVID MARQUEZ
COLORS: TAMRA BONVILLAIN
LETTERS: JOSH REED
COVER: MARQUEZ & BONVILLAIN
VARIANT COVER: KAEL NGU
ASSOCIATE EDITOR: ANDREA SHEA
EDITOR: ALEX R. CARR
GROUP EDITOR: JAMIE S. RICH
SUPERMAN CREATED BY JERRY SIEGEL & JOE SHUSTER.
BY SPECIAL ARRANGEMENT WITH THE JERRY SIEGEL FAMILY.
COME ON! I AM GRATEFUL.
UH-HUH.
LISTEN, BRUTUS, BUBBIE, IT SOUNDS LIKE THAT WORLD HAS ALREADY BEEN SPOKEN FOR, RIGHT?
I MEAN, THAT'S IT--TWO TRIPS. TWO STRIKES.
MAYBE THAT'S WHY ZUMBADO HASN'T TAKEN IT.
MAYBE IT WAS A TRAP FOR US.
BUT WE'LL FIND A WORLD WITHOUT A BUNCH OF SUPER-POWERED--
WHAT OTHER WORLD?
NO.
IT'S--THIS--THIS WORLD IS FOR US.
I'M TELLING YOU, WE FOUND IT.

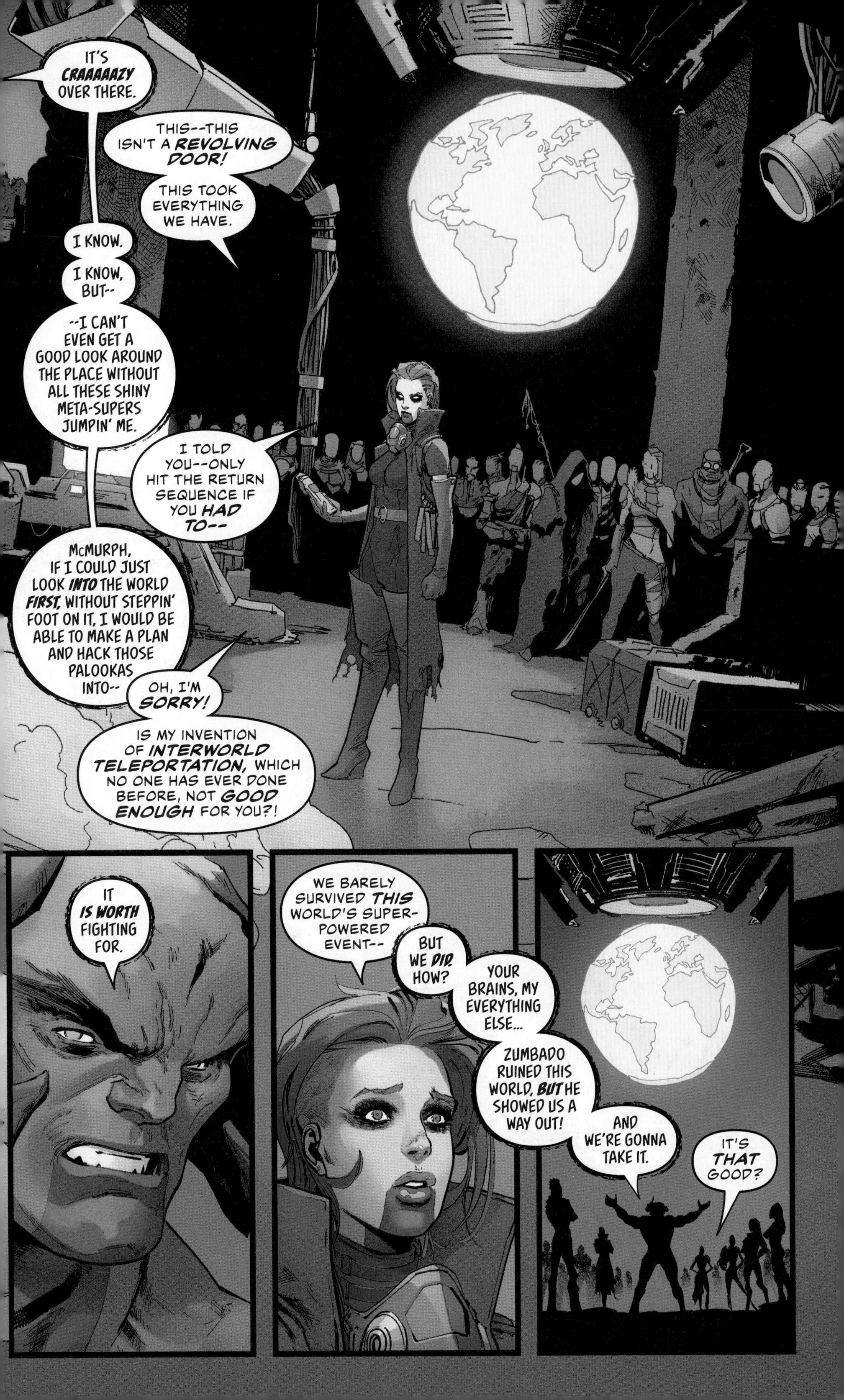
IT'S CRAAAAAZY OVER THERE.
THIS--THIS ISN'T A REVOLVING DOOR!
THIS TOOK EVERYTHING WE HAVE.
I KNOW.
I KNOW, BUT--
--I CAN'T EVEN GET A GOOD LOOK AROUND THE PLACE WITHOUT ALL THESE SHINY META-SUPERS JUMPIN' ME.
I TOLD YOU--ONLY HIT THE RETURN SEQUENCE IF YOU HAD TO--
McMURPH, IF I COULD JUST LOOK INTO THE WORLD FIRST, WITHOUT STEPPIN' FOOT ON IT, I WOULD BE ABLE TO MAKE A PLAN AND HACK THOSE PALOOKAS INTO--
OH, I'M SORRY!
IS MY INVENTION OF INTERWORLD TELEPORTATION, WHICH NO ONE HAS EVER DONE BEFORE, NOT GOOD ENOUGH FOR YOU?!
IT IS WORTH FIGHTING FOR.
WE BARELY SURVIVED THIS WORLD'S SUPER-POWERED EVENT--
BUT WE DID. HOW?
YOUR BRAINS, MY EVERYTHING ELSE...
ZUMBADO RUINED THIS WORLD, BUT HE SHOWED US A WAY OUT!
AND WE'RE GONNA TAKE IT.
IT'S THAT GOOD?

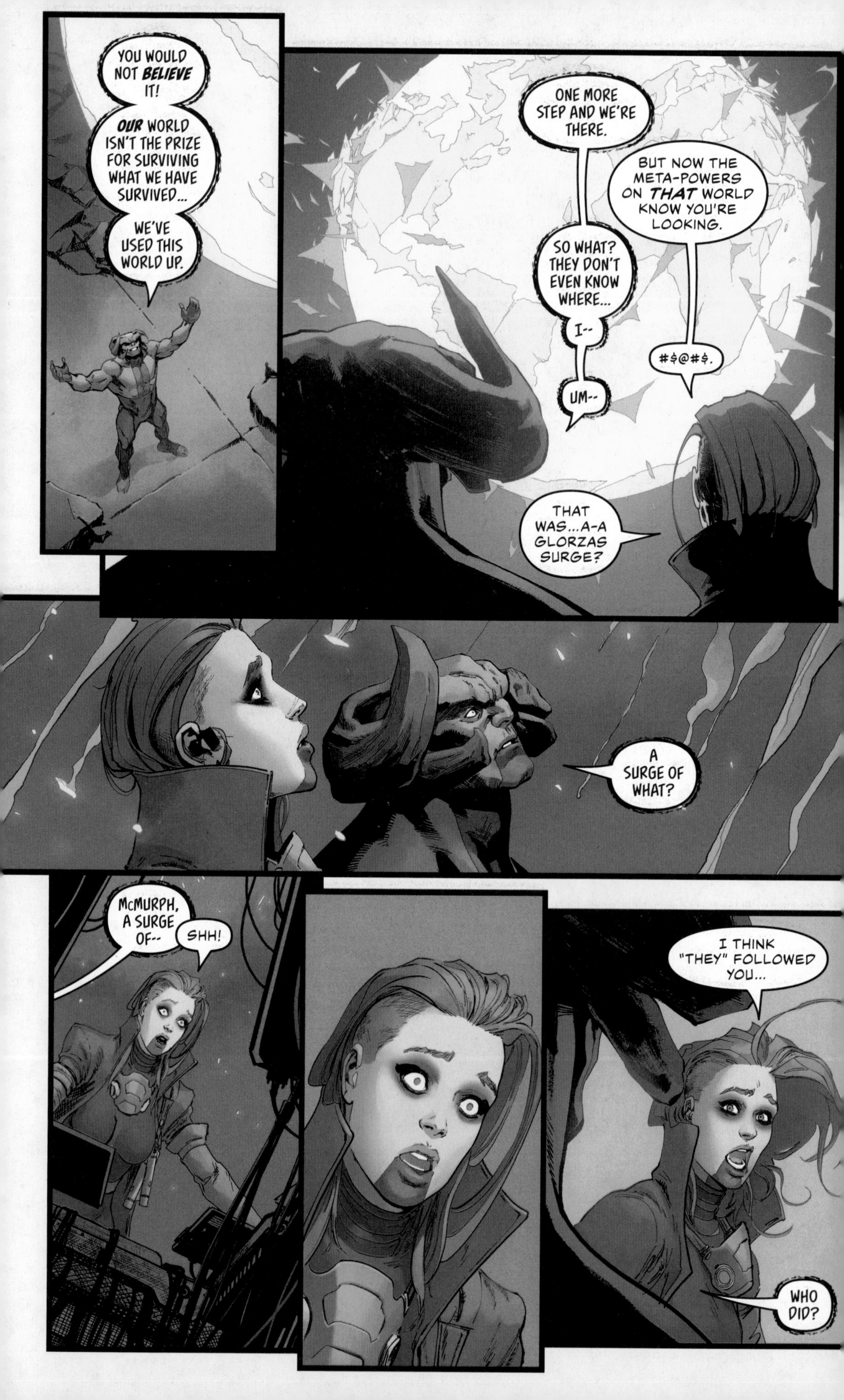
YOU WOULD NOT BELIEVE IT!
OUR WORLD ISN'T THE PRIZE FOR SURVIVING WHAT WE HAVE SURVIVED...
WE'VE USED THIS WORLD UP.
ONE MORE STEP AND WE'RE THERE.
BUT NOW THE META-POWERS ON THAT WORLD KNOW YOU'RE LOOKING.
SO WHAT? THEY DON'T EVEN KNOW WHERE...
I--
UM--
#$@#$.
THAT WAS...A-A GLORZAS SURGE?
A SURGE OF WHAT?
McMURPH, A SURGE OF--
SHH!
I THINK "THEY" FOLLOWED YOU...
WHO DID?

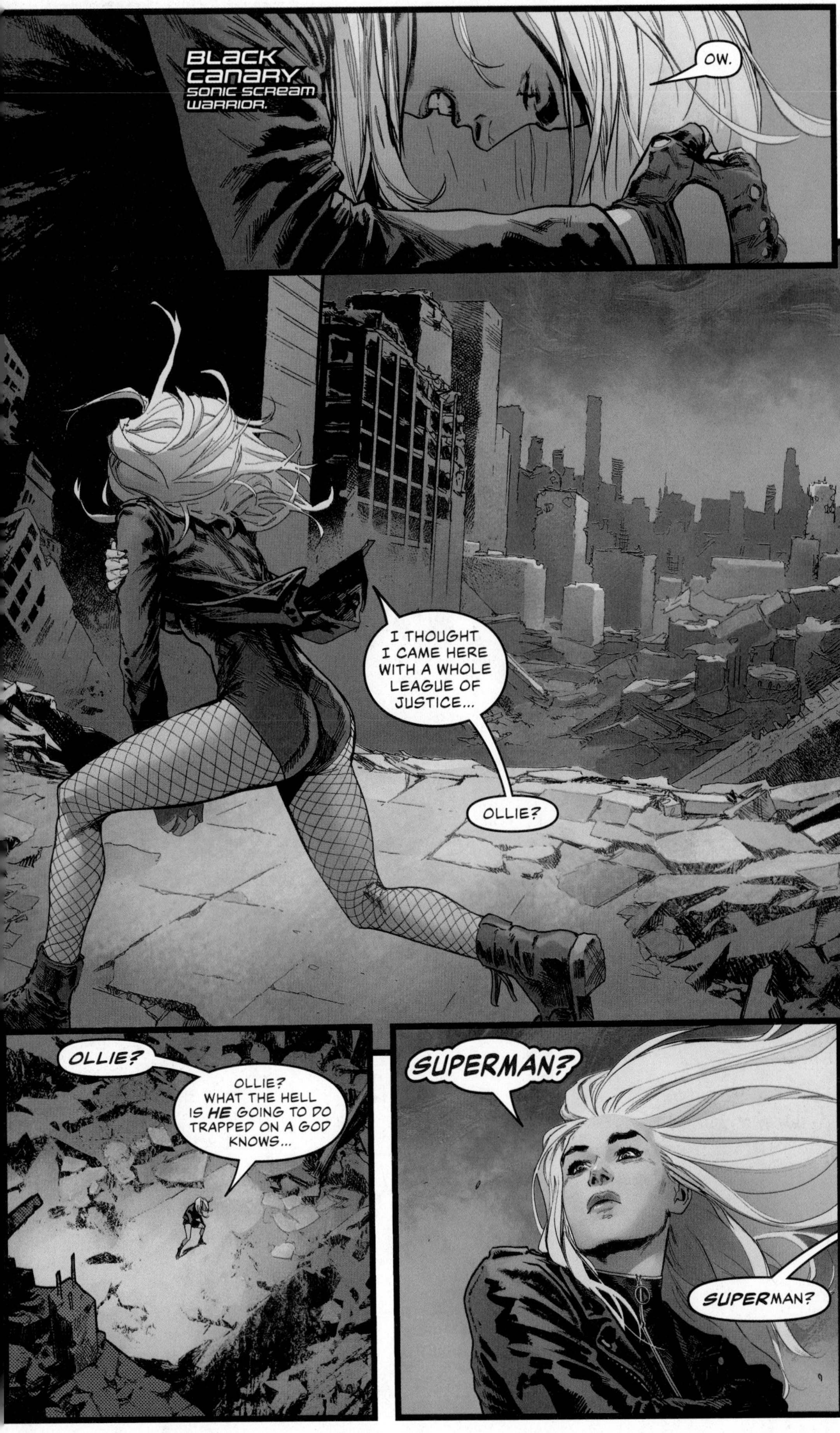
BLACK CANARY SONIC SCREAM WARRIOR.
OW.
I THOUGHT I CAME HERE WITH A WHOLE LEAGUE OF JUSTICE...
OLLIE?
OLLIE?
OLLIE? WHAT THE HELL IS HE GOING TO DO TRAPPED ON A GOD KNOWS...
SUPERMAN?
SUPERMAN?

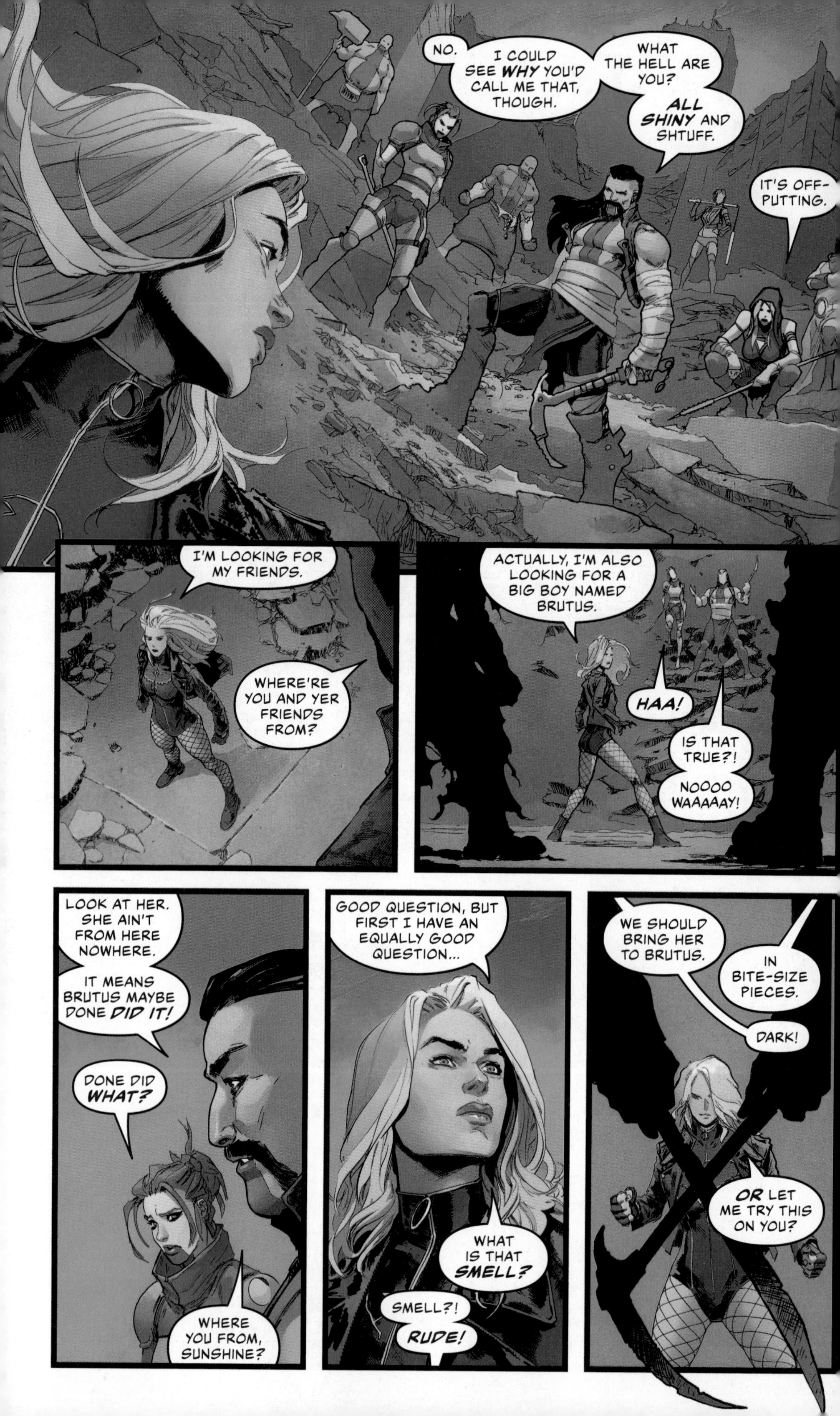
NO.
I COULD SEE WHY YOU'D CALL ME THAT, THOUGH.
WHAT THE HELL ARE YOU?
ALL SHINY AND SHTUFF.
IT'S OFF-PUTTING.
I'M LOOKING FOR MY FRIENDS.
WHERE'RE YOU AND YER FRIENDS FROM?
ACTUALLY, I'M ALSO LOOKING FOR A BIG BOY NAMED BRUTUS.
HAA!
IS THAT TRUE?!
NOOOO WAAAAAY!
LOOK AT HER. SHE AIN'T FROM HERE NOWHERE.
IT MEANS BRUTUS MAYBE DONE DID IT!
DONE DID WHAT?
WHERE YOU FROM, SUNSHINE?
GOOD QUESTION, BUT FIRST I HAVE AN EQUALLY GOOD QUESTION...
WHAT IS THAT SMELL?
SMELL?!
RUDE!
WE SHOULD BRING HER TO BRUTUS.
IN BITE-SIZE PIECES.
DARK!
OR LET ME TRY THIS ON YOU?

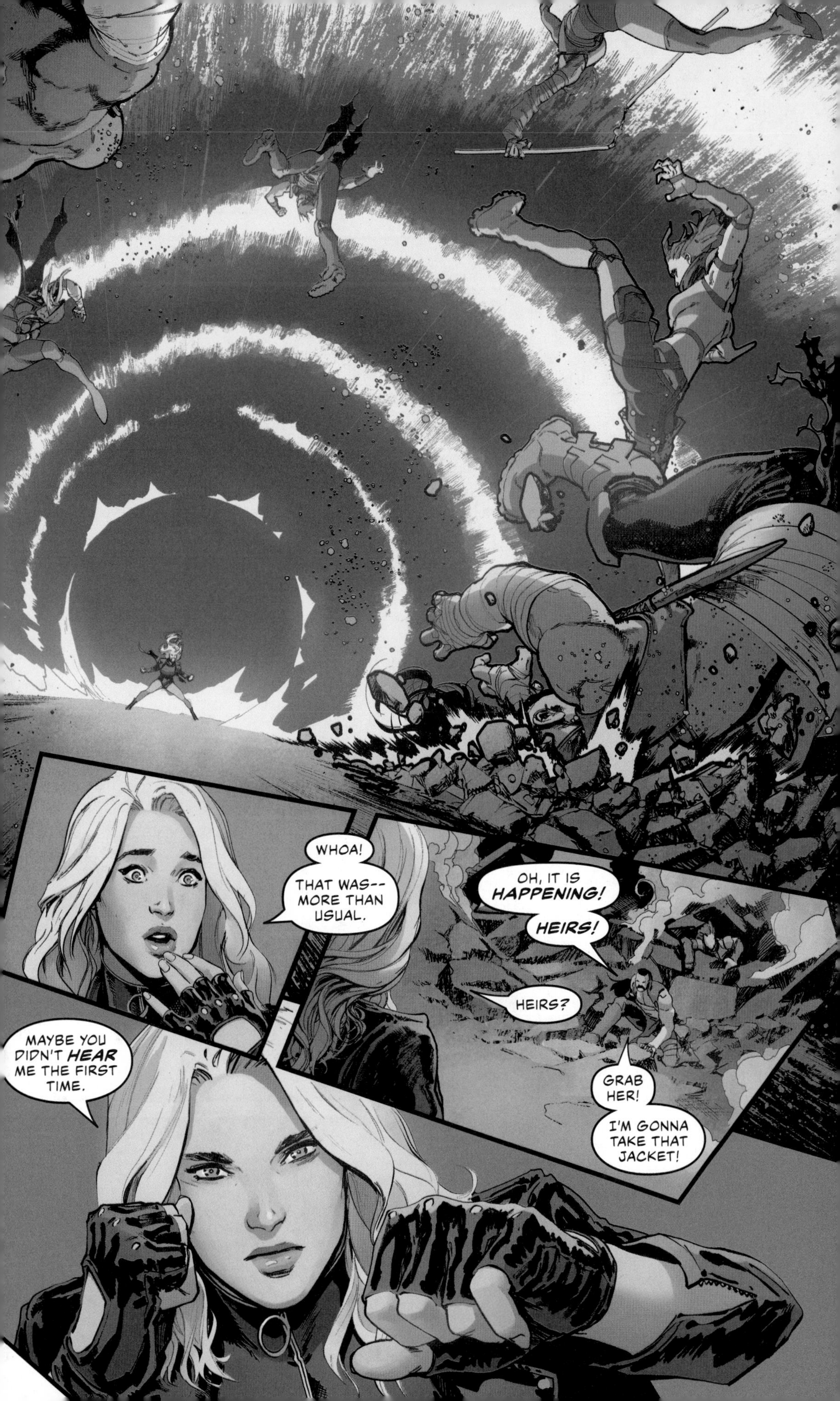

WHOA!
THAT WAS-- MORE THAN USUAL.
OH, IT IS **HAPPENING!**
HEIRS!
HEIRS?
GRAB HER!
I'M GONNA TAKE THAT JACKET!
MAYBE YOU DIDN'T **HEAR** ME THE FIRST TIME.

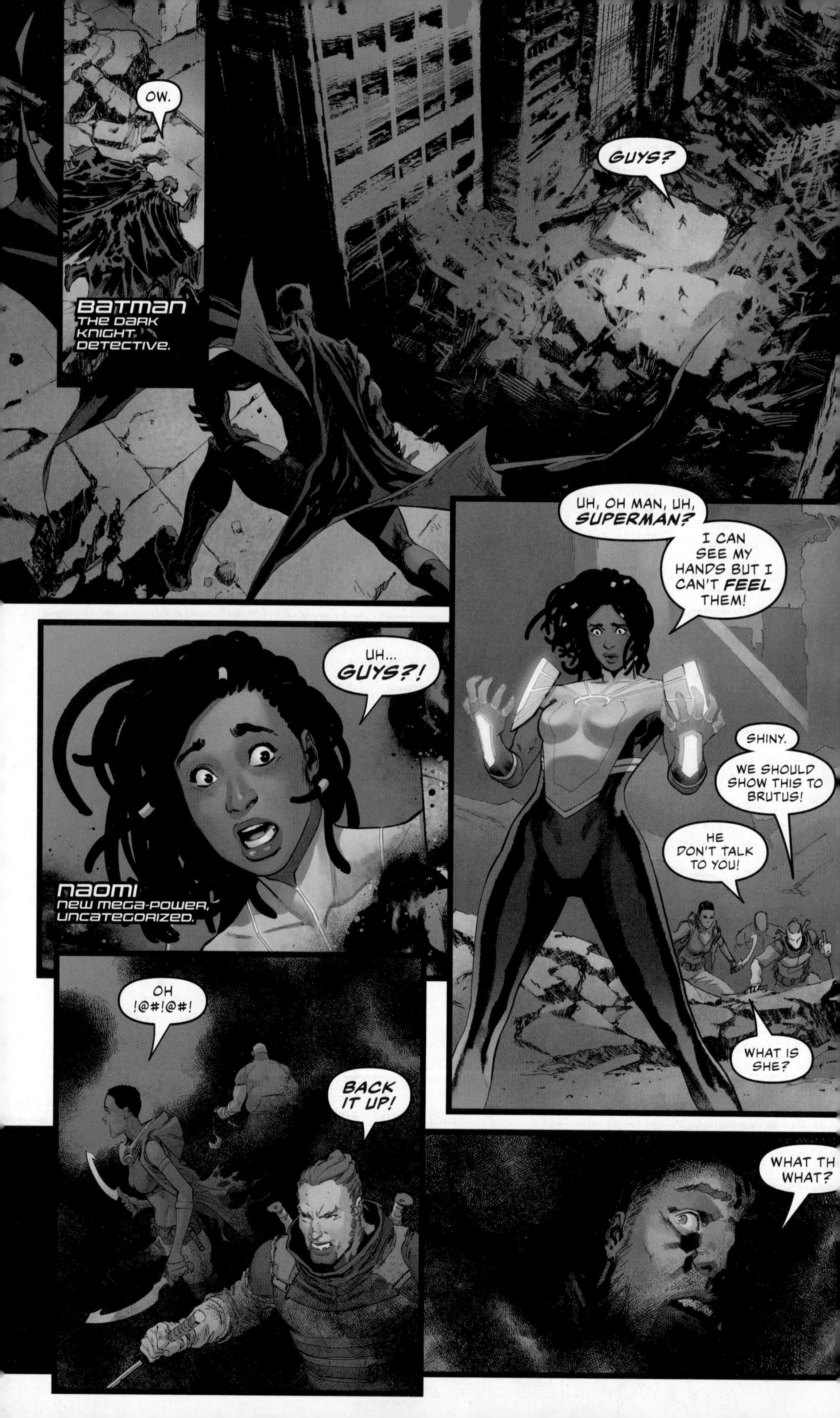

OW.
BATMAN
THE DARK KNIGHT DETECTIVE.
GUYS?
UH... GUYS?!
NAOMI
NEW MEGA-POWER, UNCATEGORIZED.
UH, OH MAN, UH, SUPERMAN?
I CAN SEE MY HANDS BUT I CAN'T FEEL THEM!
SHINY.
WE SHOULD SHOW THIS TO BRUTUS!
HE DON'T TALK TO YOU!
WHAT IS SHE?
OH !@#!@#!
BACK IT UP!
WHAT TH WHAT?

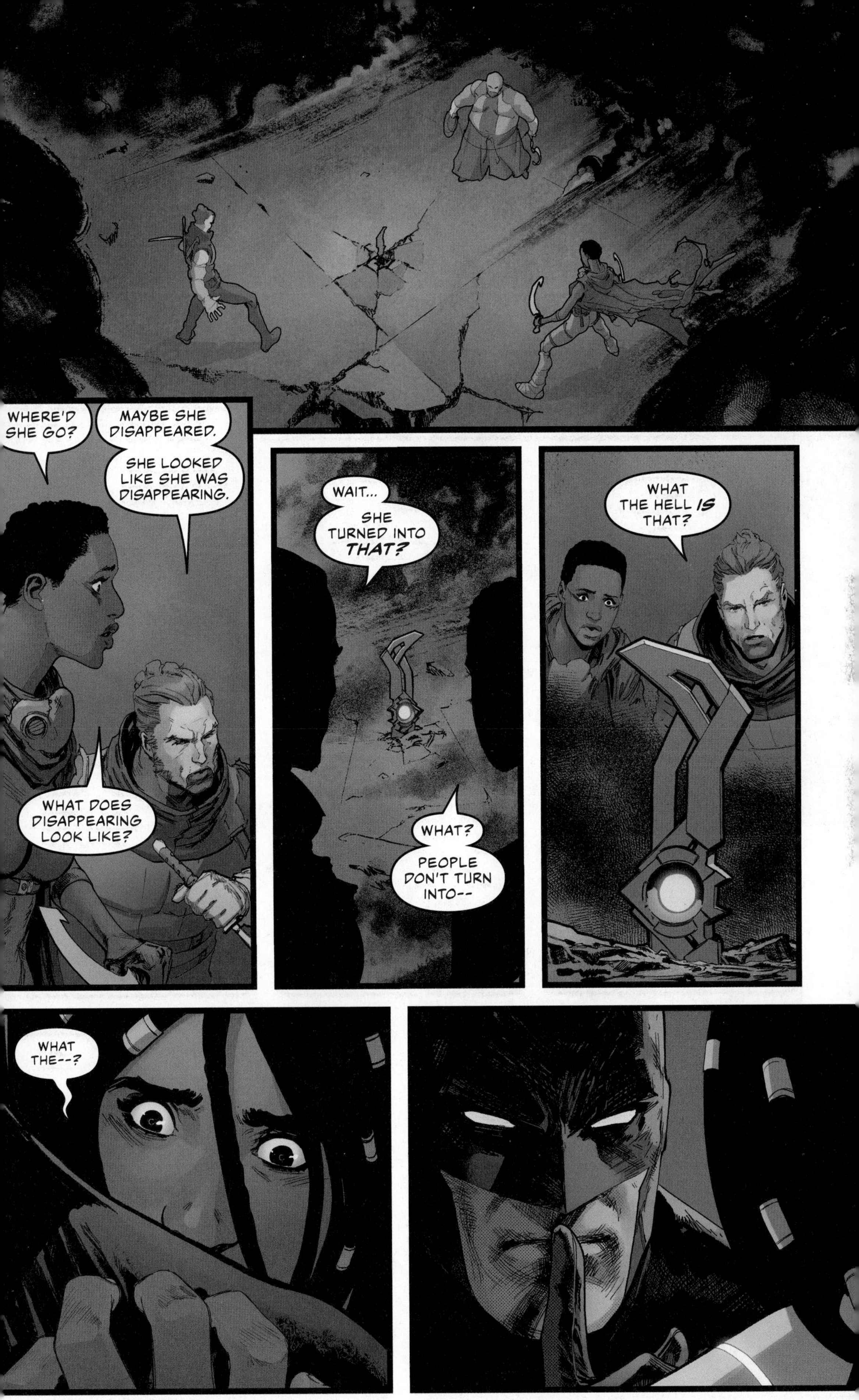
WHERE'D SHE GO?
MAYBE SHE DISAPPEARED.
SHE LOOKED LIKE SHE WAS DISAPPEARING.
WHAT DOES DISAPPEARING LOOK LIKE?
WAIT...
SHE TURNED INTO *THAT?*
WHAT?
PEOPLE DON'T TURN INTO--
WHAT THE HELL *IS* THAT?
WHAT THE--?

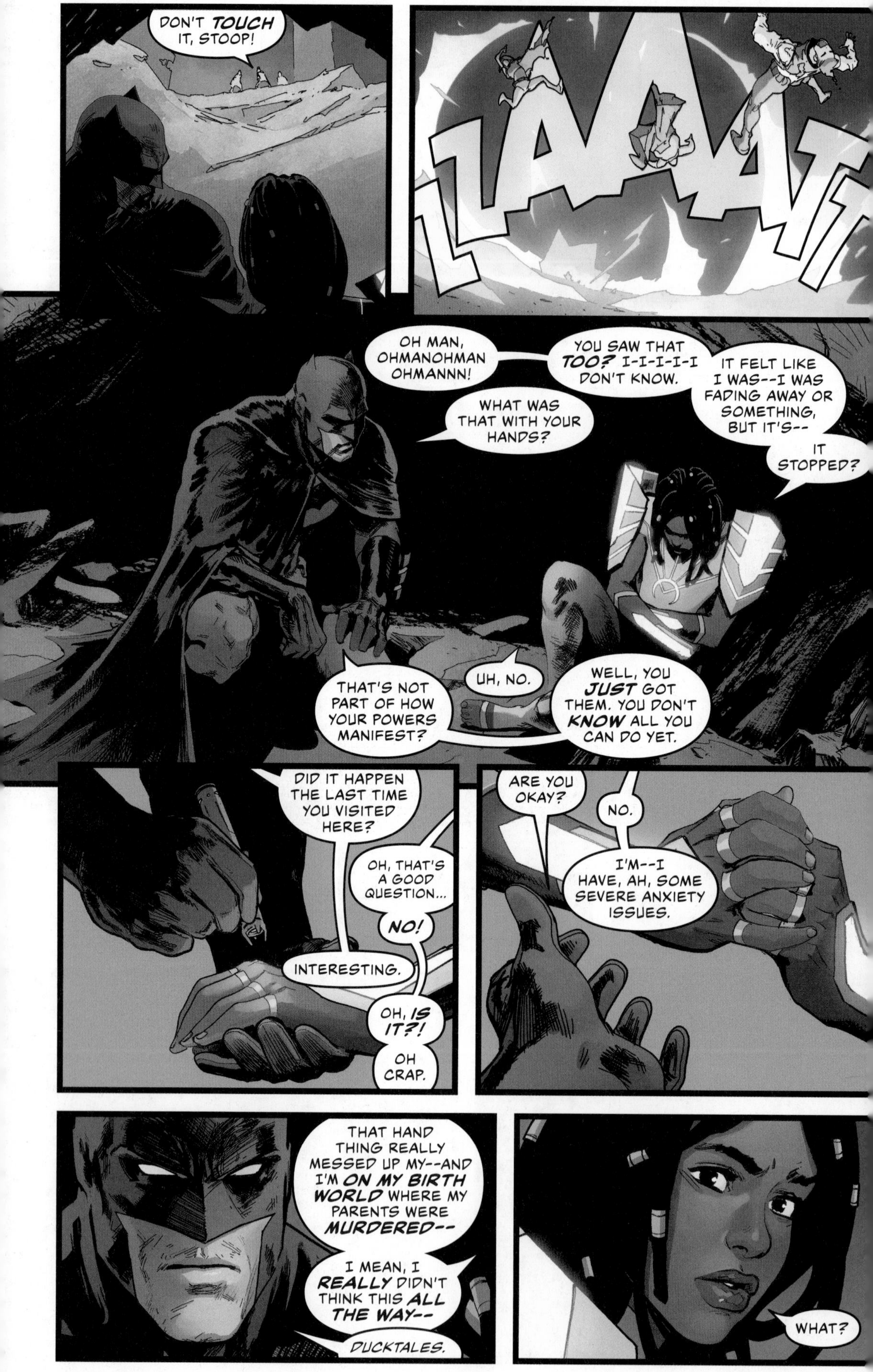

DON'T TOUCH IT, STOOP!
ZZAAAT!
OH MAN, OHMANOHMAN OHMANNN!
YOU SAW THAT TOO? I-I-I-I-I DON'T KNOW.
IT FELT LIKE I WAS--I WAS FADING AWAY OR SOMETHING, BUT IT'S--
WHAT WAS THAT WITH YOUR HANDS?
IT STOPPED?
THAT'S NOT PART OF HOW YOUR POWERS MANIFEST?
UH, NO.
WELL, YOU JUST GOT THEM. YOU DON'T KNOW ALL YOU CAN DO YET.
DID IT HAPPEN THE LAST TIME YOU VISITED HERE?
OH, THAT'S A GOOD QUESTION...
NO!
INTERESTING.
OH, IS IT?!
OH CRAP.
ARE YOU OKAY?
NO.
I'M--I HAVE, AH, SOME SEVERE ANXIETY ISSUES.
THAT HAND THING REALLY MESSED UP MY--AND I'M ON MY BIRTH WORLD WHERE MY PARENTS WERE MURDERED--
I MEAN, I REALLY DIDN'T THINK THIS ALL THE WAY--
DUCKTALES.
WHAT?

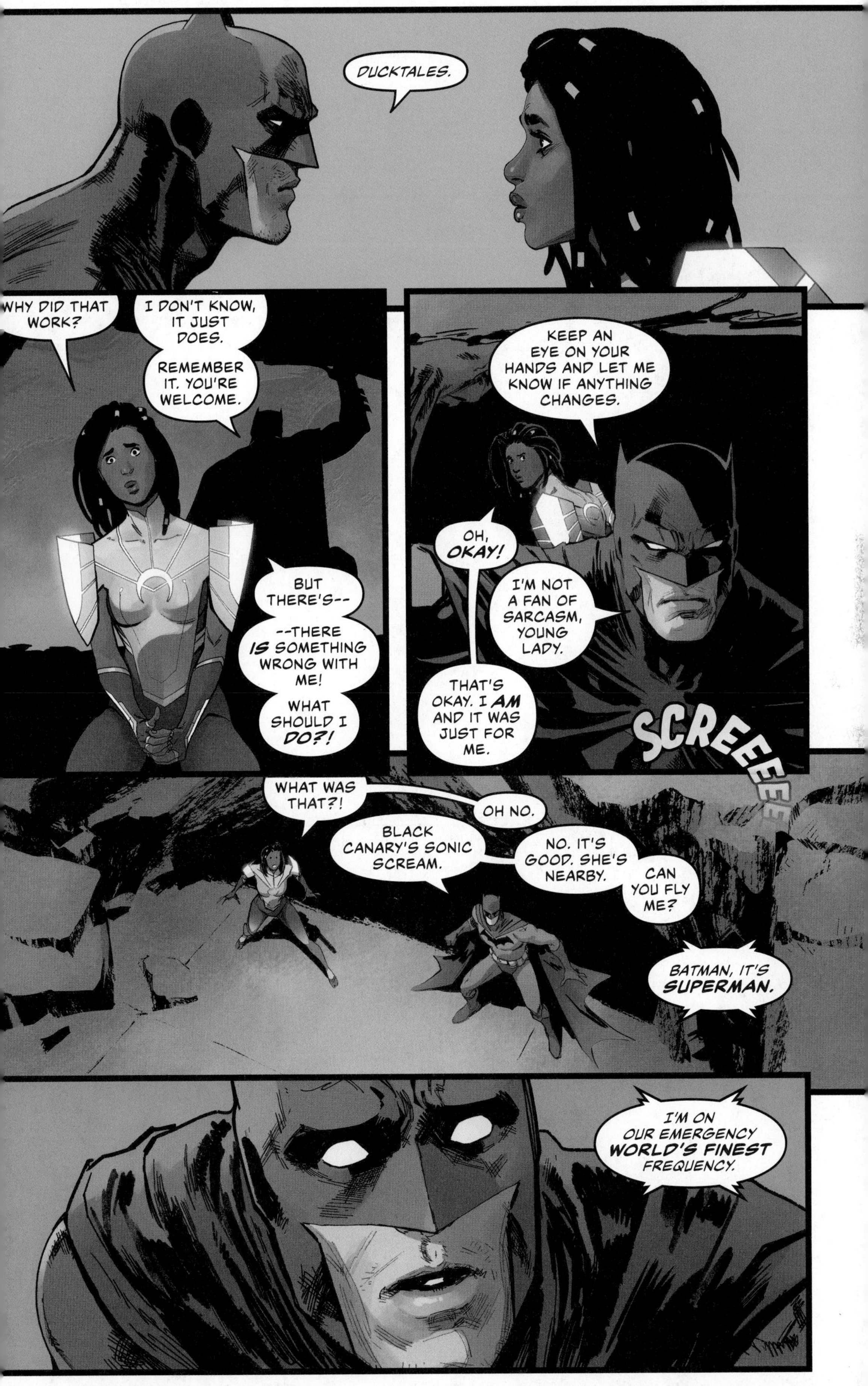
DUCKTALES.
WHY DID THAT WORK?
I DON'T KNOW, IT JUST DOES.
REMEMBER IT. YOU'RE WELCOME.
BUT THERE'S--
--THERE *IS* SOMETHING WRONG WITH ME!
WHAT SHOULD I *DO?!*
KEEP AN EYE ON YOUR HANDS AND LET ME KNOW IF ANYTHING CHANGES.
OH, *OKAY!*
I'M NOT A FAN OF SARCASM, YOUNG LADY.
THAT'S OKAY. I *AM* AND IT WAS JUST FOR ME.
SCREEEEE
WHAT WAS THAT?!
OH NO.
BLACK CANARY'S SONIC SCREAM.
NO. IT'S GOOD. SHE'S NEARBY.
CAN YOU FLY ME?
BATMAN, IT'S **SUPERMAN.**
I'M ON OUR EMERGENCY **WORLD'S FINEST** FREQUENCY.

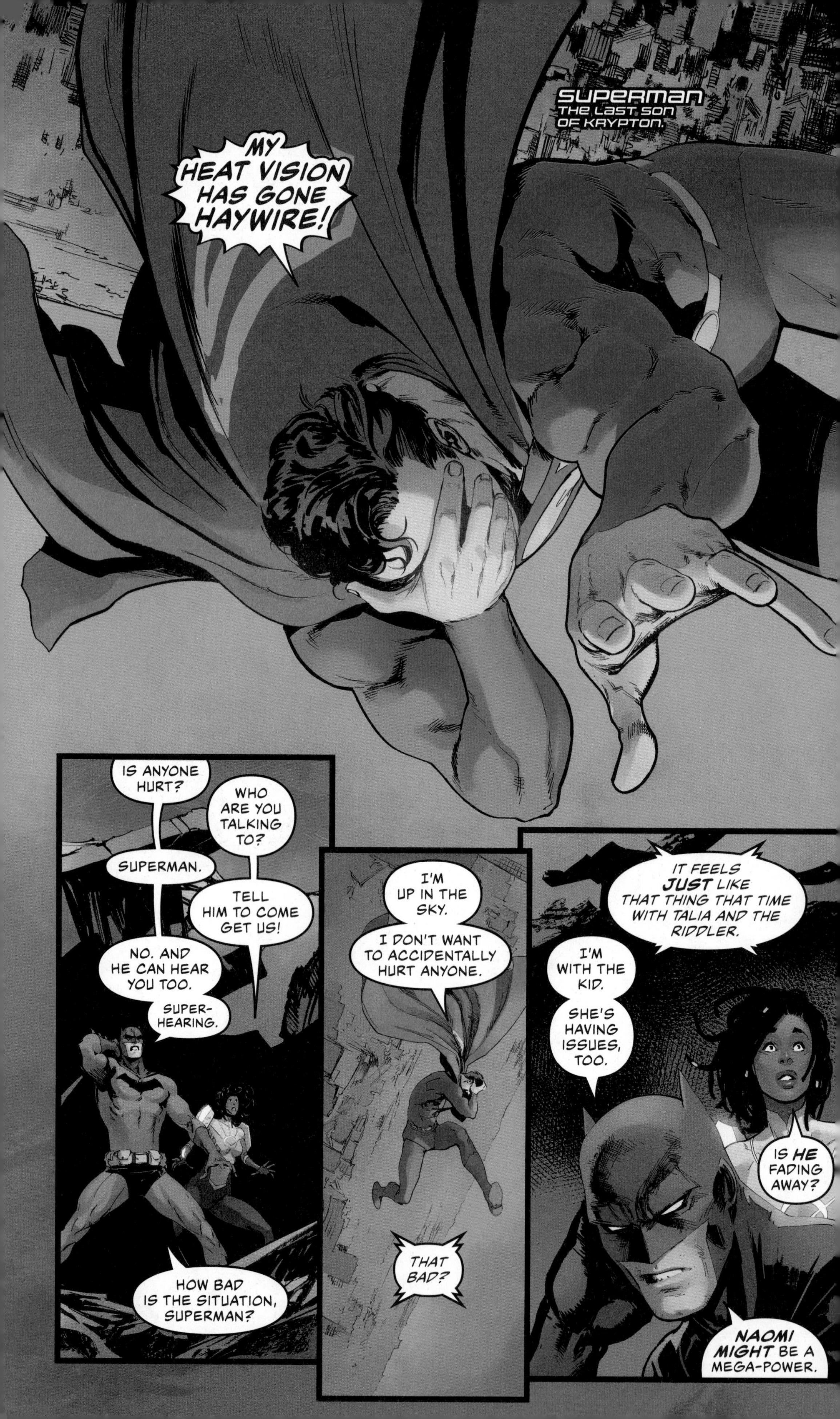
SUPERMAN
THE LAST SON OF KRYPTON.
MY HEAT VISION HAS GONE HAYWIRE!
IS ANYONE HURT?
WHO ARE YOU TALKING TO?
SUPERMAN.
TELL HIM TO COME GET US!
NO. AND HE CAN HEAR YOU TOO.
SUPER-HEARING.
HOW BAD IS THE SITUATION, SUPERMAN?
I'M UP IN THE SKY.
I DON'T WANT TO ACCIDENTALLY HURT ANYONE.
THAT BAD?
IT FEELS JUST LIKE THAT THING THAT TIME WITH TALIA AND THE RIDDLER.
I'M WITH THE KID.
SHE'S HAVING ISSUES, TOO.
IS HE FADING AWAY?
NAOMI MIGHT BE A MEGA-POWER.

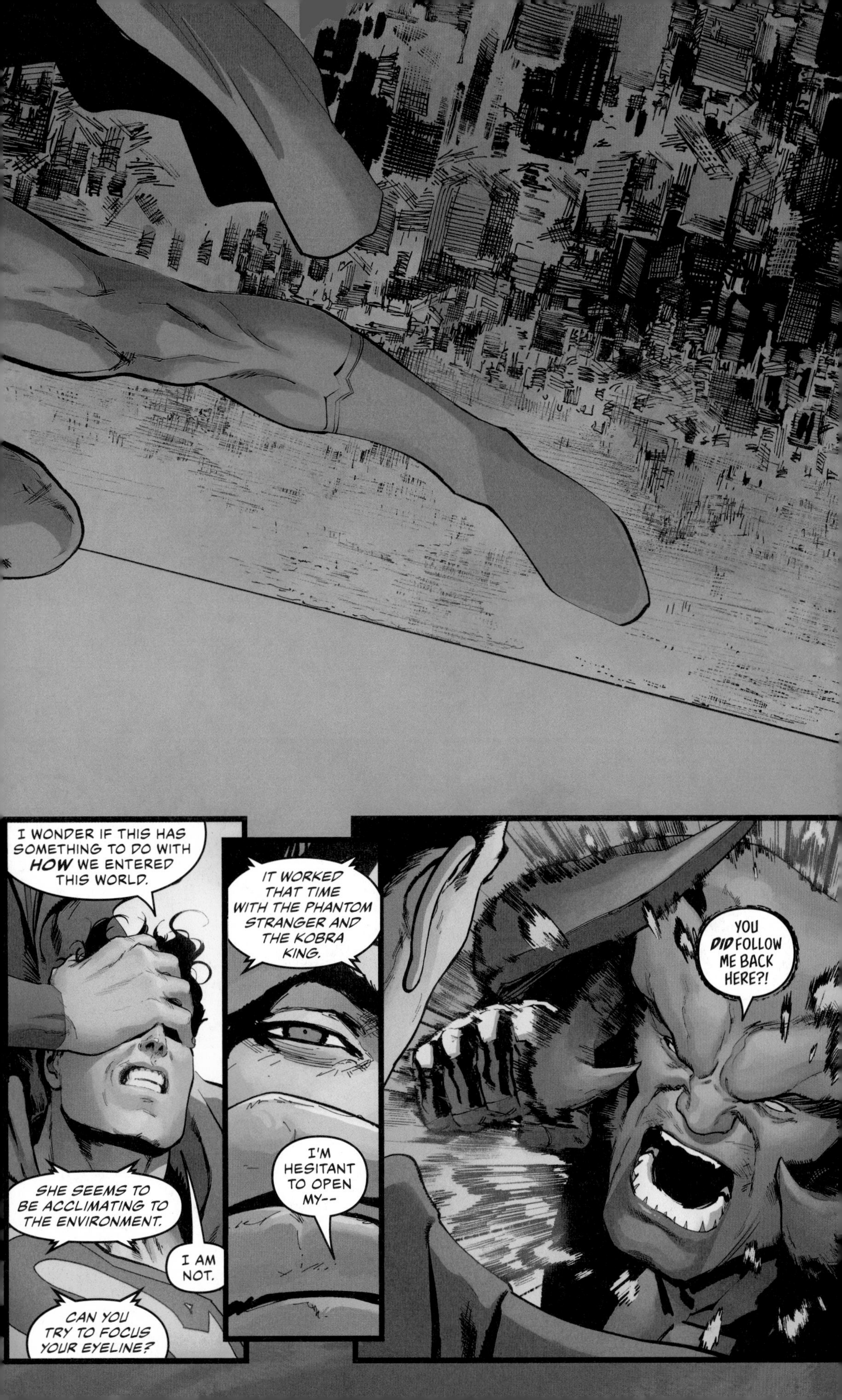

I WONDER IF THIS HAS SOMETHING TO DO WITH HOW WE ENTERED THIS WORLD.
SHE SEEMS TO BE ACCLIMATING TO THE ENVIRONMENT.
I AM NOT.
CAN YOU TRY TO FOCUS YOUR EYELINE?
IT WORKED THAT TIME WITH THE PHANTOM STRANGER AND THE KOBRA KING.
I'M HESITANT TO OPEN MY--
YOU DID FOLLOW ME BACK HERE?!

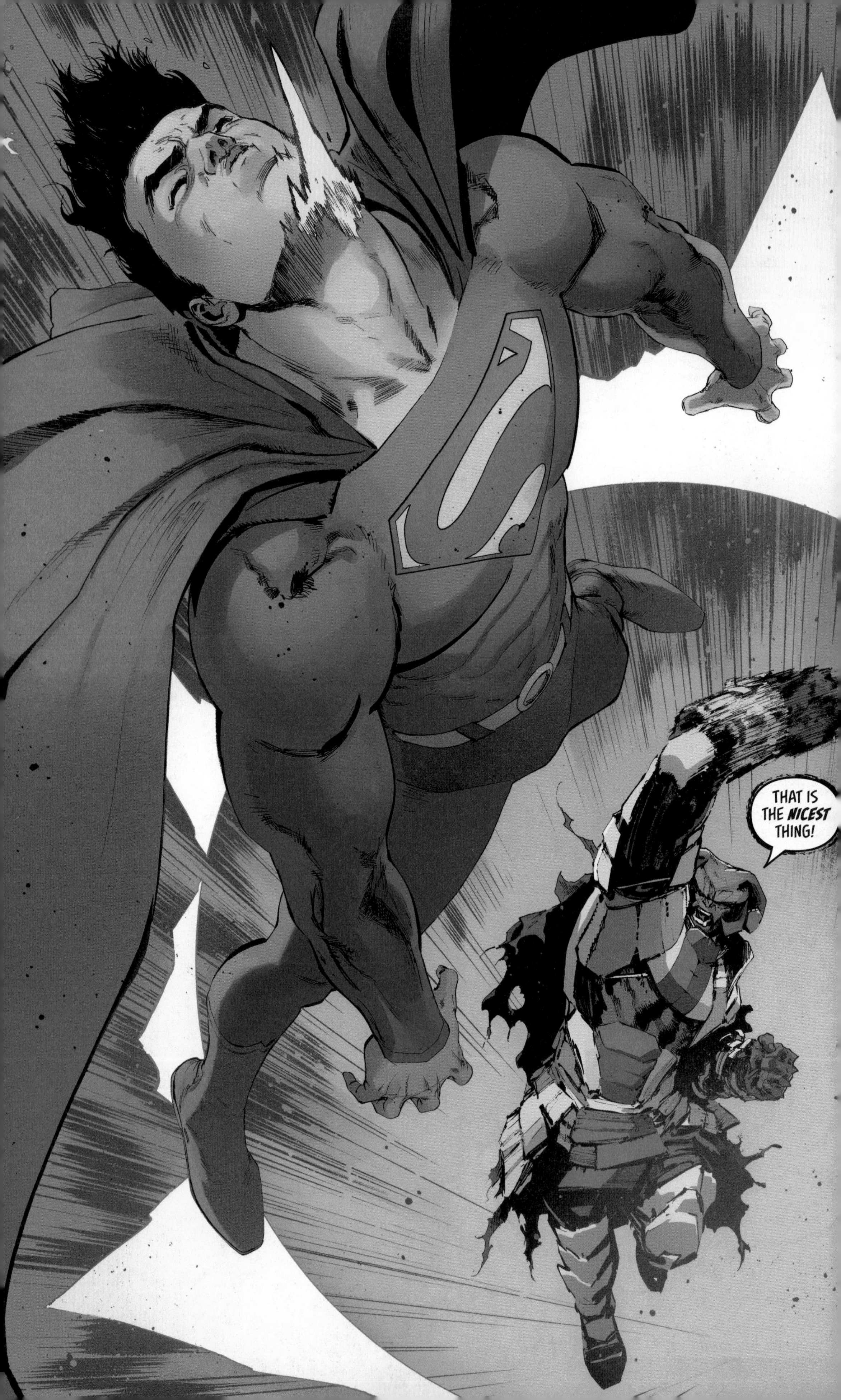
THAT IS THE NICEST THING!

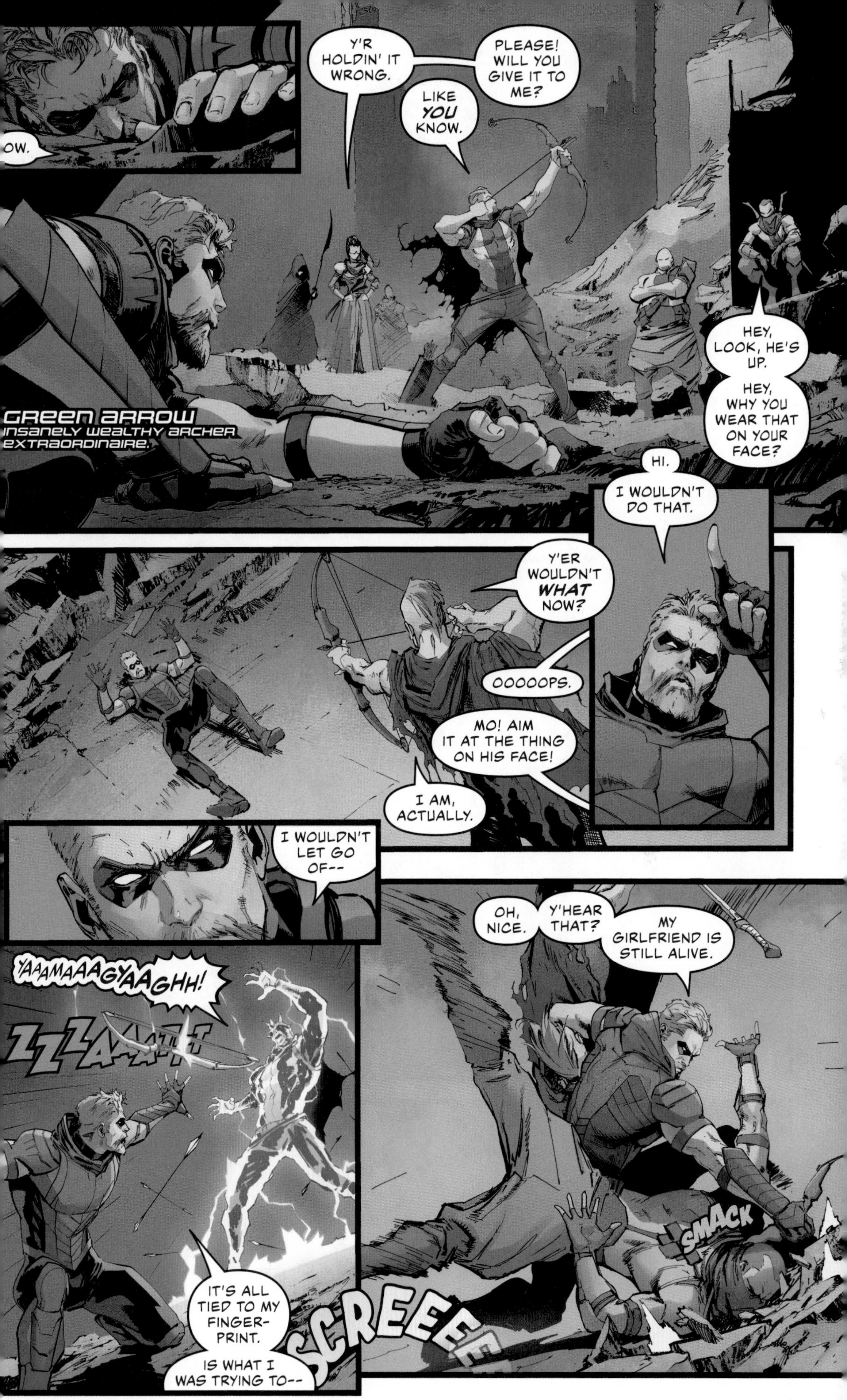
OW.
Y'R HOLDIN' IT WRONG.
PLEASE! WILL YOU GIVE IT TO ME?
LIKE *YOU* KNOW.
GREEN ARROW
INSANELY WEALTHY ARCHER EXTRAORDINAIRE.
HEY, LOOK, HE'S UP.
HEY, WHY YOU WEAR THAT ON YOUR FACE?
HI.
I WOULDN'T DO THAT.
Y'ER WOULDN'T *WHAT* NOW?
OOOOOPS.
MO! AIM IT AT THE THING ON HIS FACE!
I AM, ACTUALLY.
I WOULDN'T LET GO OF--
YAAAMAAAGYAAGHH!
ZZZAAAT
IT'S ALL TIED TO MY FINGER-PRINT.
IS WHAT I WAS TRYING TO--
SCREEEE
OH, NICE.
Y'HEAR THAT?
MY GIRLFRIEND IS STILL ALIVE.
SMACK

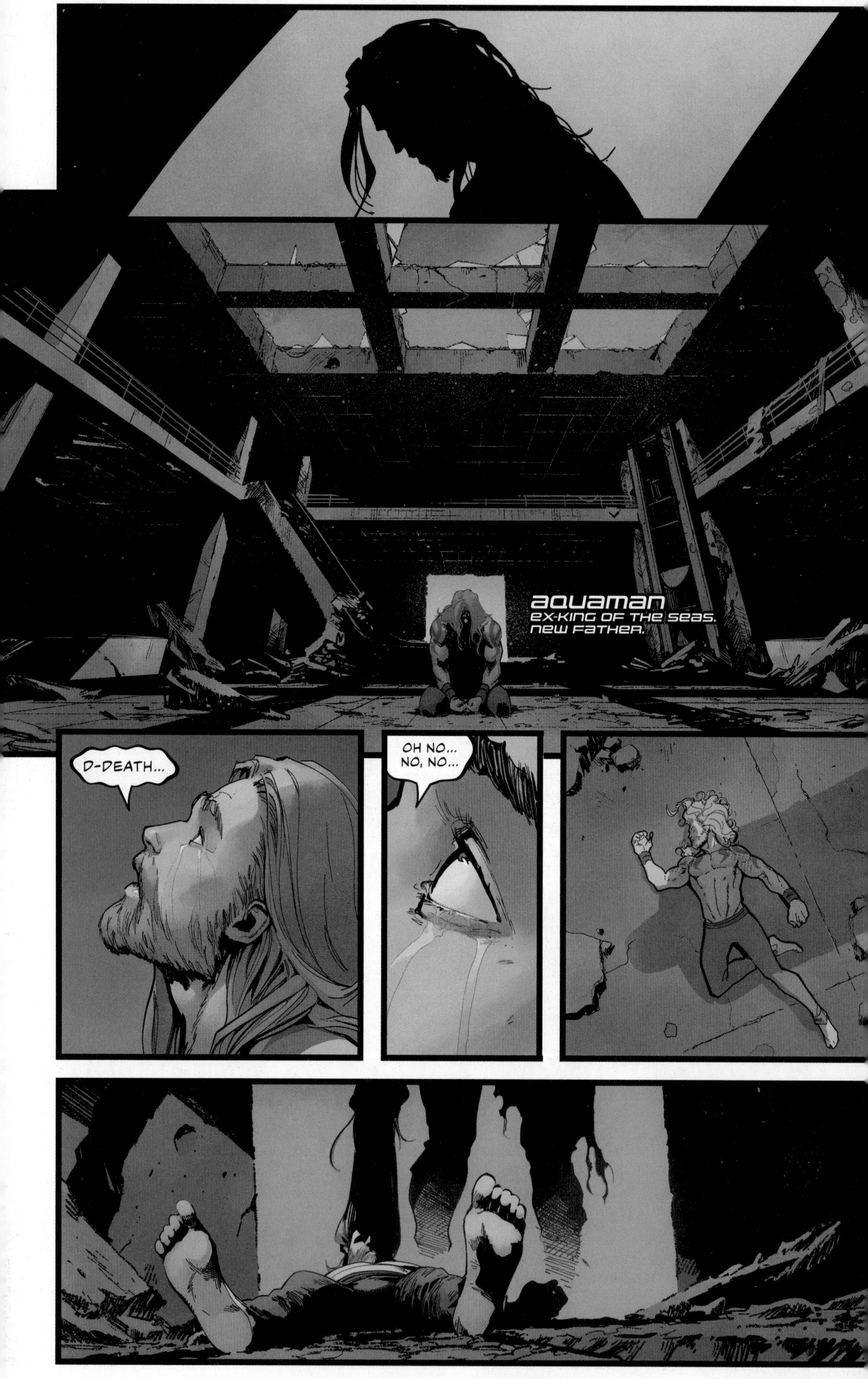
AQUAMAN
EX-KING OF THE SEAS.
NEW FATHER.
D-DEATH...
OH NO...
NO, NO...

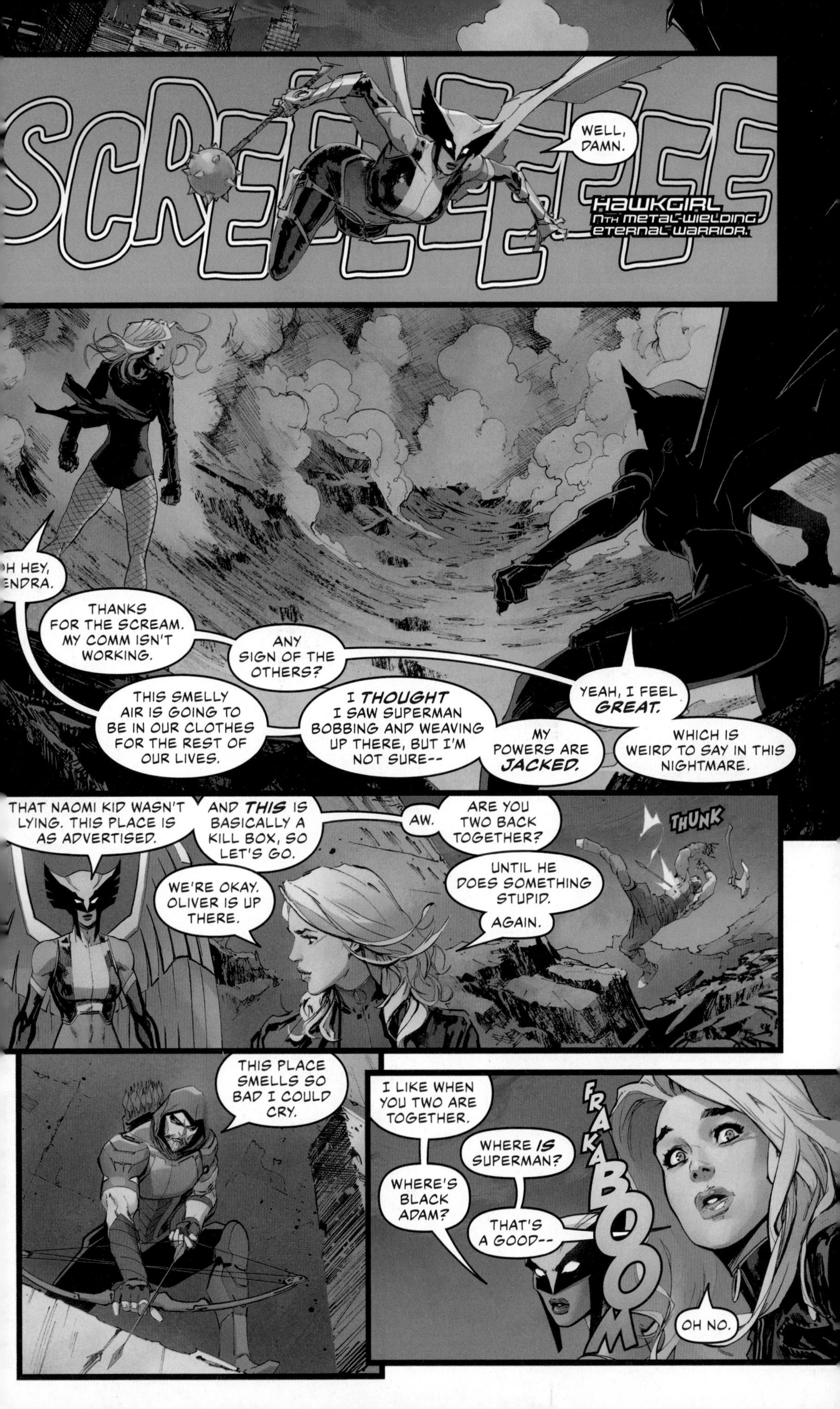
SCREEEEEEE
WELL, DAMN.
HAWKGIRL
NTH METAL-WIELDING ETERNAL WARRIOR.
OH HEY, ENDRA.
THANKS FOR THE SCREAM. MY COMM ISN'T WORKING.
ANY SIGN OF THE OTHERS?
YEAH, I FEEL GREAT.
THIS SMELLY AIR IS GOING TO BE IN OUR CLOTHES FOR THE REST OF OUR LIVES.
I THOUGHT I SAW SUPERMAN BOBBING AND WEAVING UP THERE, BUT I'M NOT SURE--
MY POWERS ARE JACKED.
WHICH IS WEIRD TO SAY IN THIS NIGHTMARE.
THAT NAOMI KID WASN'T LYING. THIS PLACE IS AS ADVERTISED.
AND THIS IS BASICALLY A KILL BOX, SO LET'S GO.
AW.
ARE YOU TWO BACK TOGETHER?
THUNK
WE'RE OKAY. OLIVER IS UP THERE.
UNTIL HE DOES SOMETHING STUPID.
AGAIN.
THIS PLACE SMELLS SO BAD I COULD CRY.
I LIKE WHEN YOU TWO ARE TOGETHER.
WHERE IS SUPERMAN?
WHERE'S BLACK ADAM?
THAT'S A GOOD--
FRAKABOOOM
OH NO.

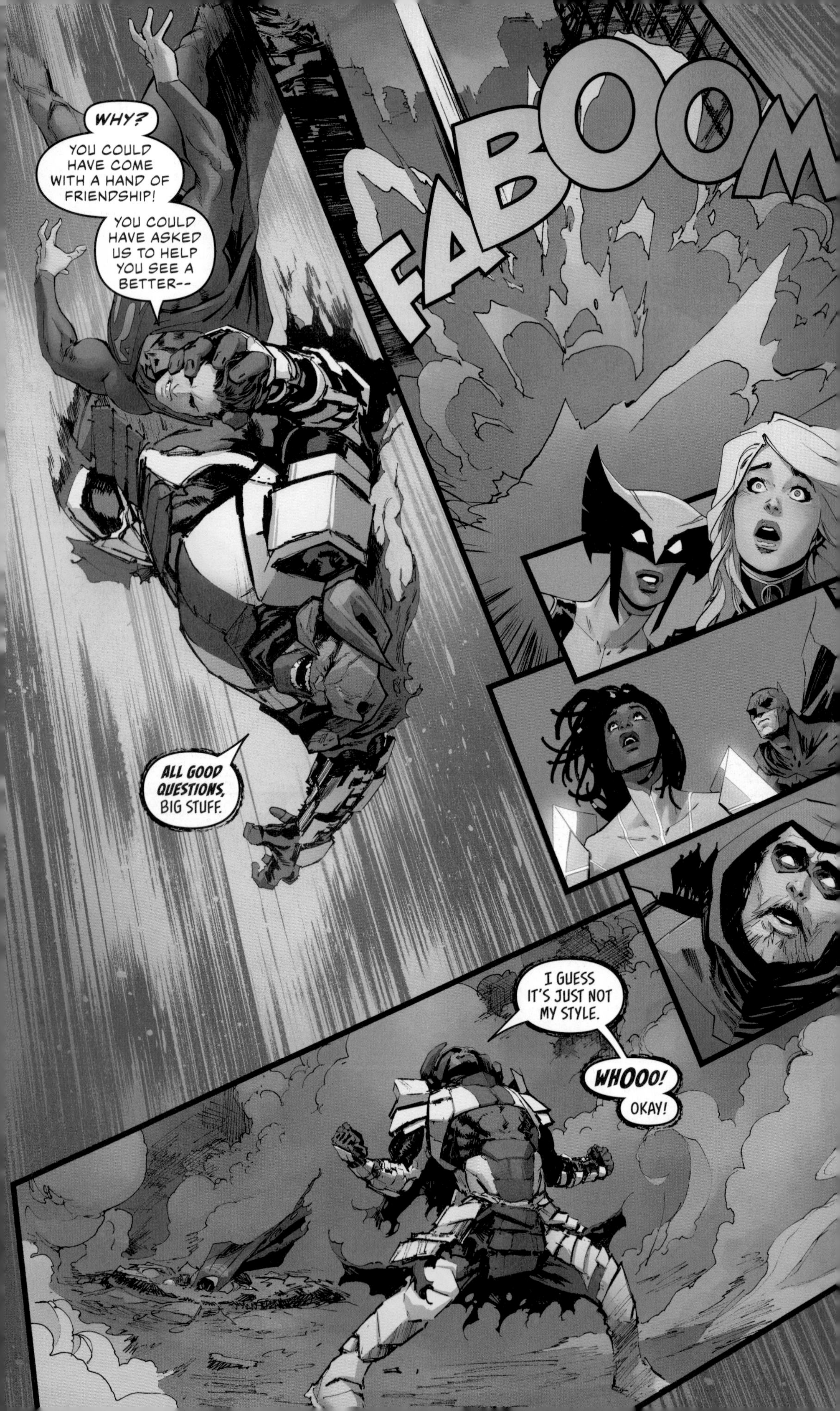

WHY?
YOU COULD HAVE COME WITH A HAND OF FRIENDSHIP!
YOU COULD HAVE ASKED US TO HELP YOU SEE A BETTER--
FABOOM
ALL GOOD QUESTIONS, BIG STUFF.
I GUESS IT'S JUST NOT MY STYLE.
WHOOO!
OKAY!

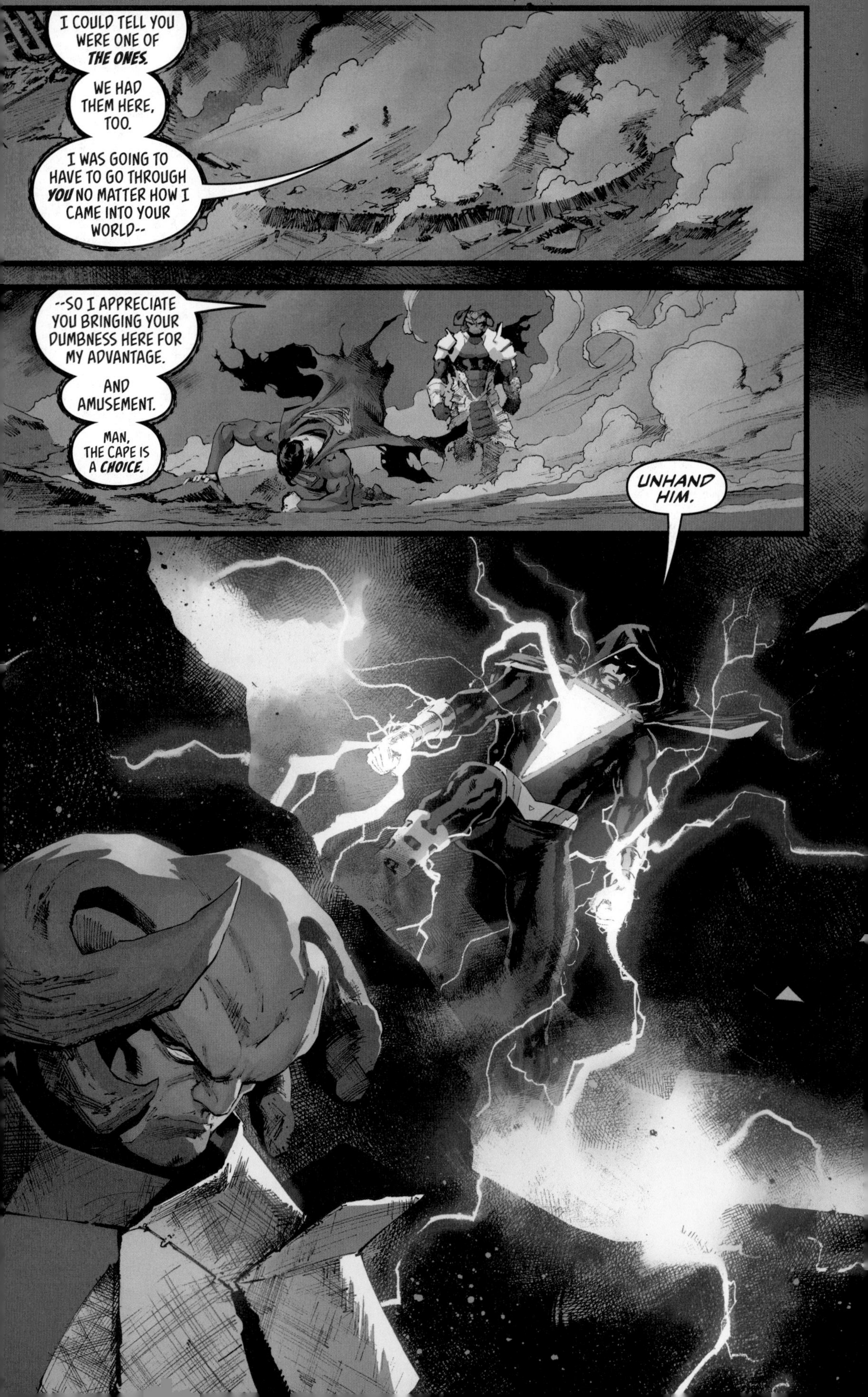
I COULD TELL YOU WERE ONE OF *THE ONES.*
WE HAD THEM HERE, TOO.
I WAS GOING TO HAVE TO GO THROUGH *YOU* NO MATTER HOW I CAME INTO YOUR WORLD--
--SO I APPRECIATE YOU BRINGING YOUR DUMBNESS HERE FOR MY ADVANTAGE.
AND AMUSEMENT.
MAN, THE CAPE IS A *CHOICE.*
UNHAND HIM.

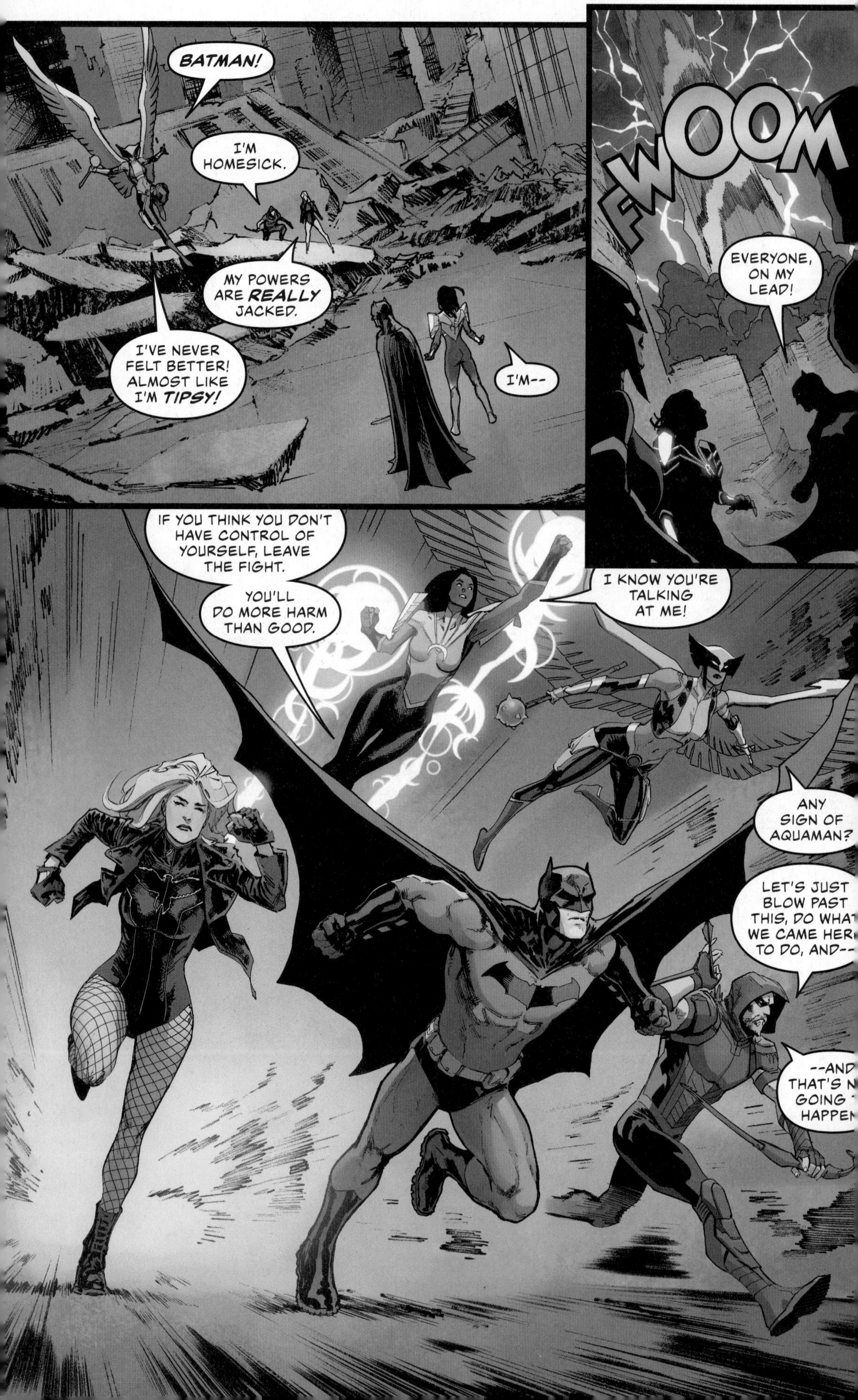
BATMAN!
I'M HOMESICK.
MY POWERS ARE REALLY JACKED.
I'VE NEVER FELT BETTER! ALMOST LIKE I'M TIPSY!
I'M--
FWOOOM
EVERYONE, ON MY LEAD!
IF YOU THINK YOU DON'T HAVE CONTROL OF YOURSELF, LEAVE THE FIGHT.
YOU'LL DO MORE HARM THAN GOOD.
I KNOW YOU'RE TALKING AT ME!
ANY SIGN OF AQUAMAN?
LET'S JUST BLOW PAST THIS, DO WHAT WE CAME HERE TO DO, AND--
--AND THAT'S N GOING HAPPEN

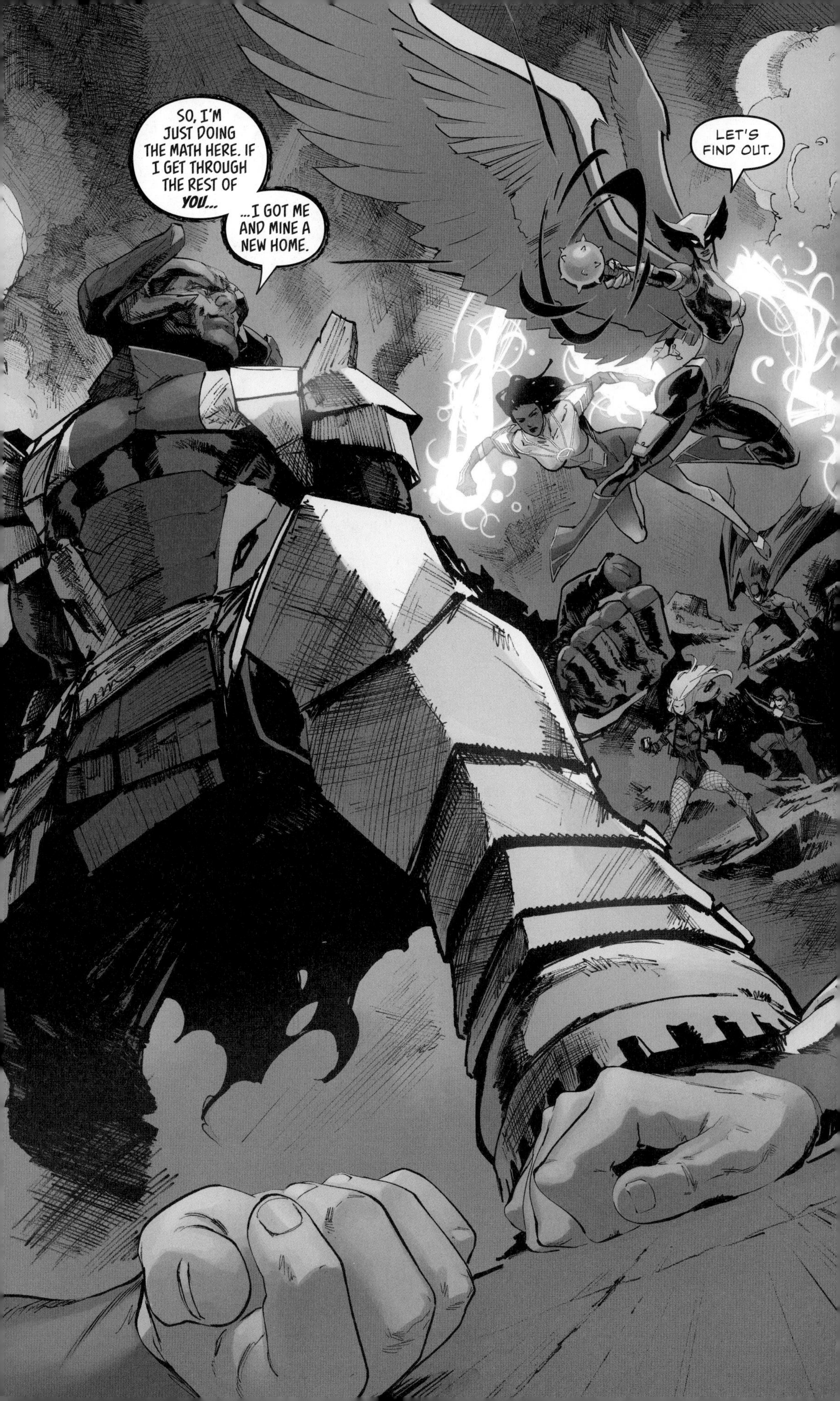
SO, I'M JUST DOING THE MATH HERE. IF I GET THROUGH THE REST OF ***YOU...***
...I GOT ME AND MINE A NEW HOME.
LET'S FIND OUT.

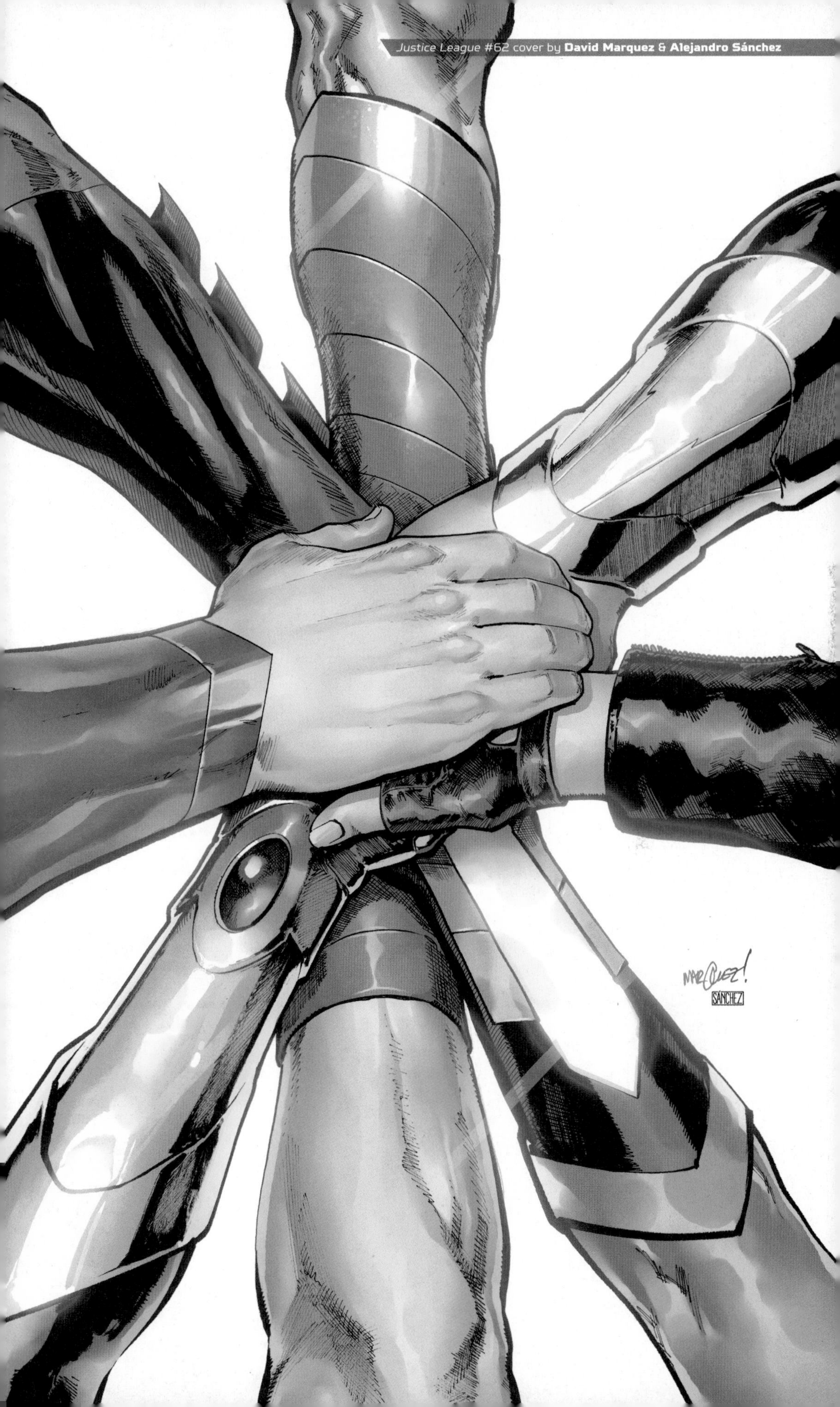
MARQUEZ!
SÁNCHEZ
Justice League #62 cover by **David Marquez & Alejandro Sánchez**

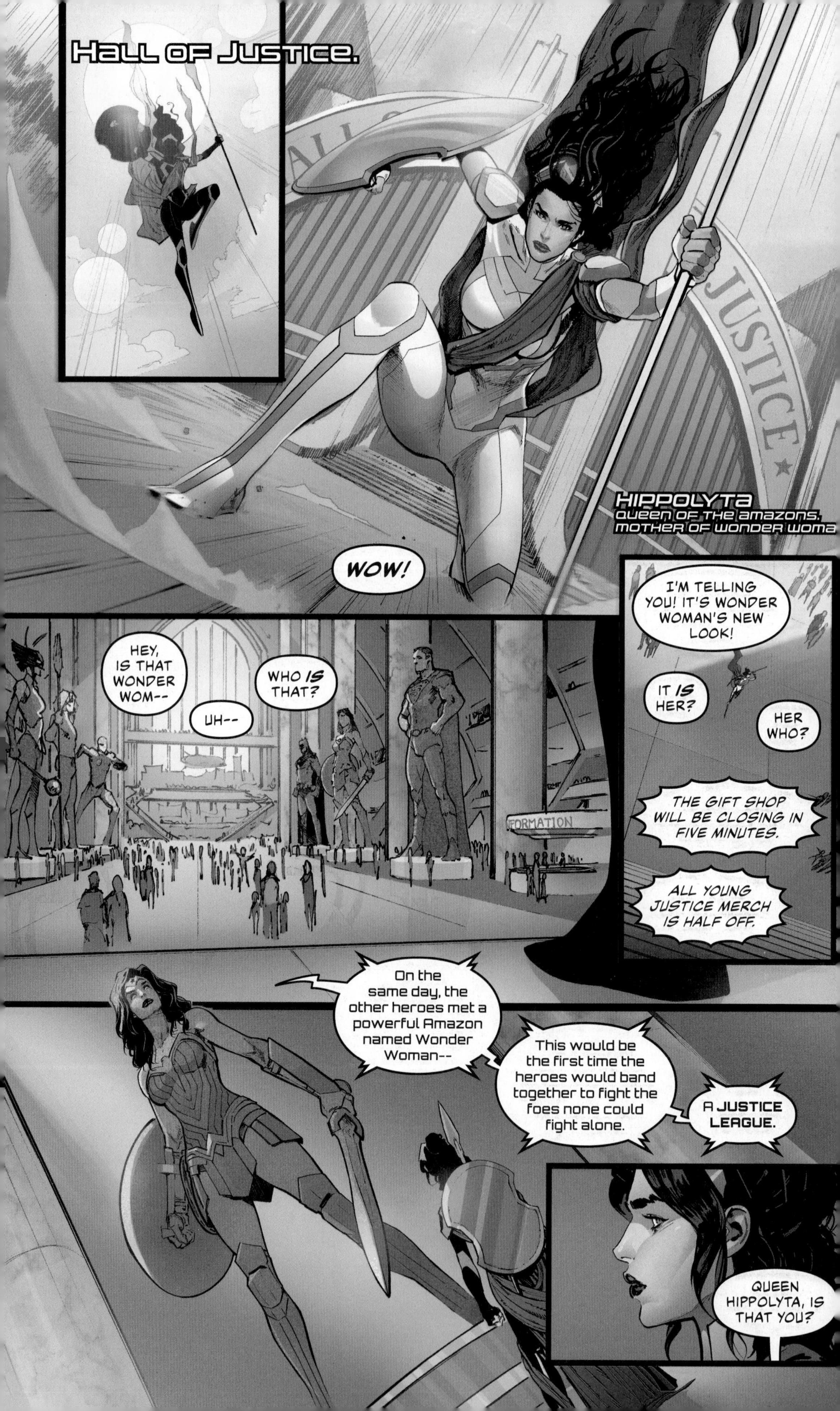
HALL OF JUSTICE.
HIPPOLYTA
QUEEN OF THE AMAZONS.
MOTHER OF WONDER WOMA
WOW!
I'M TELLING YOU! IT'S WONDER WOMAN'S NEW LOOK!
IT *IS* HER?
HER WHO?
THE GIFT SHOP WILL BE CLOSING IN FIVE MINUTES.
ALL YOUNG JUSTICE MERCH IS HALF OFF.
HEY, IS THAT WONDER WOM--
UH--
WHO *IS* THAT?
FORMATION
On the same day, the other heroes met a powerful Amazon named Wonder Woman--
This would be the first time the heroes would band together to fight the foes none could fight alone.
A **JUSTICE LEAGUE.**
QUEEN HIPPOLYTA, IS THAT YOU?

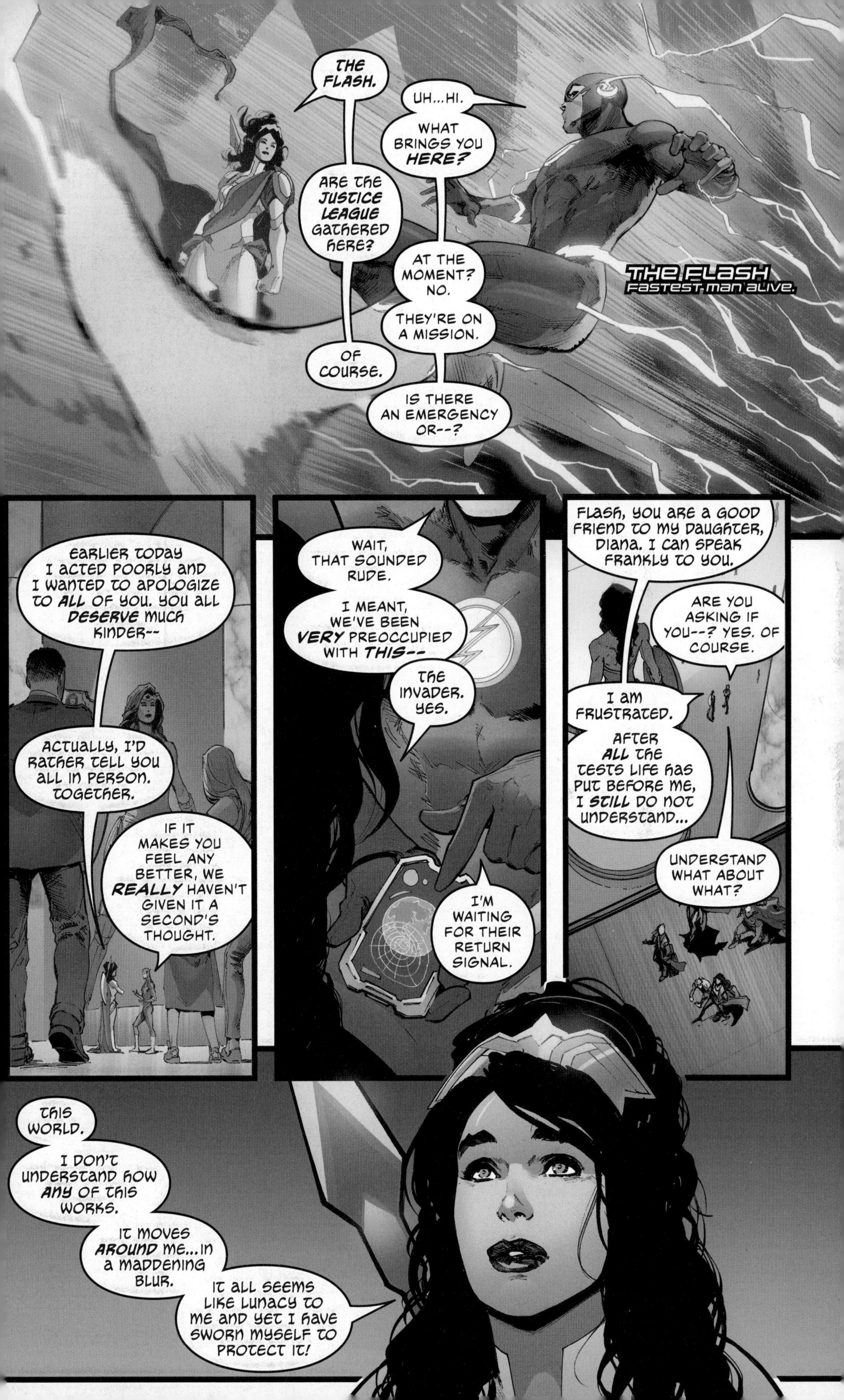
THE FLASH.
UH...HI.
WHAT BRINGS YOU HERE?
ARE THE JUSTICE LEAGUE GATHERED HERE?
AT THE MOMENT? NO.
THEY'RE ON A MISSION.
OF COURSE.
IS THERE AN EMERGENCY OR--?
THE FLASH
FASTEST MAN ALIVE.
EARLIER TODAY I ACTED POORLY AND I WANTED TO APOLOGIZE TO ALL OF YOU. YOU ALL DESERVE MUCH KINDER--
ACTUALLY, I'D RATHER TELL YOU ALL IN PERSON. TOGETHER.
IF IT MAKES YOU FEEL ANY BETTER, WE REALLY HAVEN'T GIVEN IT A SECOND'S THOUGHT.
WAIT, THAT SOUNDED RUDE.
I MEANT, WE'VE BEEN VERY PREOCCUPIED WITH THIS--
THE INVADER. YES.
I'M WAITING FOR THEIR RETURN SIGNAL.
FLASH, YOU ARE A GOOD FRIEND TO MY DAUGHTER, DIANA. I CAN SPEAK FRANKLY TO YOU.
ARE YOU ASKING IF YOU--? YES. OF COURSE.
I AM FRUSTRATED.
AFTER ALL THE TESTS LIFE HAS PUT BEFORE ME, I STILL DO NOT UNDERSTAND...
UNDERSTAND WHAT ABOUT WHAT?
THIS WORLD.
I DON'T UNDERSTAND HOW ANY OF THIS WORKS.
IT MOVES AROUND ME...IN A MADDENING BLUR.
IT ALL SEEMS LIKE LUNACY TO ME AND YET I HAVE SWORN MYSELF TO PROTECT IT!

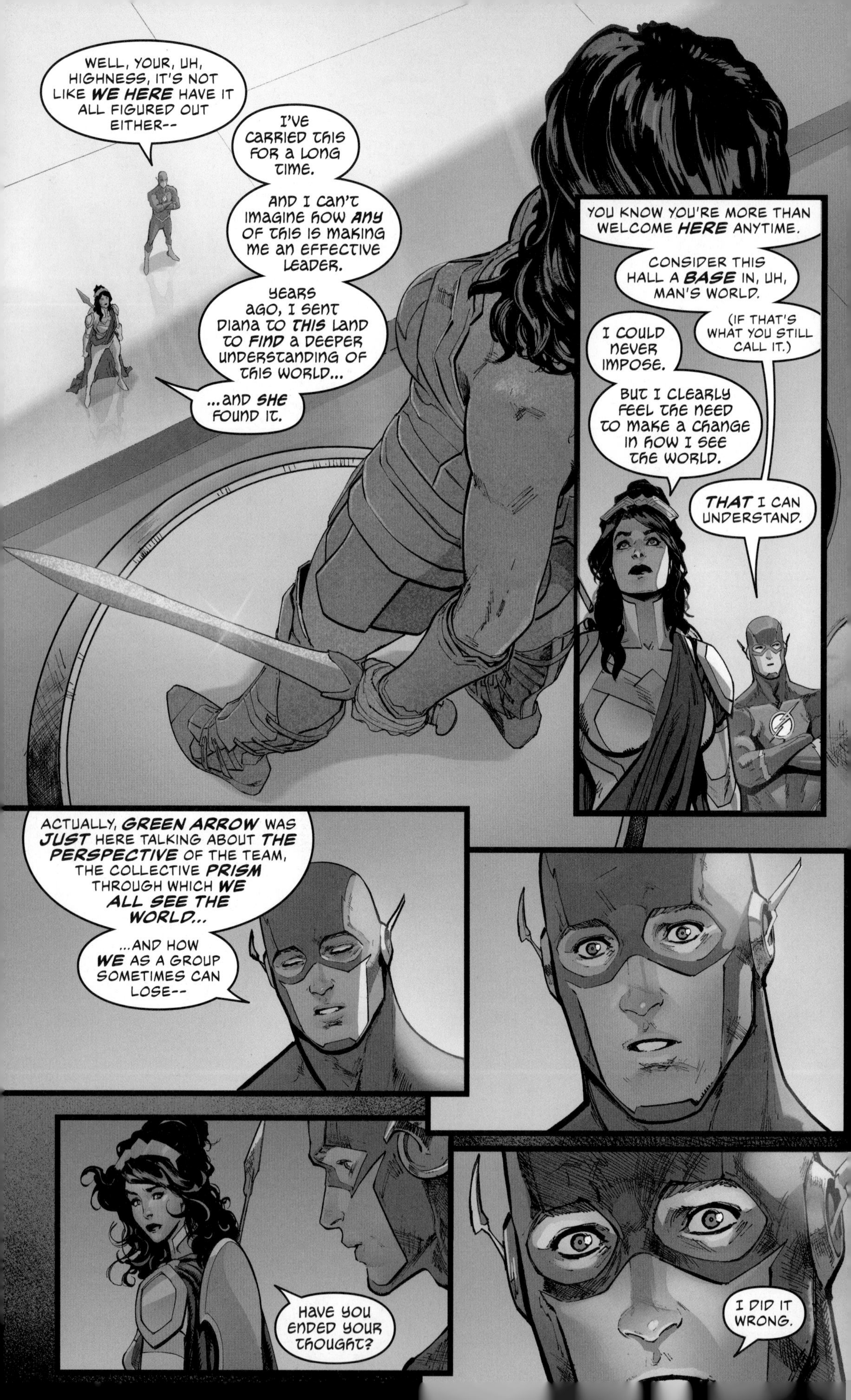
WELL, YOUR, UH, HIGHNESS, IT'S NOT LIKE WE HERE HAVE IT ALL FIGURED OUT EITHER--
I'VE CARRIED THIS FOR A LONG TIME.
AND I CAN'T IMAGINE HOW ANY OF THIS IS MAKING ME AN EFFECTIVE LEADER.
YEARS AGO, I SENT DIANA TO THIS LAND TO FIND A DEEPER UNDERSTANDING OF THIS WORLD...
...AND SHE FOUND IT.
YOU KNOW YOU'RE MORE THAN WELCOME HERE ANYTIME.
CONSIDER THIS HALL A BASE IN, UH, MAN'S WORLD.
(IF THAT'S WHAT YOU STILL CALL IT.)
I COULD NEVER IMPOSE.
BUT I CLEARLY FEEL THE NEED TO MAKE A CHANGE IN HOW I SEE THE WORLD.
THAT I CAN UNDERSTAND.
ACTUALLY, GREEN ARROW WAS JUST HERE TALKING ABOUT THE PERSPECTIVE OF THE TEAM, THE COLLECTIVE PRISM THROUGH WHICH WE ALL SEE THE WORLD...
...AND HOW WE AS A GROUP SOMETIMES CAN LOSE--
HAVE YOU ENDED YOUR THOUGHT?
I DID IT WRONG.

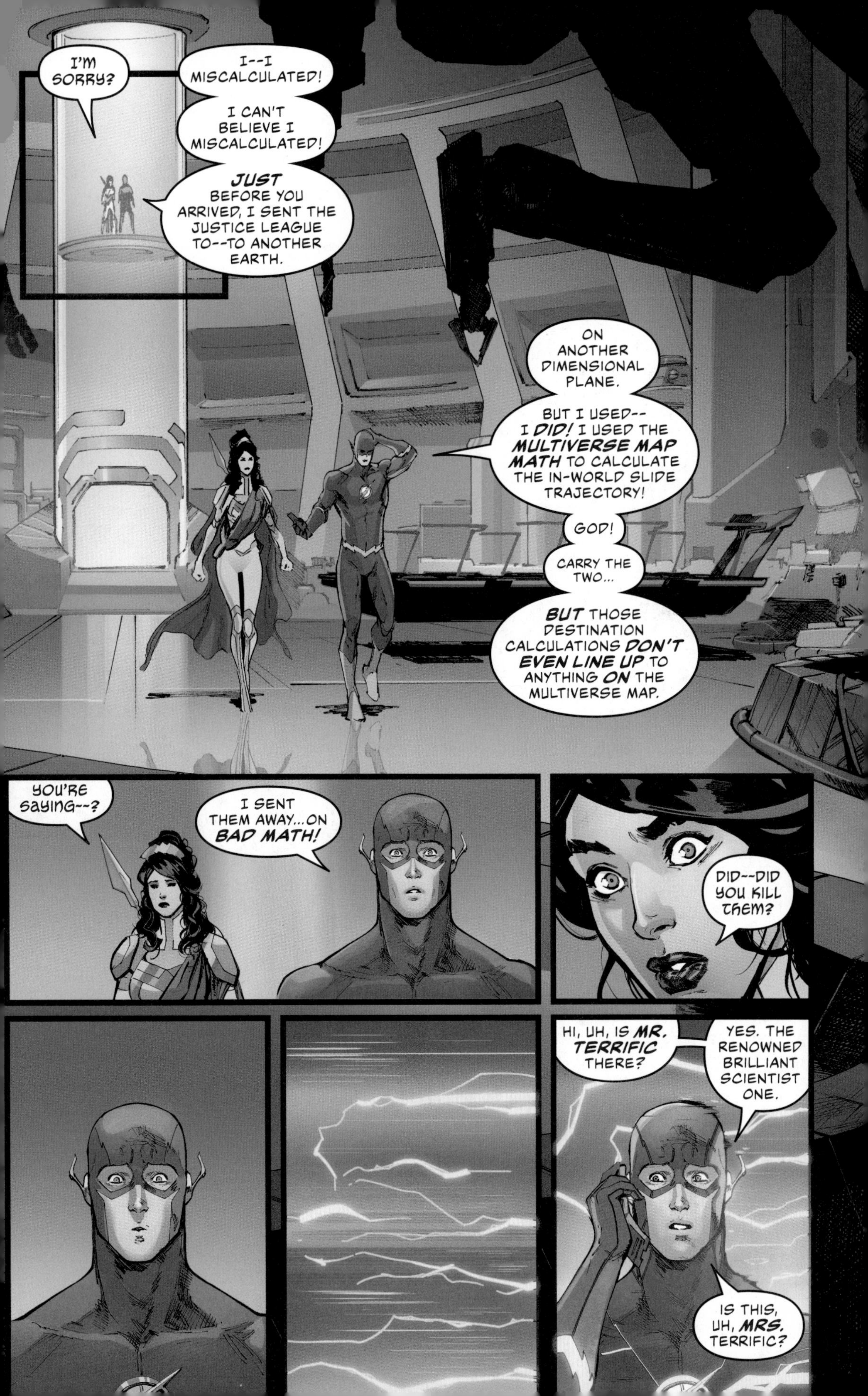

I'M SORRY?
I--I MISCALCULATED!
I CAN'T BELIEVE I MISCALCULATED!
JUST BEFORE YOU ARRIVED, I SENT THE JUSTICE LEAGUE TO--TO ANOTHER EARTH.
ON ANOTHER DIMENSIONAL PLANE.
BUT I USED-- I DID! I USED THE MULTIVERSE MAP MATH TO CALCULATE THE IN-WORLD SLIDE TRAJECTORY!
GOD!
CARRY THE TWO...
BUT THOSE DESTINATION CALCULATIONS DON'T EVEN LINE UP TO ANYTHING ON THE MULTIVERSE MAP.
YOU'RE SAYING--?
I SENT THEM AWAY...ON BAD MATH!
DID--DID YOU KILL THEM?
HI, UH, IS MR. TERRIFIC THERE?
YES. THE RENOWNED BRILLIANT SCIENTIST ONE.
IS THIS, UH, MRS. TERRIFIC?

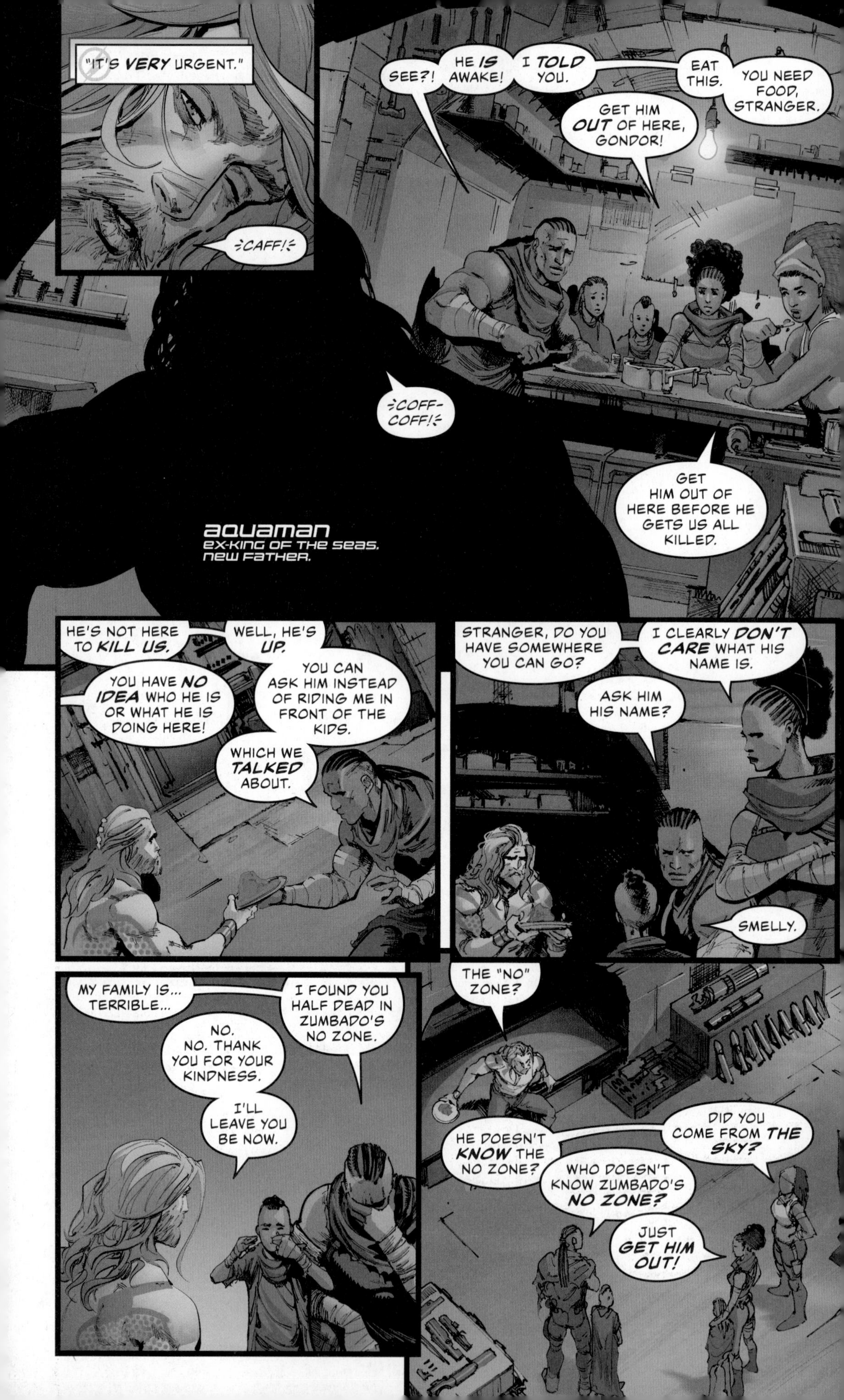
"IT'S VERY URGENT."
CAFF!
SEE?!
HE IS AWAKE!
I TOLD YOU.
EAT THIS.
YOU NEED FOOD, STRANGER.
GET HIM OUT OF HERE, GONDOR!
COFF-COFF!
GET HIM OUT OF HERE BEFORE HE GETS US ALL KILLED.
aquaman
ex-king of the seas.
new father.
HE'S NOT HERE TO KILL US.
WELL, HE'S UP.
YOU HAVE NO IDEA WHO HE IS OR WHAT HE IS DOING HERE!
YOU CAN ASK HIM INSTEAD OF RIDING ME IN FRONT OF THE KIDS.
WHICH WE TALKED ABOUT.
STRANGER, DO YOU HAVE SOMEWHERE YOU CAN GO?
I CLEARLY DON'T CARE WHAT HIS NAME IS.
ASK HIM HIS NAME?
SMELLY.
MY FAMILY IS... TERRIBLE...
I FOUND YOU HALF DEAD IN ZUMBADO'S NO ZONE.
NO. NO. THANK YOU FOR YOUR KINDNESS.
I'LL LEAVE YOU BE NOW.
THE "NO" ZONE?
HE DOESN'T KNOW THE NO ZONE?
DID YOU COME FROM THE SKY?
WHO DOESN'T KNOW ZUMBADO'S NO ZONE?
JUST GET HIM OUT!

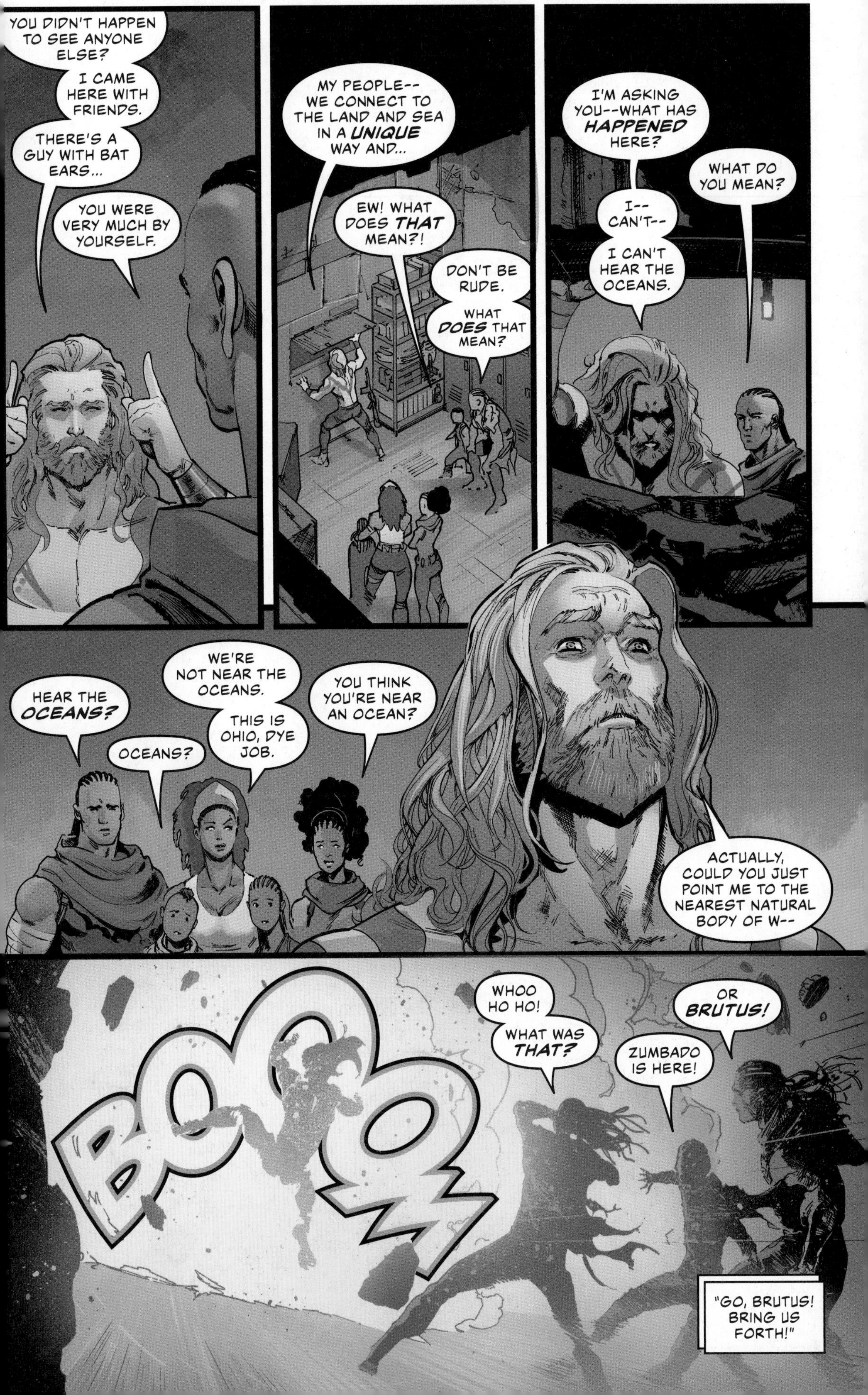

YOU DIDN'T HAPPEN TO SEE ANYONE ELSE?
I CAME HERE WITH FRIENDS.
THERE'S A GUY WITH BAT EARS...
YOU WERE VERY MUCH BY YOURSELF.
MY PEOPLE-- WE CONNECT TO THE LAND AND SEA IN A UNIQUE WAY AND...
EW! WHAT DOES THAT MEAN?!
DON'T BE RUDE.
WHAT DOES THAT MEAN?
I'M ASKING YOU--WHAT HAS HAPPENED HERE?
WHAT DO YOU MEAN?
I-- CAN'T--
I CAN'T HEAR THE OCEANS.
HEAR THE OCEANS?
OCEANS?
WE'RE NOT NEAR THE OCEANS.
THIS IS OHIO, DYE JOB.
YOU THINK YOU'RE NEAR AN OCEAN?
ACTUALLY, COULD YOU JUST POINT ME TO THE NEAREST NATURAL BODY OF W--
BOOOM
WHOO HO HO!
WHAT WAS THAT?
OR BRUTUS!
ZUMBADO IS HERE!
"GO, BRUTUS! BRING US FORTH!"

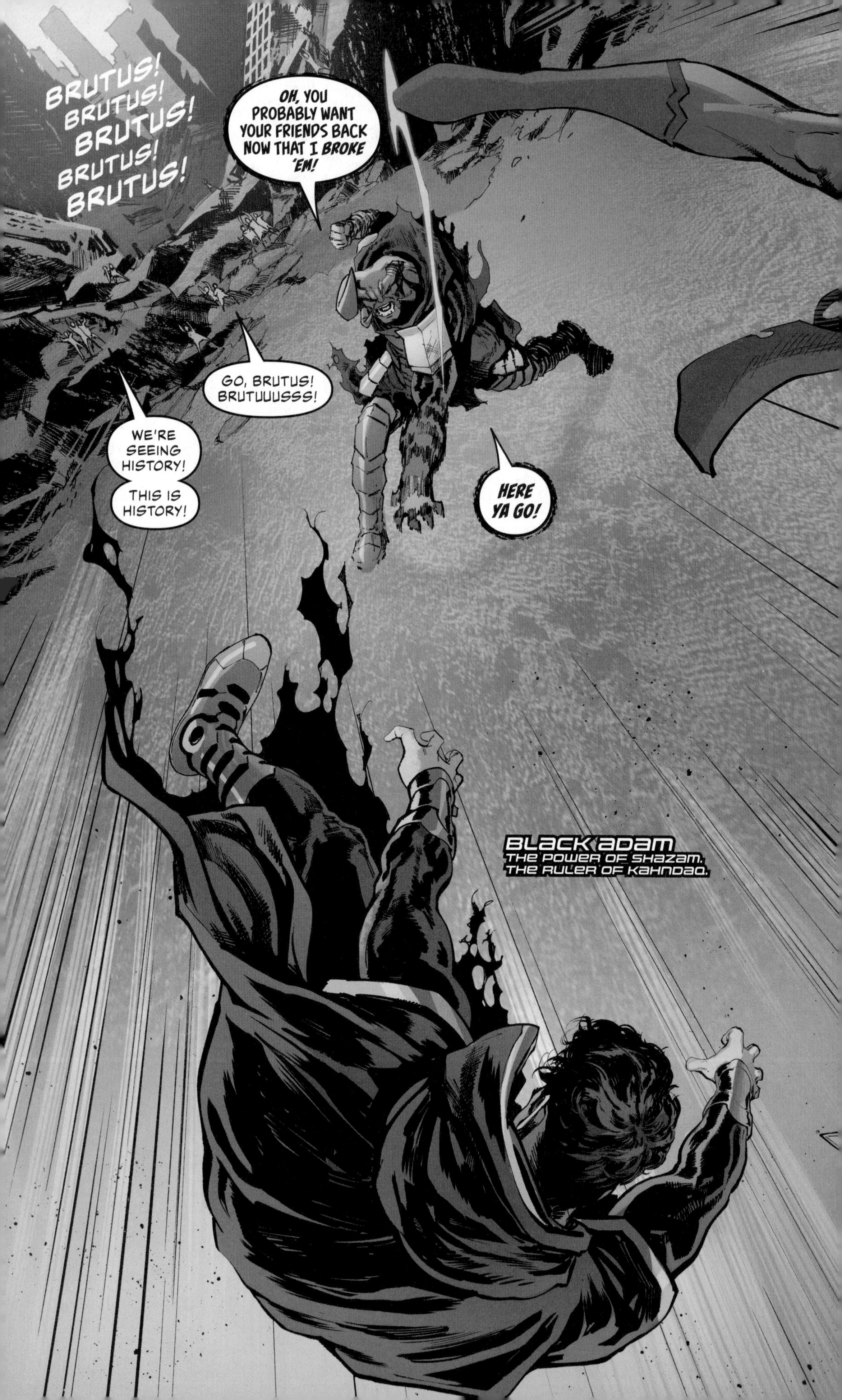
BRUTUS! BRUTUS! BRUTUS! BRUTUS! BRUTUS!
OH, YOU PROBABLY WANT YOUR FRIENDS BACK NOW THAT I BROKE 'EM!
GO, BRUTUS! BRUTUUUSSS!
WE'RE SEEING HISTORY!
THIS IS HISTORY!
HERE YA GO!
BLACK ADAM
THE POWER OF SHAZAM.
THE RULER OF KAHNDAQ.

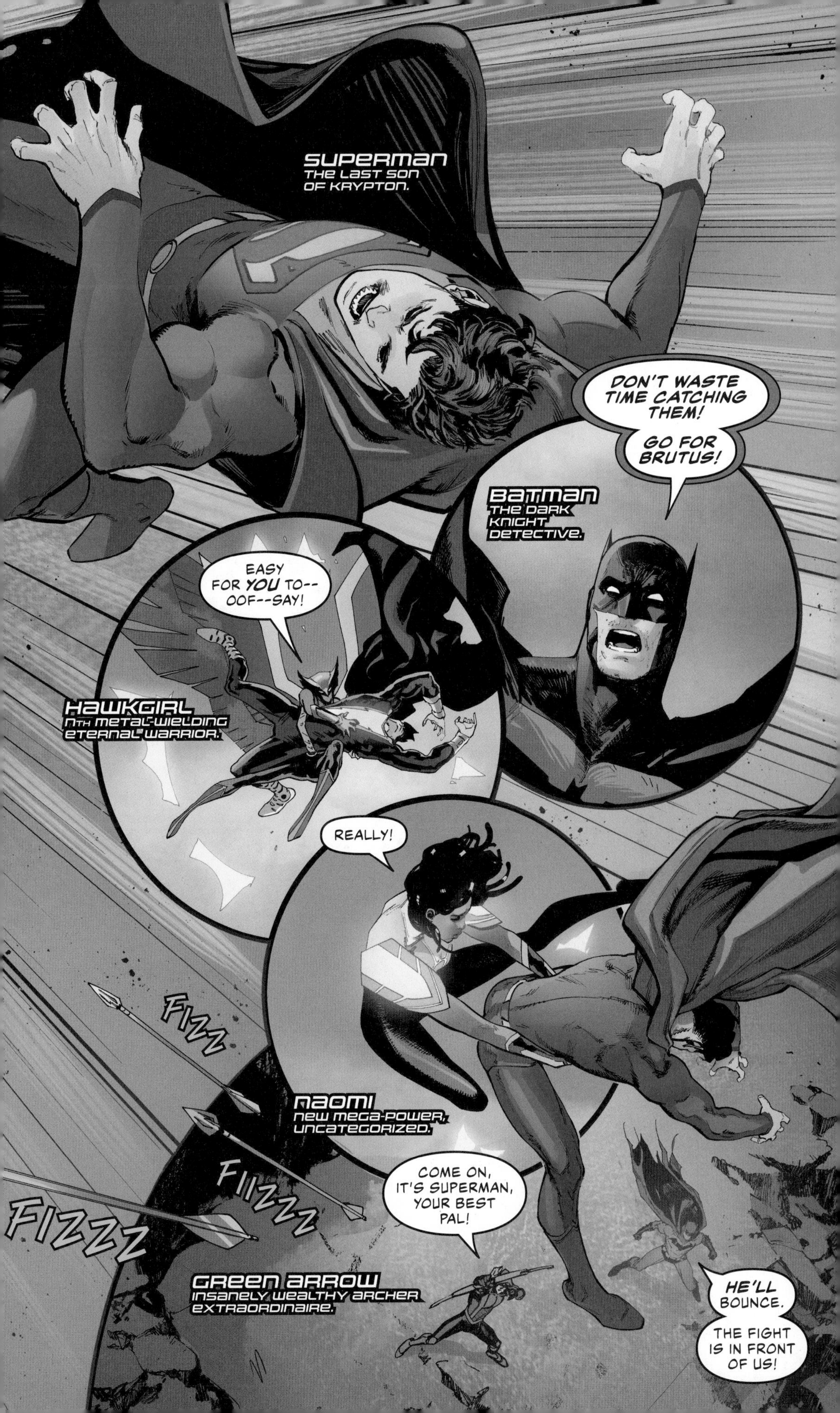
SUPERMAN
THE LAST SON OF KRYPTON.
DON'T WASTE TIME CATCHING THEM!
GO FOR BRUTUS!
BATMAN
THE DARK KNIGHT DETECTIVE.
EASY FOR YOU TO--OOF--SAY!
HAWKGIRL
NTH METAL-WIELDING ETERNAL WARRIOR.
REALLY!
FIZZ
NAOMI
NEW MEGA-POWER, UNCATEGORIZED.
FIIZZZ
FIZZZ
COME ON, IT'S SUPERMAN, YOUR BEST PAL!
GREEN ARROW
INSANELY WEALTHY ARCHER EXTRAORDINAIRE.
HE'LL BOUNCE.
THE FIGHT IS IN FRONT OF US!

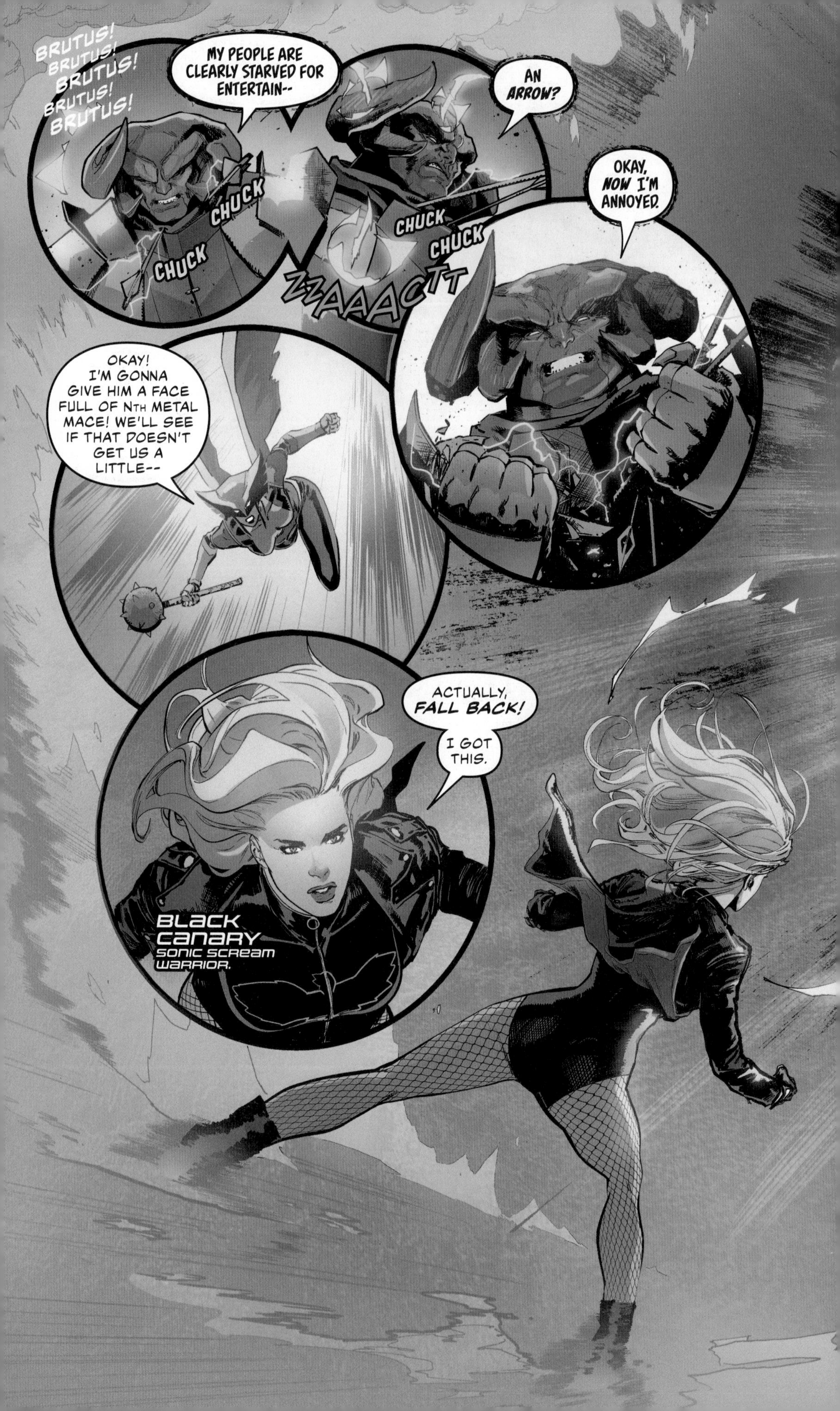
BRUTUS! BRUTUS! BRUTUS! BRUTUS! BRUTUS!
MY PEOPLE ARE CLEARLY STARVED FOR ENTERTAIN--
CHUCK
CHUCK
AN ARROW?
CHUCK
CHUCK
ZZAAACTT
OKAY, NOW I'M ANNOYED.
OKAY! I'M GONNA GIVE HIM A FACE FULL OF NTH METAL MACE! WE'LL SEE IF THAT DOESN'T GET US A LITTLE--
ACTUALLY, FALL BACK!
I GOT THIS.
BLACK CANARY
SONIC SCREAM WARRIOR.

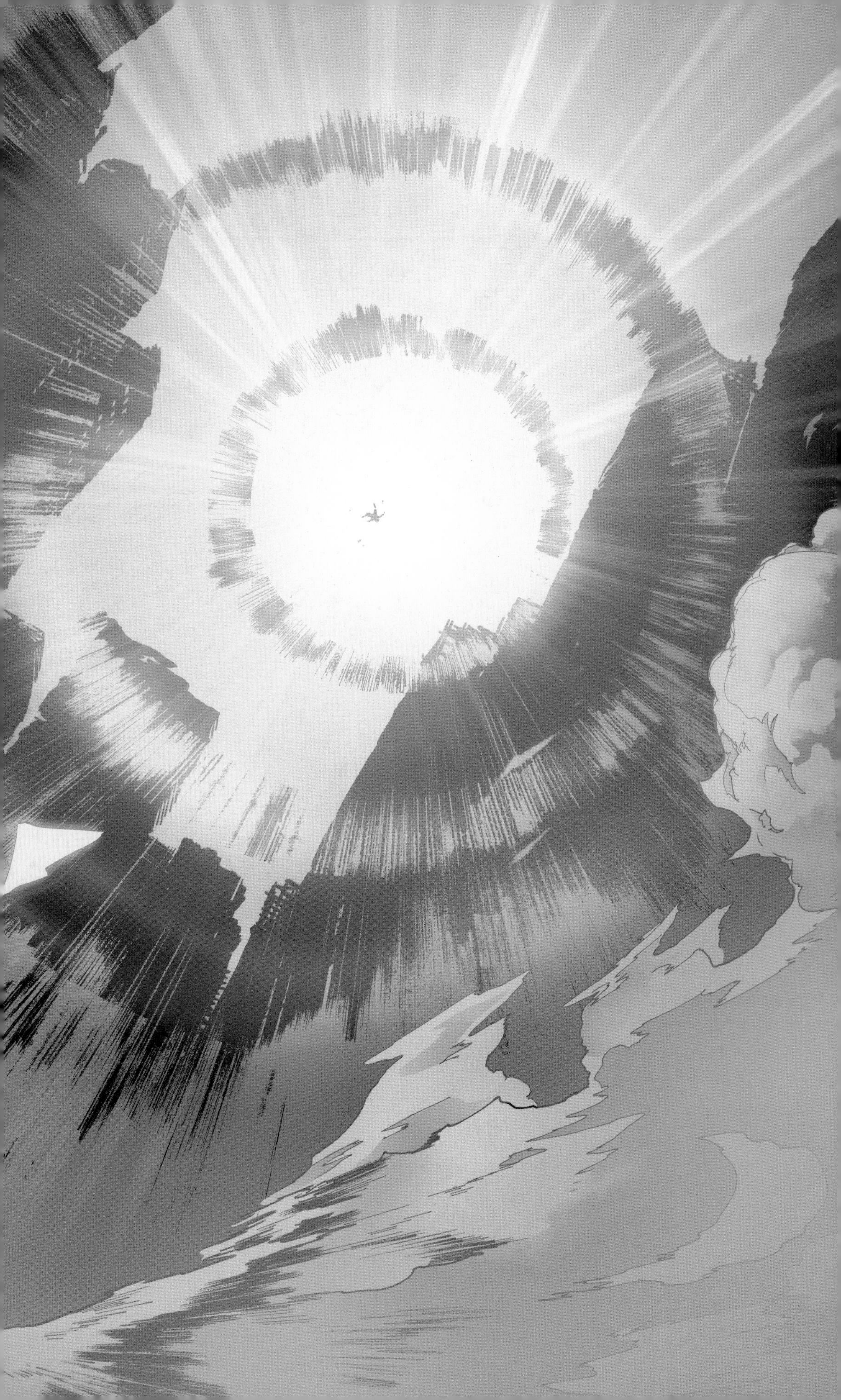

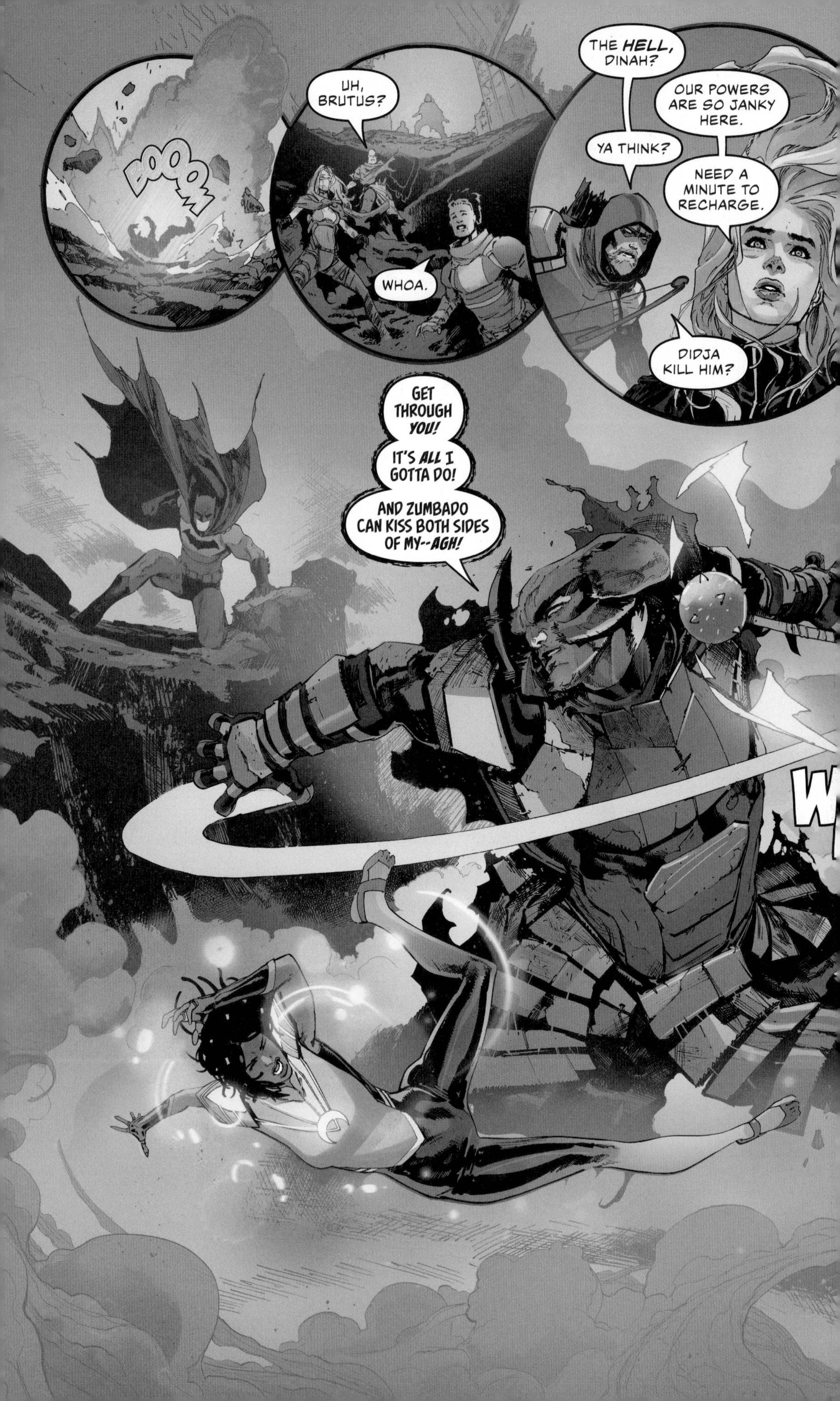
BOOOM
UH, BRUTUS?
WHOA.
THE HELL, DINAH?
YA THINK?
OUR POWERS ARE SO JANKY HERE.
NEED A MINUTE TO RECHARGE.
DIDJA KILL HIM?
GET THROUGH YOU!
IT'S ALL I GOTTA DO!
AND ZUMBADO CAN KISS BOTH SIDES OF MY--AGH!

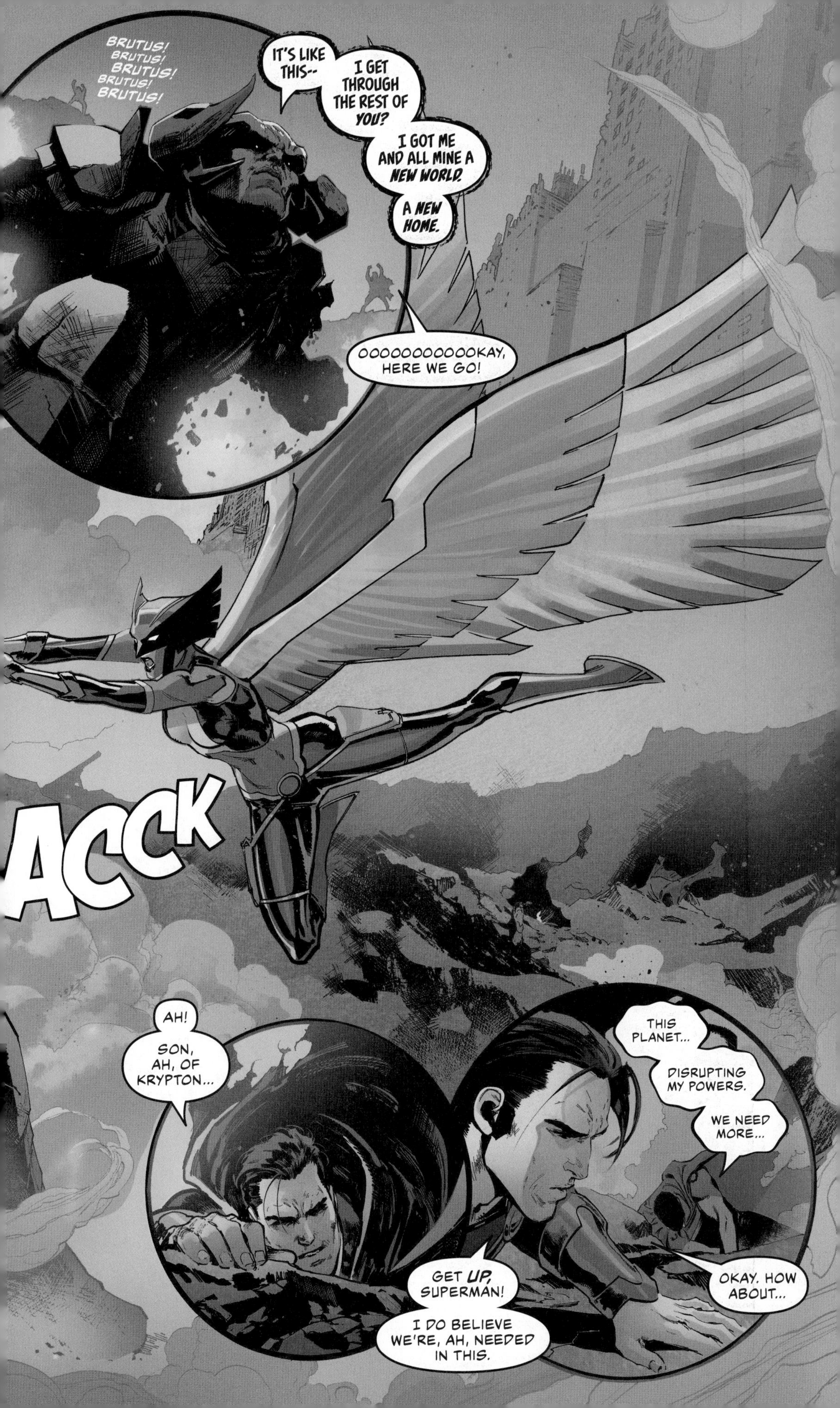
BRUTUS! BRUTUS! BRUTUS! BRUTUS! BRUTUS!
IT'S LIKE THIS--
I GET THROUGH THE REST OF YOU?
I GOT ME AND ALL MINE A NEW WORLD.
A NEW HOME.
OOOOOOOOOOOKAY, HERE WE GO!
ACCK
AH!
SON, AH, OF KRYPTON...
THIS PLANET...
DISRUPTING MY POWERS.
WE NEED MORE...
GET UP, SUPERMAN!
I DO BELIEVE WE'RE, AH, NEEDED IN THIS.
OKAY. HOW ABOUT...

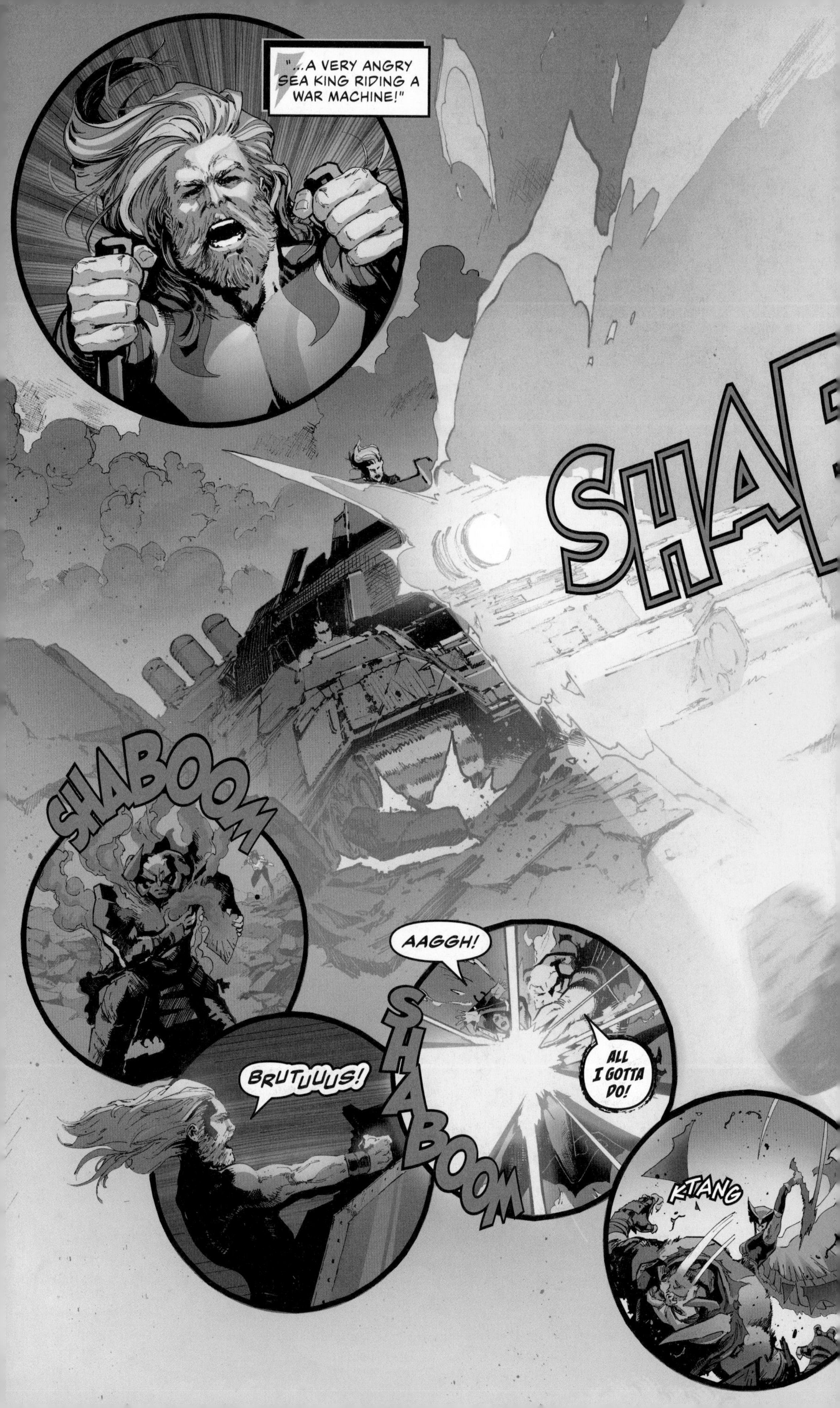
"...A VERY ANGRY SEA KING RIDING A WAR MACHINE!"
SHA
SHABOOM
AAGGH!
SHABOOM
ALL I GOTTA DO!
BRUTUUUS!
KTANG

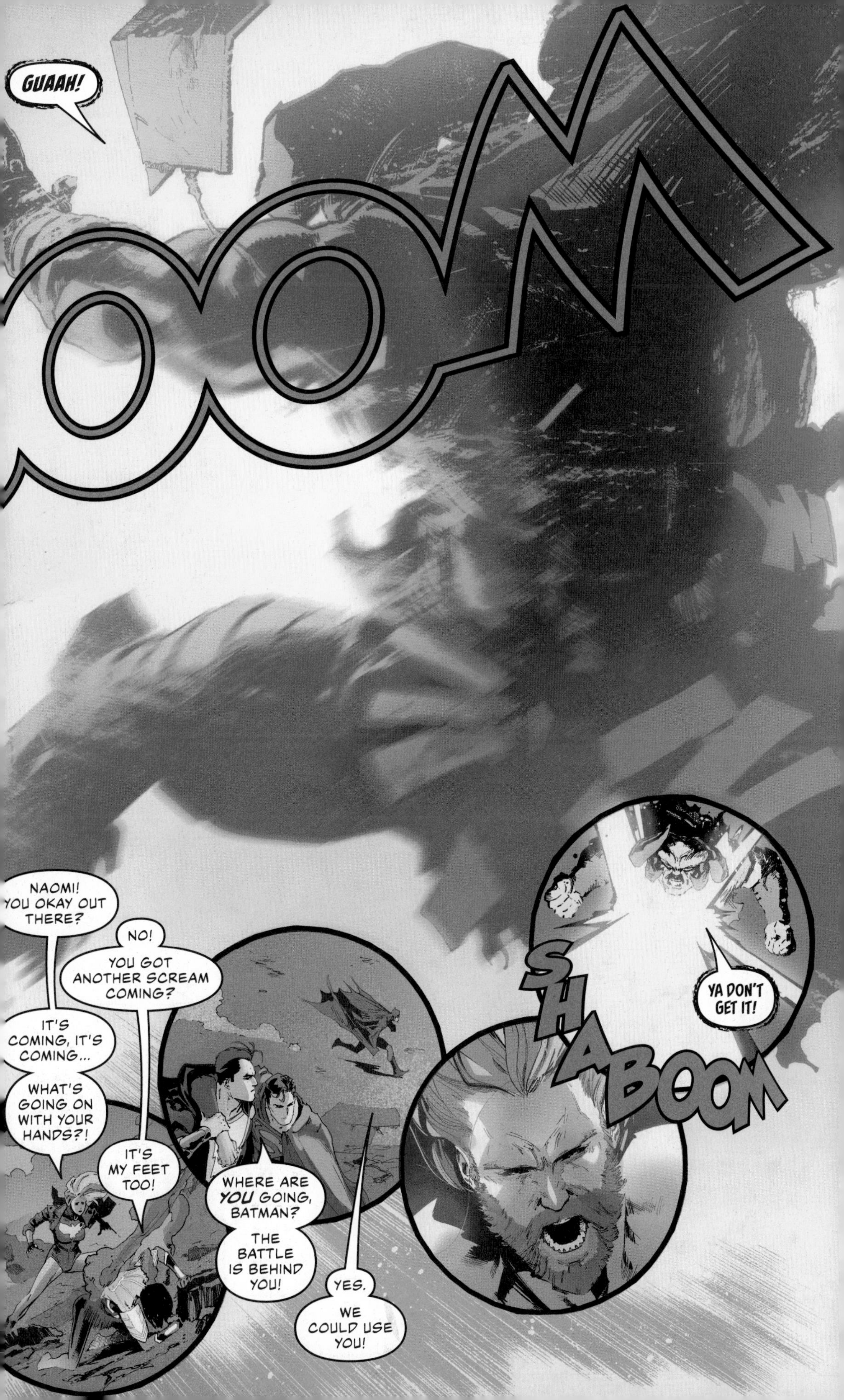
GUAAH!
OOM
NAOMI! YOU OKAY OUT THERE?
NO!
YOU GOT ANOTHER SCREAM COMING?
IT'S COMING, IT'S COMING...
WHAT'S GOING ON WITH YOUR HANDS?!
IT'S MY FEET TOO!
WHERE ARE *YOU* GOING, BATMAN?
THE BATTLE IS BEHIND YOU!
YES.
WE COULD USE YOU!
YA DON'T GET IT!
SHABOOM

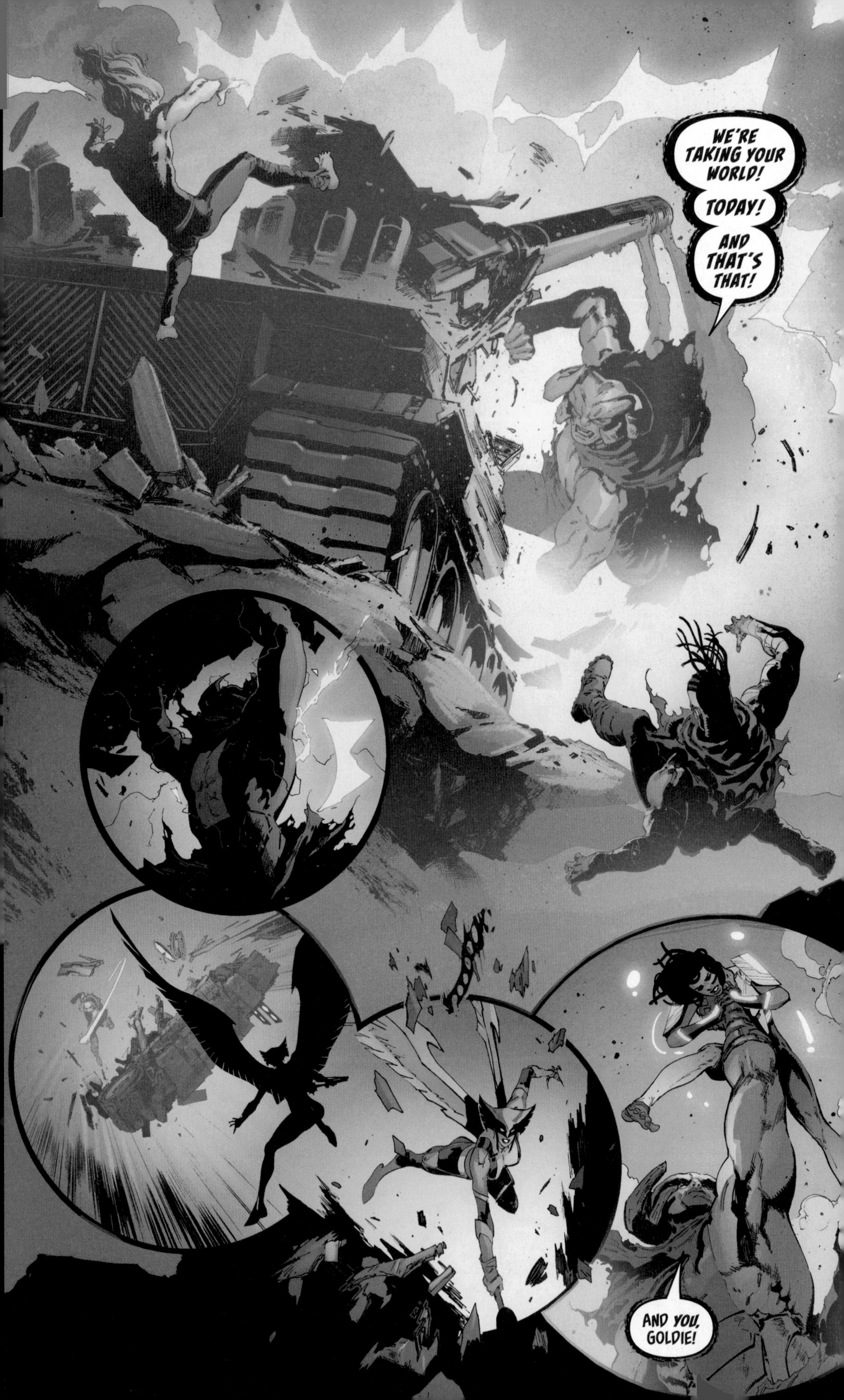
WE'RE TAKING YOUR WORLD!
TODAY!
AND THAT'S THAT!
AND YOU, GOLDIE!

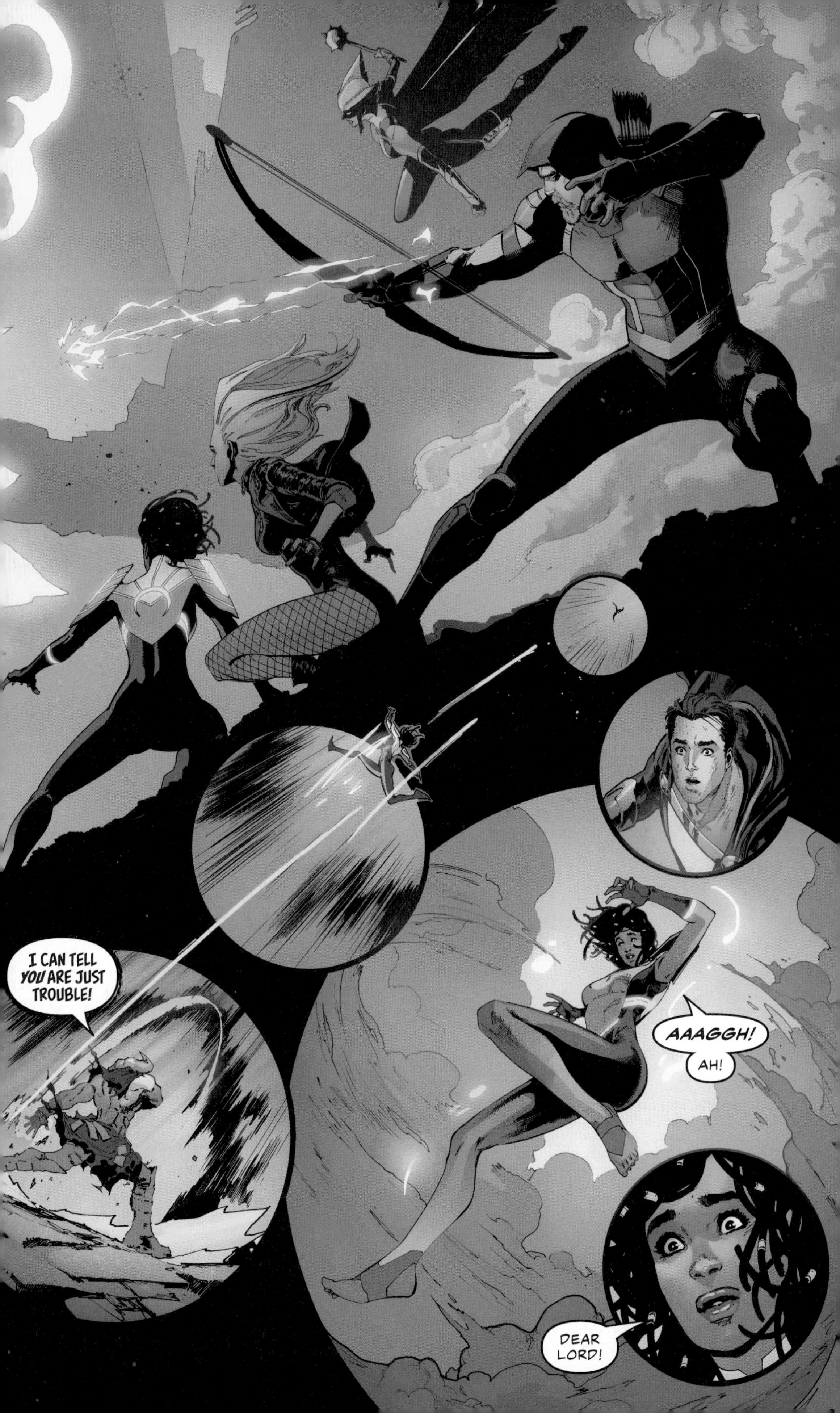
I CAN TELL YOU ARE JUST TROUBLE!
AAAGGH!
AH!
DEAR LORD!

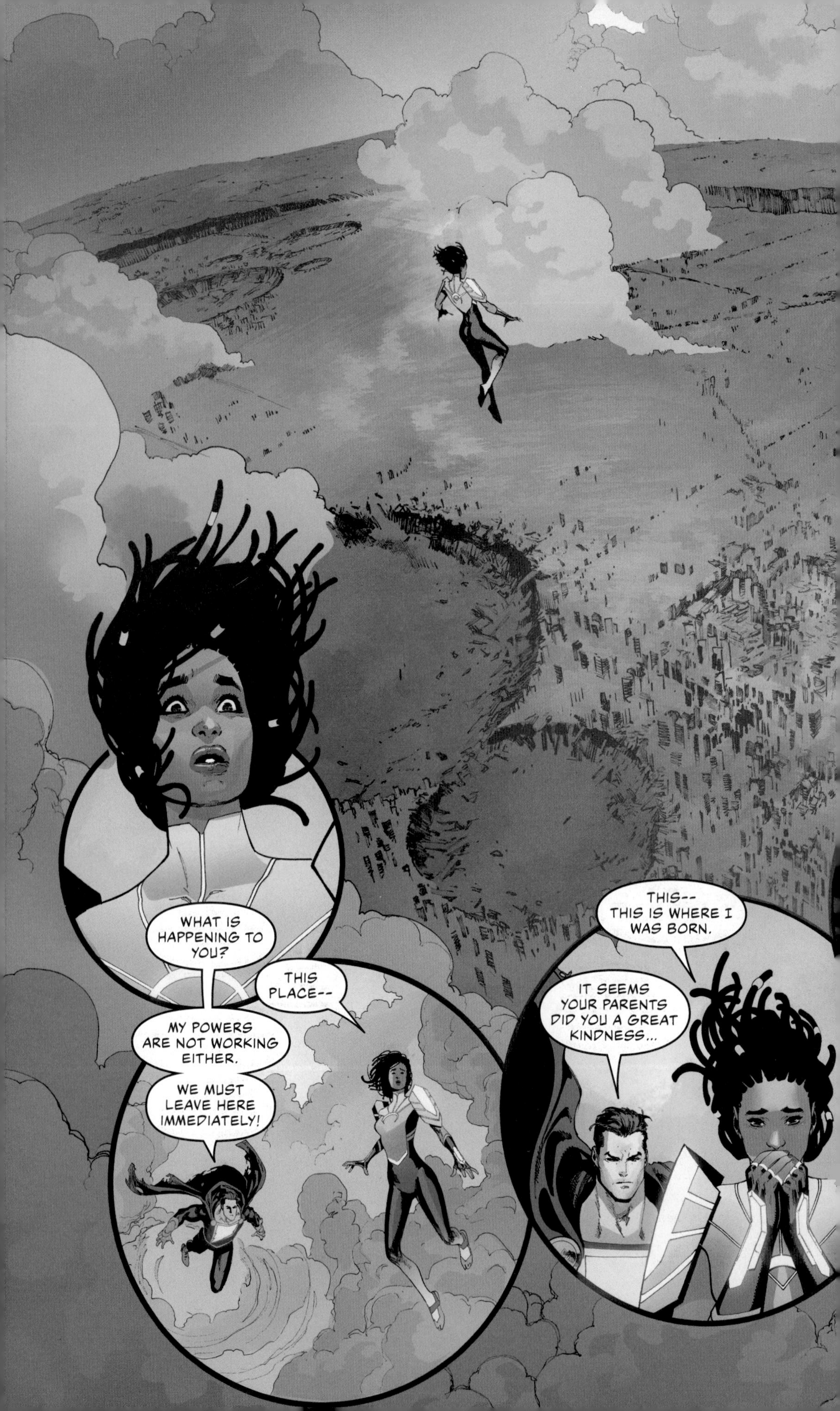
WHAT IS HAPPENING TO YOU?
THIS PLACE--
MY POWERS ARE NOT WORKING EITHER.
WE MUST LEAVE HERE IMMEDIATELY!
THIS-- THIS IS WHERE I WAS BORN.
IT SEEMS YOUR PARENTS DID YOU A GREAT KINDNESS...

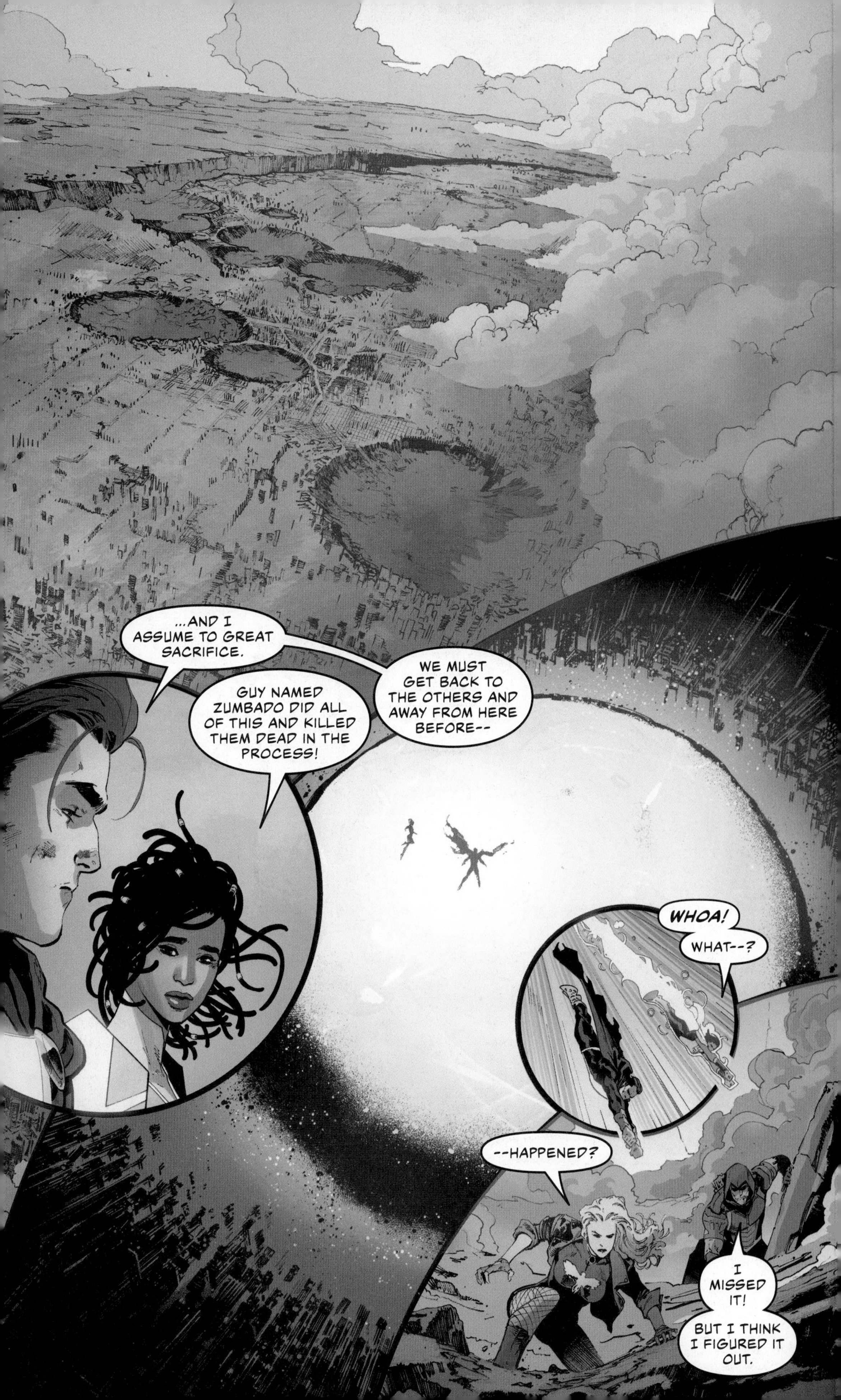
...AND I ASSUME TO GREAT SACRIFICE.
GUY NAMED ZUMBADO DID ALL OF THIS AND KILLED THEM DEAD IN THE PROCESS!
WE MUST GET BACK TO THE OTHERS AND AWAY FROM HERE BEFORE--
WHOA!
WHAT--?
--HAPPENED?
I MISSED IT!
BUT I THINK I FIGURED IT OUT.

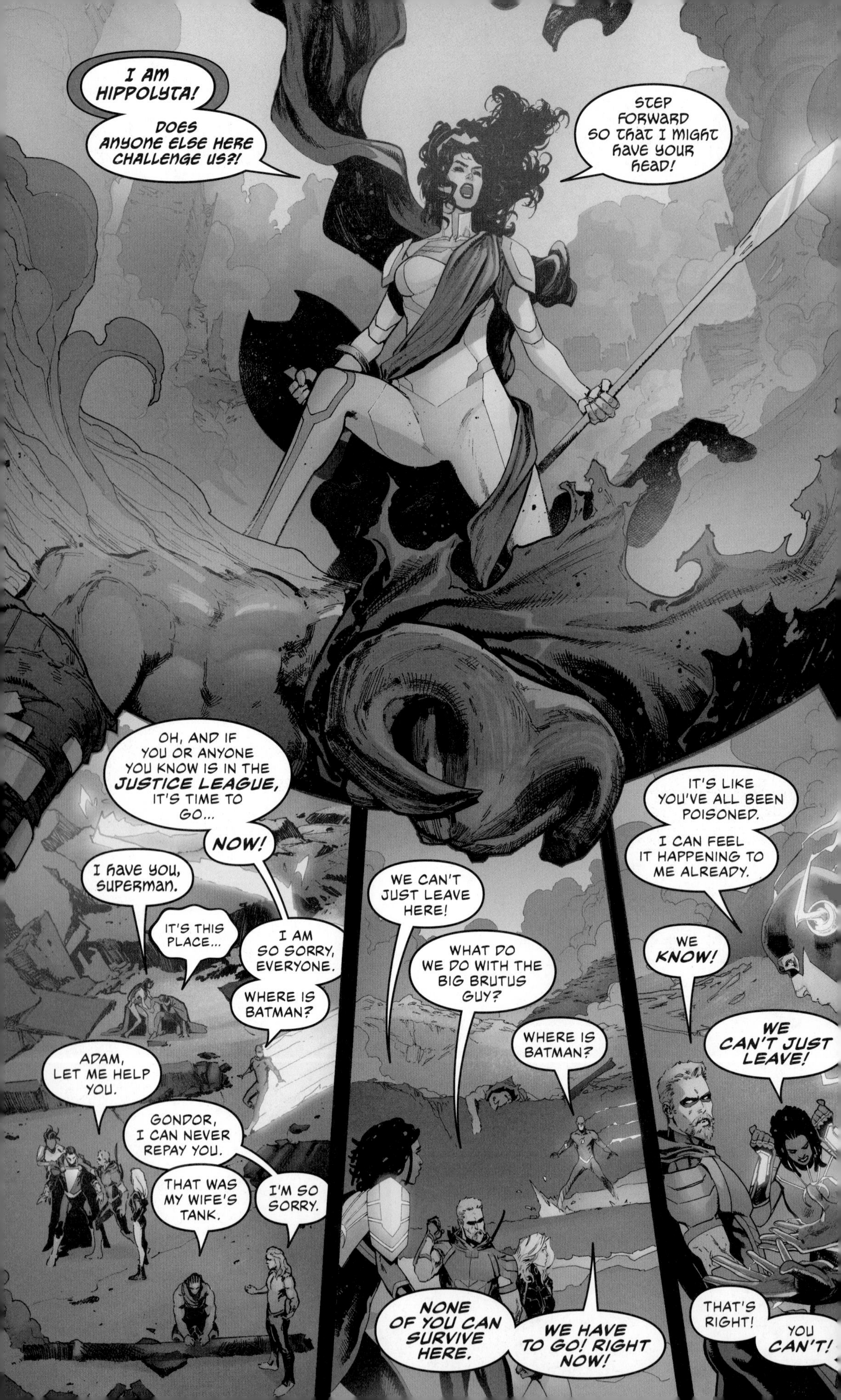
I AM HIPPOLYTA!
DOES ANYONE ELSE HERE CHALLENGE US?!
STEP FORWARD SO THAT I MIGHT HAVE YOUR HEAD!
OH, AND IF YOU OR ANYONE YOU KNOW IS IN THE JUSTICE LEAGUE, IT'S TIME TO GO...
NOW!
I HAVE YOU, SUPERMAN.
IT'S THIS PLACE...
I AM SO SORRY, EVERYONE.
WHERE IS BATMAN?
ADAM, LET ME HELP YOU.
GONDOR, I CAN NEVER REPAY YOU.
THAT WAS MY WIFE'S TANK.
I'M SO SORRY.
WE CAN'T JUST LEAVE HERE!
WHAT DO WE DO WITH THE BIG BRUTUS GUY?
WHERE IS BATMAN?
NONE OF YOU CAN SURVIVE HERE.
WE HAVE TO GO! RIGHT NOW!
IT'S LIKE YOU'VE ALL BEEN POISONED.
I CAN FEEL IT HAPPENING TO ME ALREADY.
WE KNOW!
WE CAN'T JUST LEAVE!
THAT'S RIGHT!
YOU CAN'T!

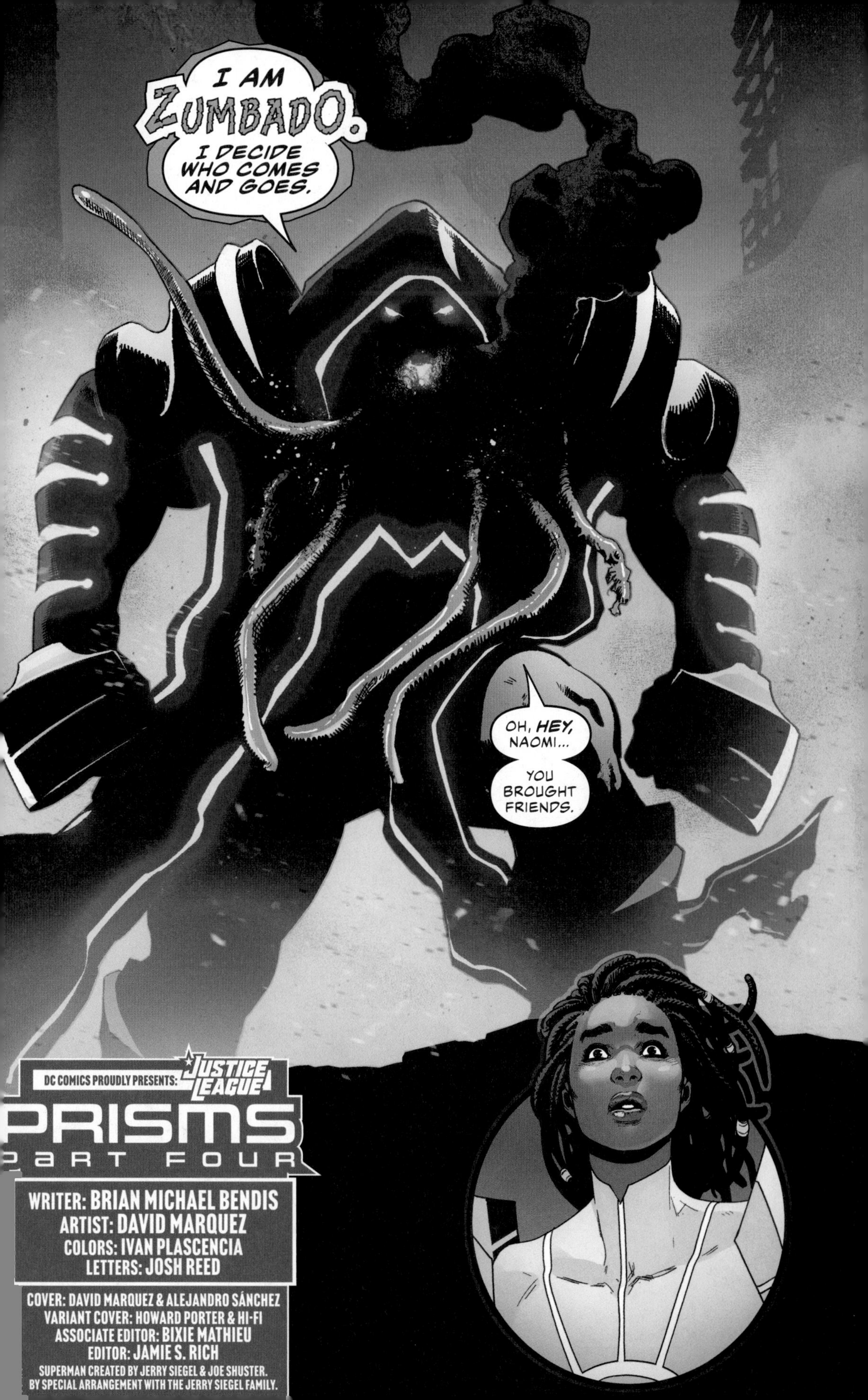
I AM ZUMBADO. I DECIDE WHO COMES AND GOES.
OH, HEY, NAOMI...
YOU BROUGHT FRIENDS.
DC COMICS PROUDLY PRESENTS: JUSTICE LEAGUE
PRISMS PART FOUR
WRITER: BRIAN MICHAEL BENDIS
ARTIST: DAVID MARQUEZ
COLORS: IVAN PLASCENCIA
LETTERS: JOSH REED
COVER: DAVID MARQUEZ & ALEJANDRO SÁNCHEZ
VARIANT COVER: HOWARD PORTER & HI-FI
ASSOCIATE EDITOR: BIXIE MATHIEU
EDITOR: JAMIE S. RICH
SUPERMAN CREATED BY JERRY SIEGEL & JOE SHUSTER.
BY SPECIAL ARRANGEMENT WITH THE JERRY SIEGEL FAMILY.

Justice League #63 cover by **David Marquez & Alejandro Sánchez**

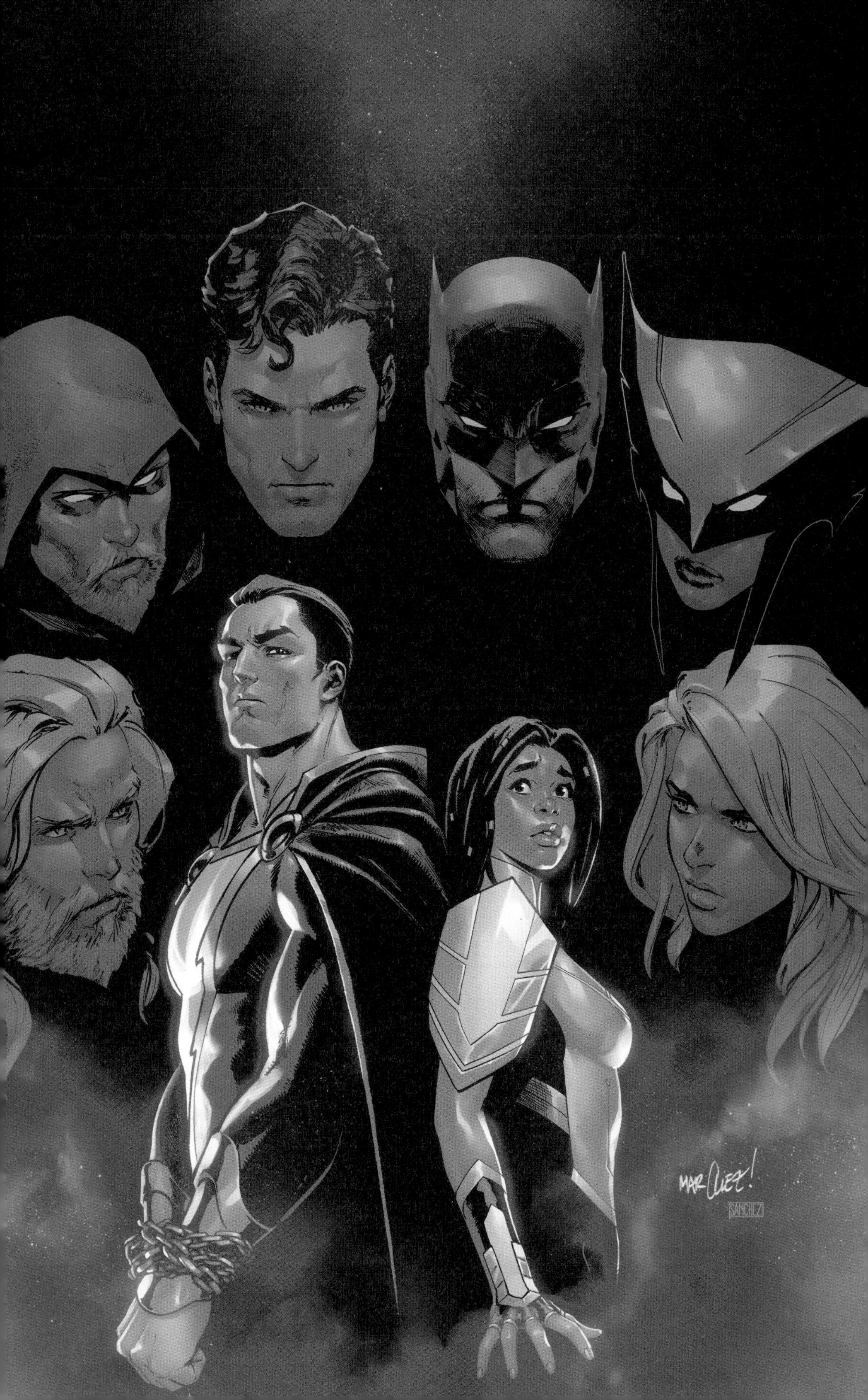
MARQUEZ!
SANCHEZ

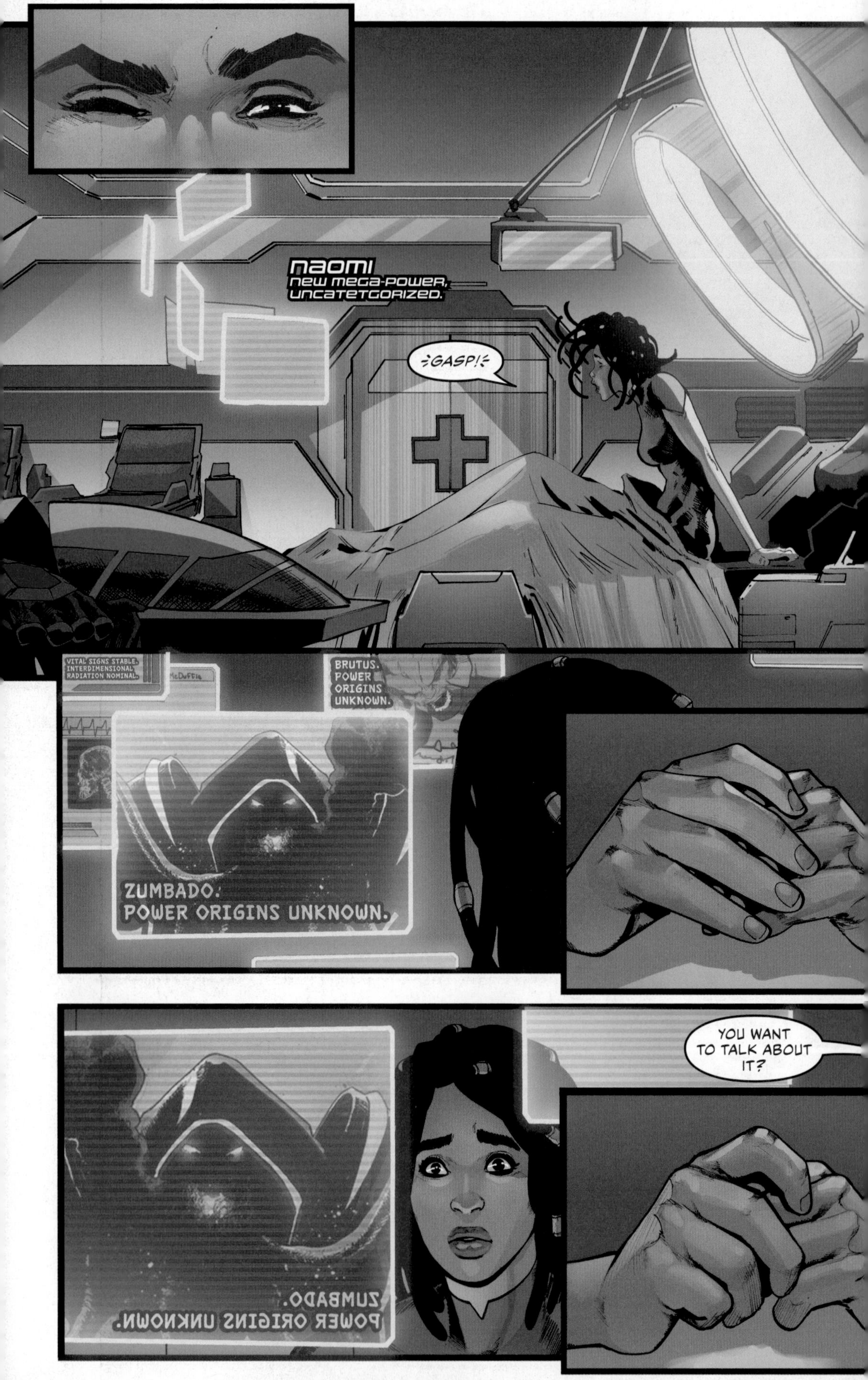

NAOMI
NEW MEGA-POWER, UNCATETGORIZED.
GASP!
VITAL SIGNS STABLE. INTERDIMENSIONAL RADIATION NOMINAL.
BRUTUS. POWER ORIGINS UNKNOWN.
ZUMBADO. POWER ORIGINS UNKNOWN.
YOU WANT TO TALK ABOUT IT?

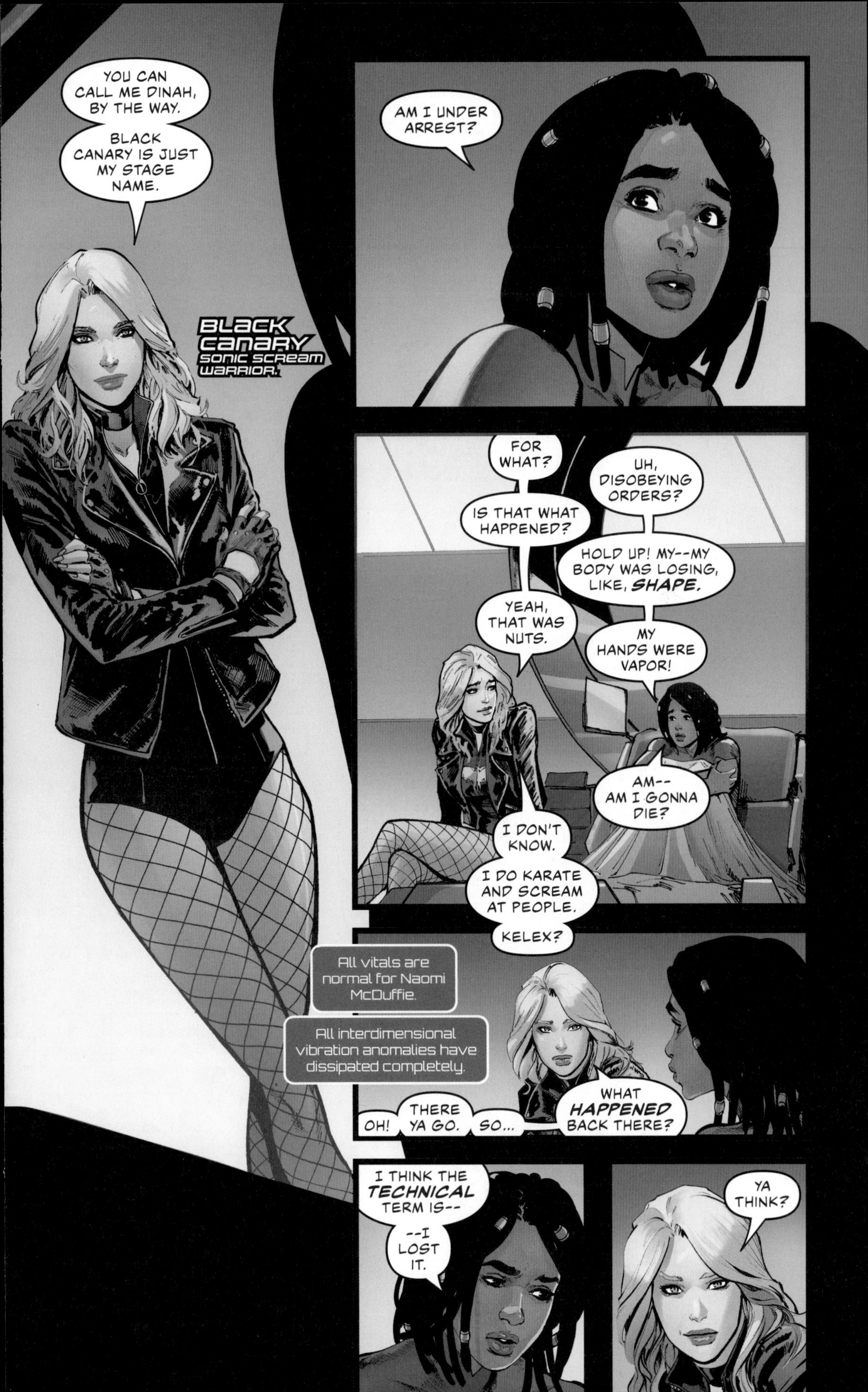
YOU CAN CALL ME DINAH, BY THE WAY.
BLACK CANARY IS JUST MY STAGE NAME.
BLACK CANARY SONIC SCREAM WARRIOR.
AM I UNDER ARREST?
FOR WHAT?
UH, DISOBEYING ORDERS?
IS THAT WHAT HAPPENED?
HOLD UP! MY--MY BODY WAS LOSING, LIKE, SHAPE.
YEAH, THAT WAS NUTS.
MY HANDS WERE VAPOR!
AM--AM I GONNA DIE?
I DON'T KNOW.
I DO KARATE AND SCREAM AT PEOPLE.
KELEX?
All vitals are normal for Naomi McDuffie.
All interdimensional vibration anomalies have dissipated completely.
OH!
THERE YA GO.
SO...
WHAT HAPPENED BACK THERE?
I THINK THE TECHNICAL TERM IS--
--I LOST IT.
YA THINK?

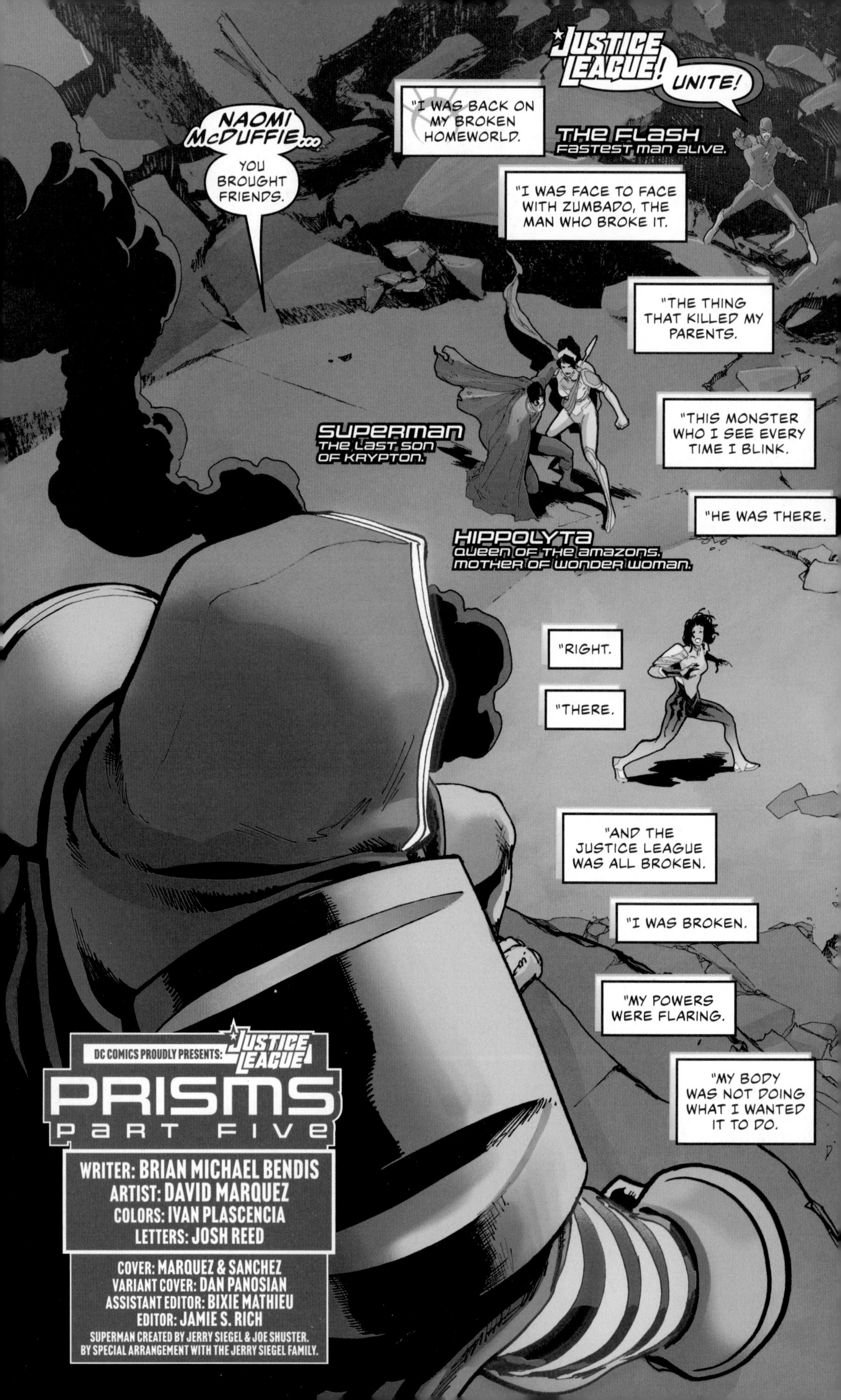

NAOMI McDUFFIE...
YOU BROUGHT FRIENDS.
"I WAS BACK ON MY BROKEN HOMEWORLD.
JUSTICE LEAGUE! UNITE!
THE FLASH FASTEST MAN ALIVE.
"I WAS FACE TO FACE WITH ZUMBADO, THE MAN WHO BROKE IT.
"THE THING THAT KILLED MY PARENTS.
"THIS MONSTER WHO I SEE EVERY TIME I BLINK.
SUPERMAN THE LAST SON OF KRYPTON.
"HE WAS THERE.
HIPPOLYTA QUEEN OF THE AMAZONS. MOTHER OF WONDER WOMAN.
"RIGHT.
"THERE.
"AND THE JUSTICE LEAGUE WAS ALL BROKEN.
"I WAS BROKEN.
"MY POWERS WERE FLARING.
"MY BODY WAS NOT DOING WHAT I WANTED IT TO DO.
DC COMICS PROUDLY PRESENTS: JUSTICE LEAGUE
PRISMS
PART FIVE
WRITER: BRIAN MICHAEL BENDIS
ARTIST: DAVID MARQUEZ
COLORS: IVAN PLASCENCIA
LETTERS: JOSH REED
COVER: MARQUEZ & SANCHEZ
VARIANT COVER: DAN PANOSIAN
ASSISTANT EDITOR: BIXIE MATHIEU
EDITOR: JAMIE S. RICH
SUPERMAN CREATED BY JERRY SIEGEL & JOE SHUSTER.
BY SPECIAL ARRANGEMENT WITH THE JERRY SIEGEL FAMILY.

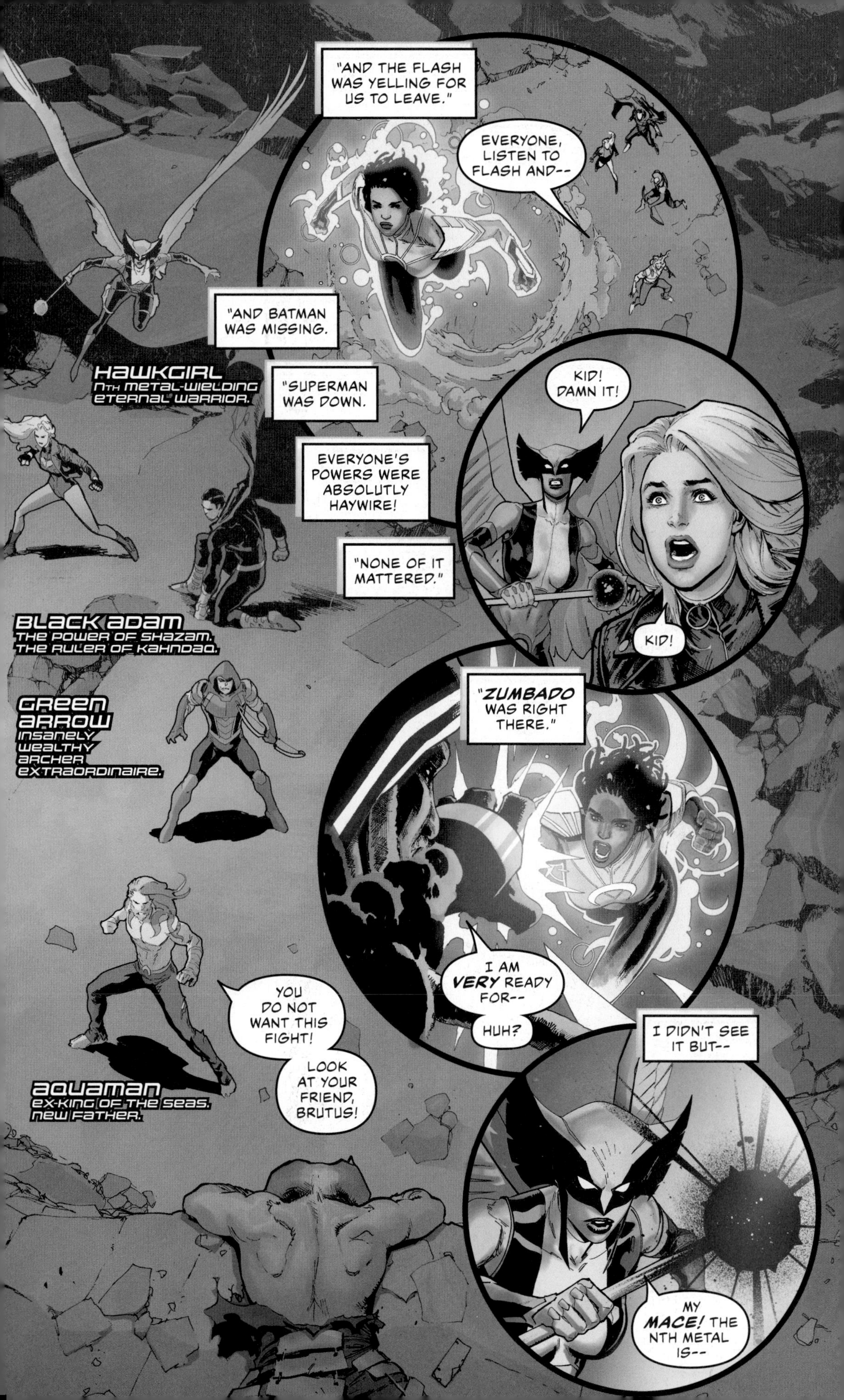

"AND THE FLASH WAS YELLING FOR US TO LEAVE."
EVERYONE, LISTEN TO FLASH AND--
"AND BATMAN WAS MISSING.
HAWKGIRL
NTH METAL-WIELDING ETERNAL WARRIOR.
"SUPERMAN WAS DOWN.
KID! DAMN IT!
EVERYONE'S POWERS WERE ABSOLUTLY HAYWIRE!
"NONE OF IT MATTERED."
KID!
BLACK ADAM
THE POWER OF SHAZAM. THE RULER OF KAHNDAQ.
GREEN ARROW
INSANELY WEALTHY ARCHER EXTRAORDINAIRE.
"ZUMBADO WAS RIGHT THERE."
I AM VERY READY FOR--
HUH?
YOU DO NOT WANT THIS FIGHT!
LOOK AT YOUR FRIEND, BRUTUS!
AQUAMAN
EX-KING OF THE SEAS. NEW FATHER.
I DIDN'T SEE IT BUT--
MY MACE! THE NTH METAL IS--

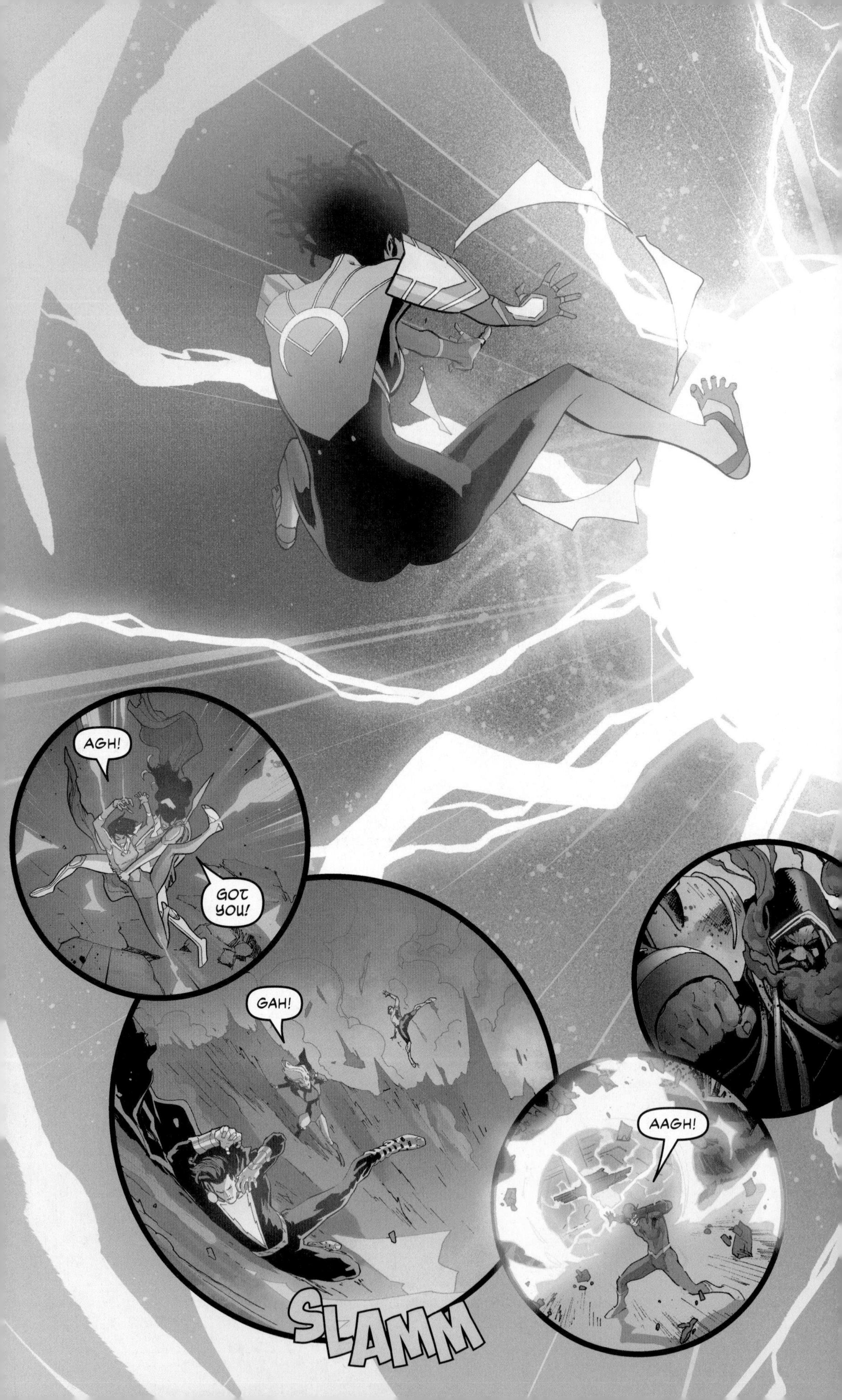
AGH!
GOT YOU!
GAH!
AAGH!
SLAMM

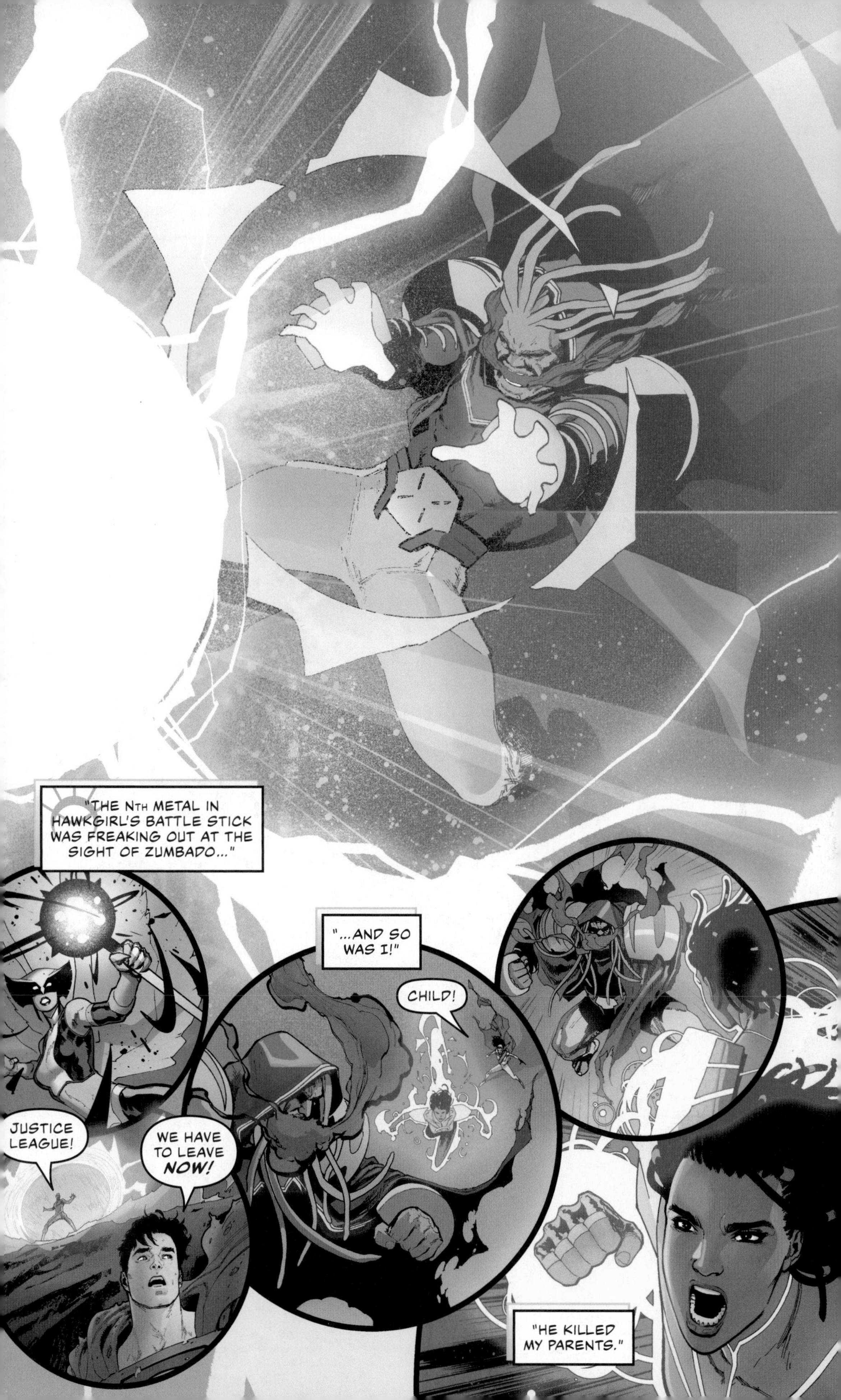
"THE NTH METAL IN HAWKGIRL'S BATTLE STICK WAS FREAKING OUT AT THE SIGHT OF ZUMBADO..."
"...AND SO WAS I!"
CHILD!
JUSTICE LEAGUE!
WE HAVE TO LEAVE NOW!
"HE KILLED MY PARENTS."

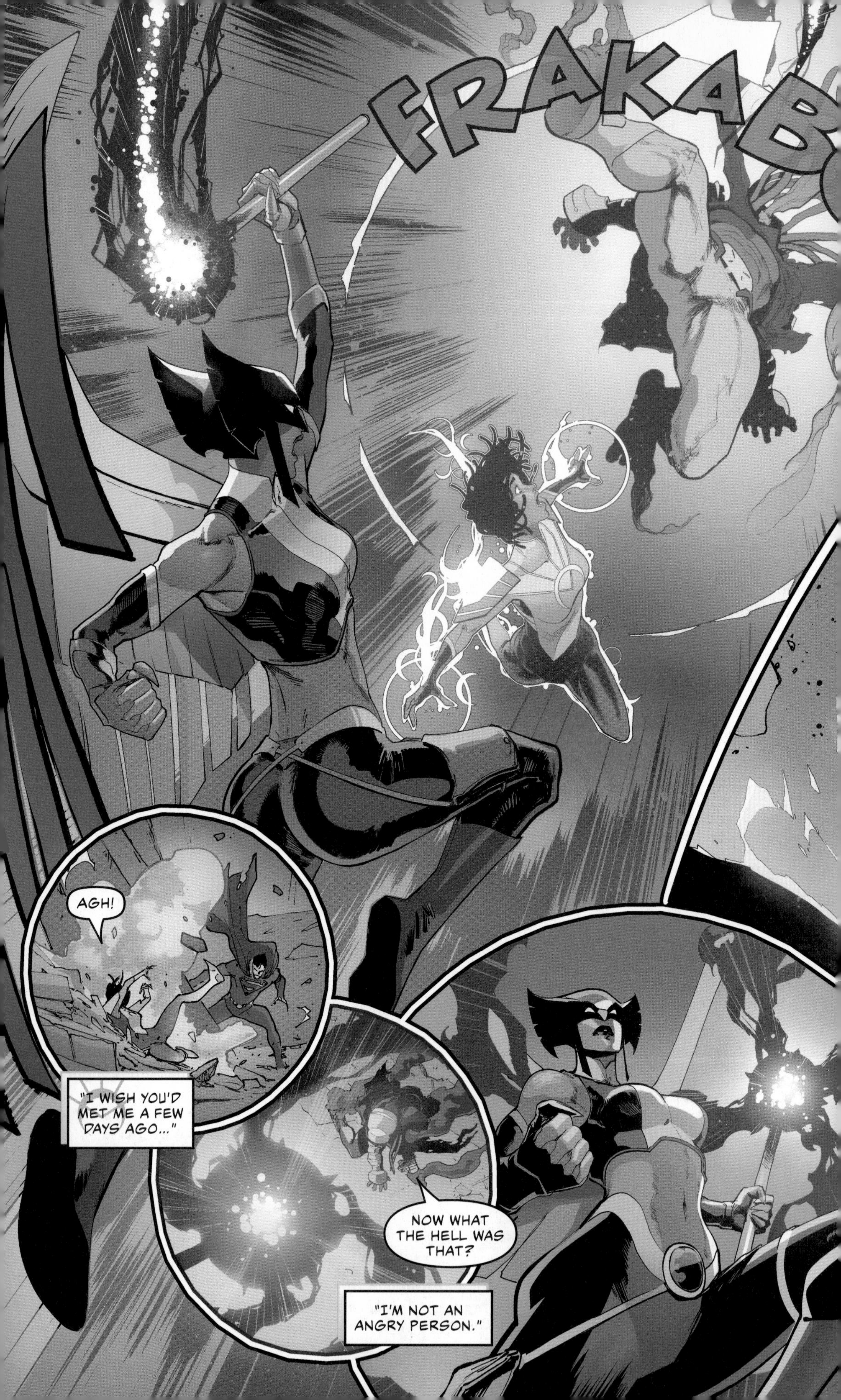
FRAKAB
AGH!
"I WISH YOU'D MET ME A FEW DAYS AGO..."
NOW WHAT THE HELL WAS THAT?
"I'M NOT AN ANGRY PERSON."

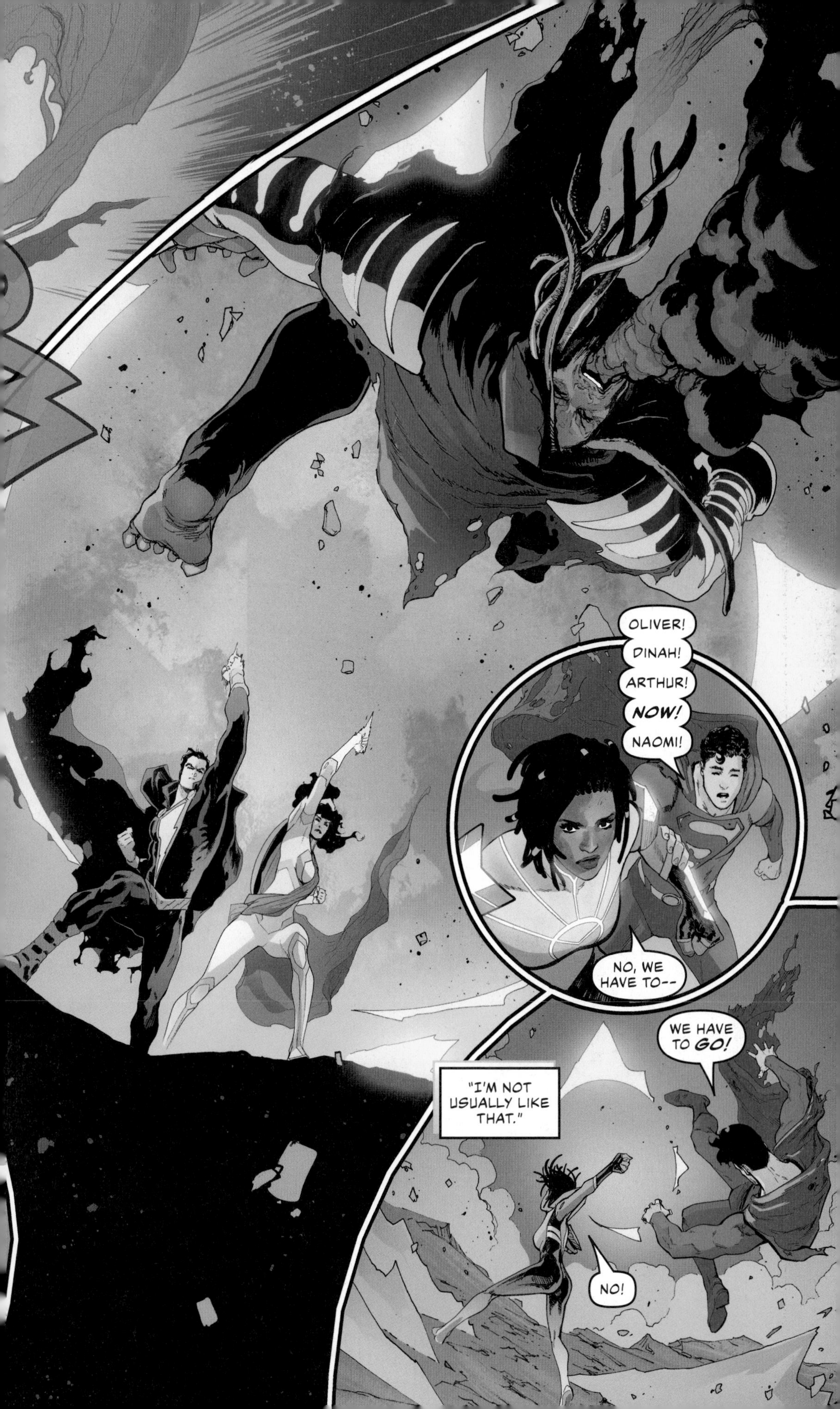
OLIVER!
DINAH!
ARTHUR!
NOW!
NAOMI!
NO, WE HAVE TO--
WE HAVE TO GO!
"I'M NOT USUALLY LIKE THAT."
NO!

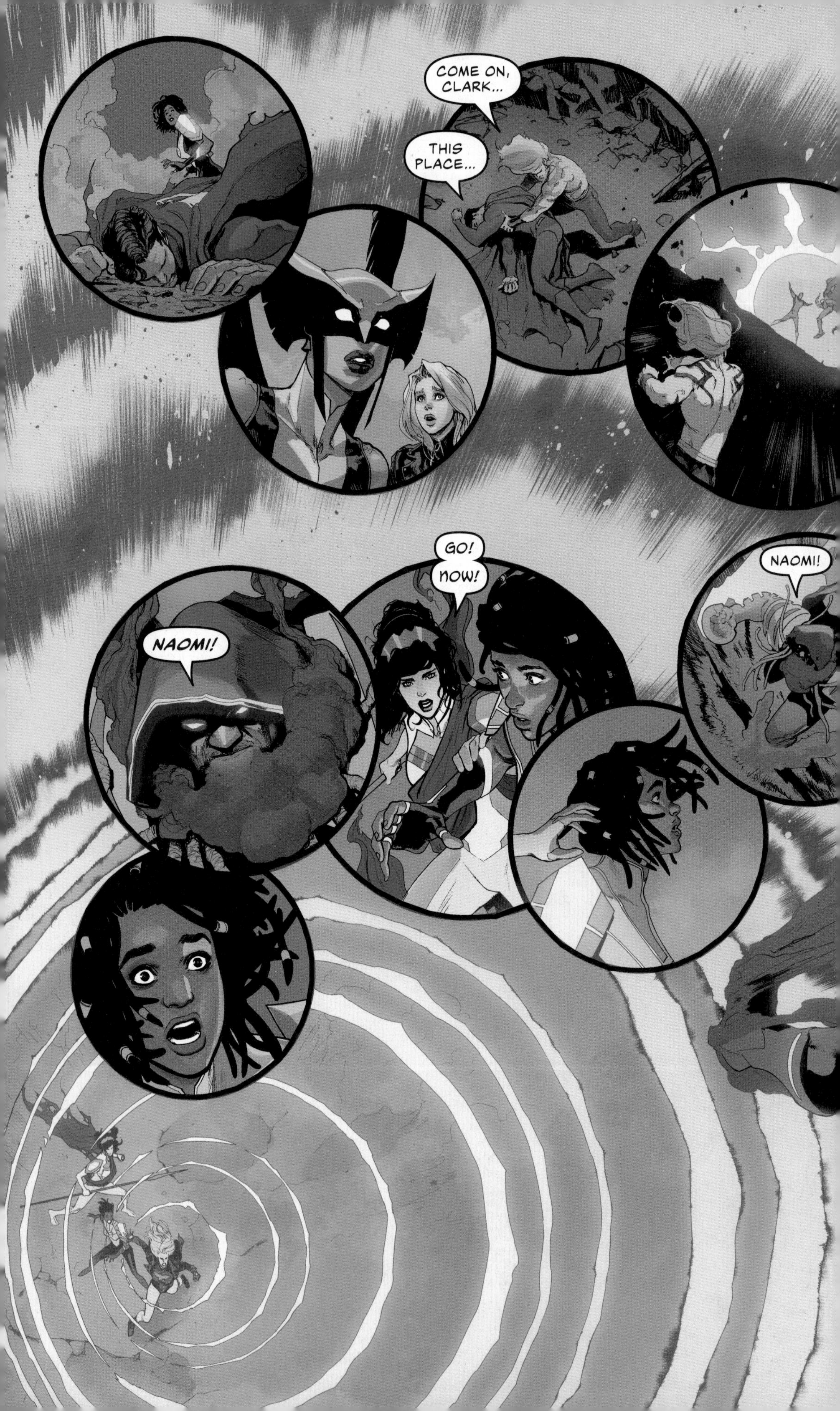
COME ON, CLARK...
THIS PLACE...
GO! NOW!
NAOMI!
NAOMI!

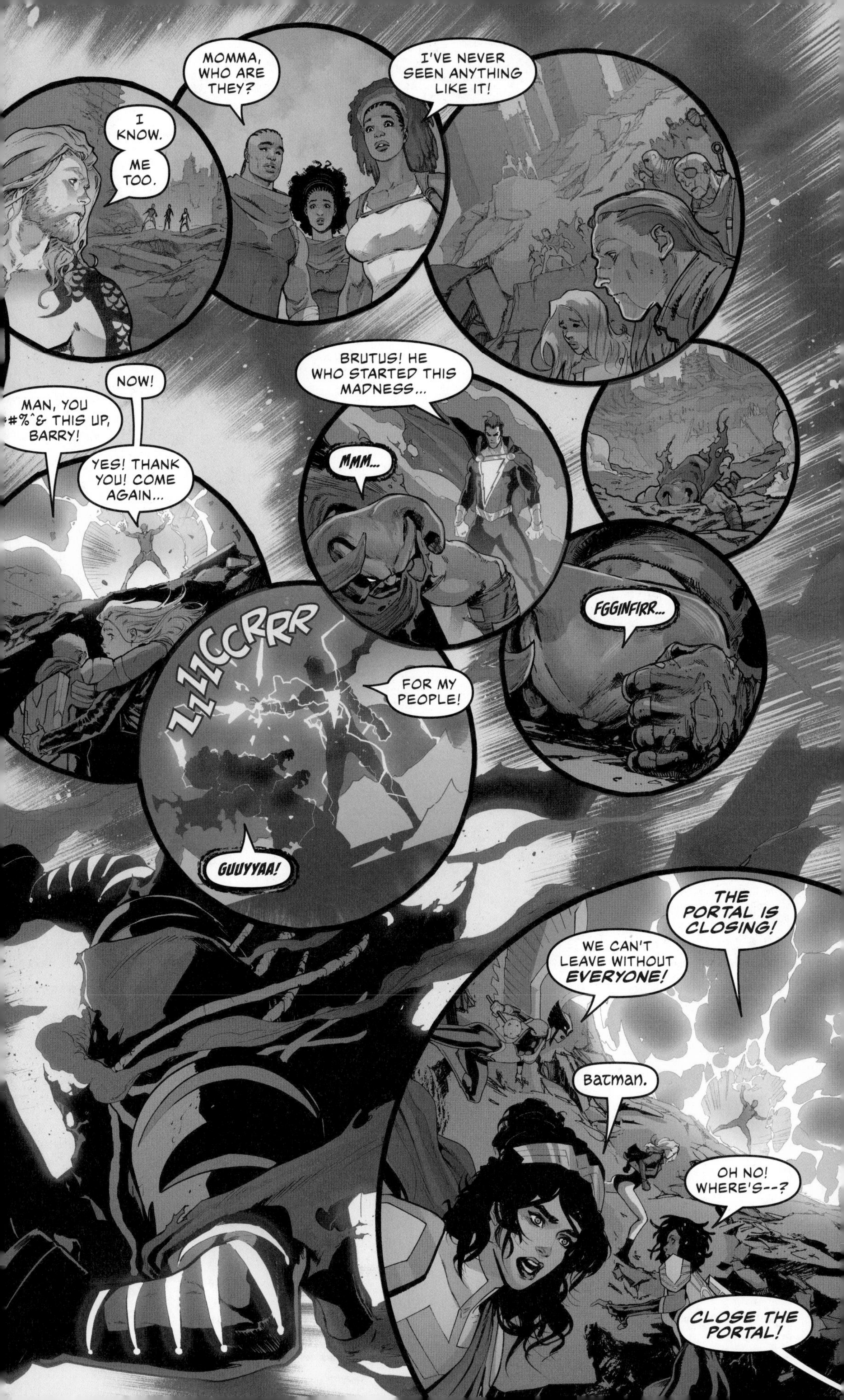
I KNOW.
ME TOO.
MOMMA, WHO ARE THEY?
I'VE NEVER SEEN ANYTHING LIKE IT!
MAN, YOU #%^& THIS UP, BARRY!
NOW!
YES! THANK YOU! COME AGAIN...
BRUTUS! HE WHO STARTED THIS MADNESS...
MMM...
FGGINFIRR...
ZZZCCRRR
FOR MY PEOPLE!
GUUYYAA!
THE PORTAL IS CLOSING!
WE CAN'T LEAVE WITHOUT EVERYONE!
Batman.
OH NO! WHERE'S--?
CLOSE THE PORTAL!

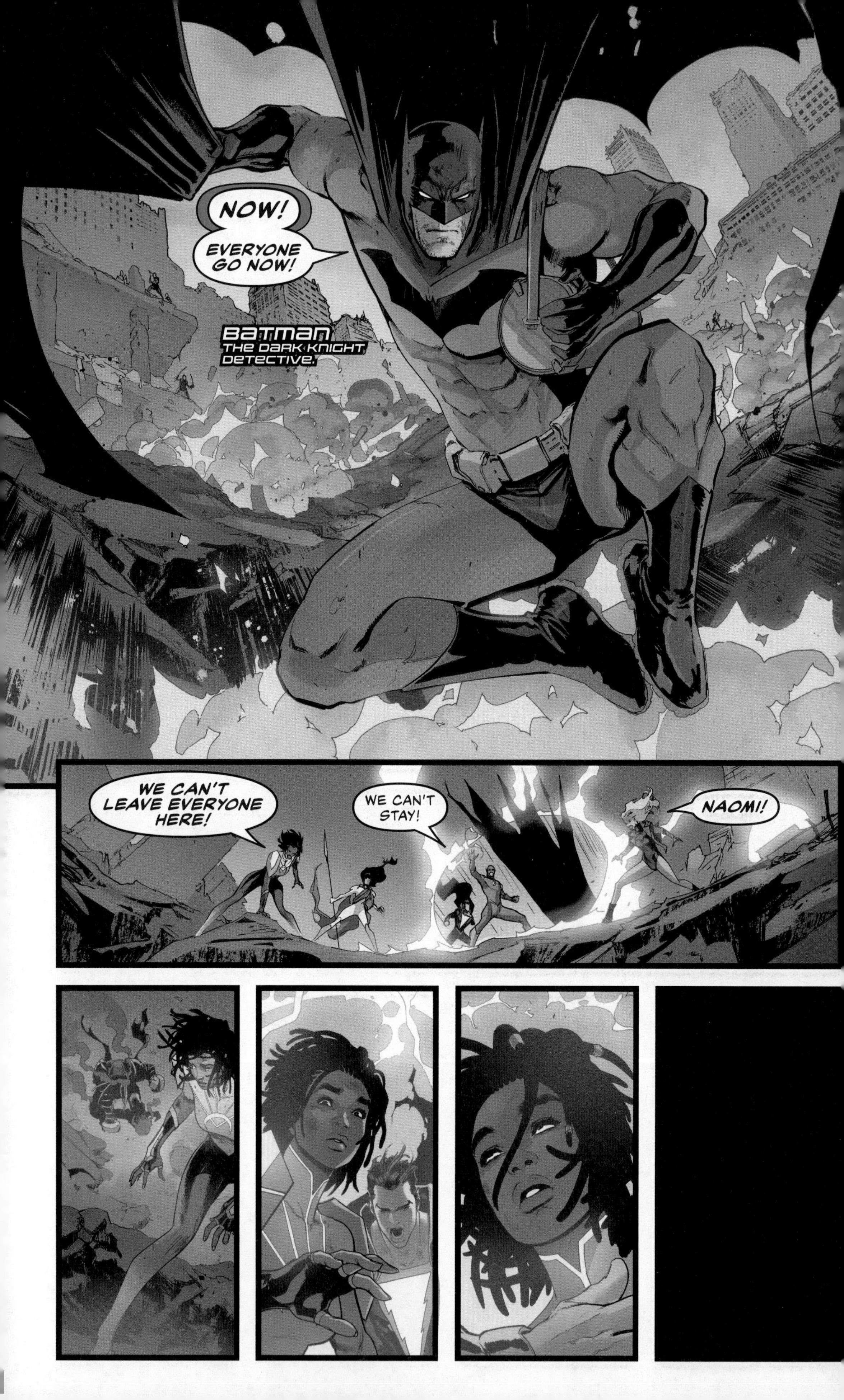
NOW!
EVERYONE GO NOW!
BATMAN THE DARK KNIGHT DETECTIVE.
WE CAN'T LEAVE EVERYONE HERE!
WE CAN'T STAY!
NAOMI!

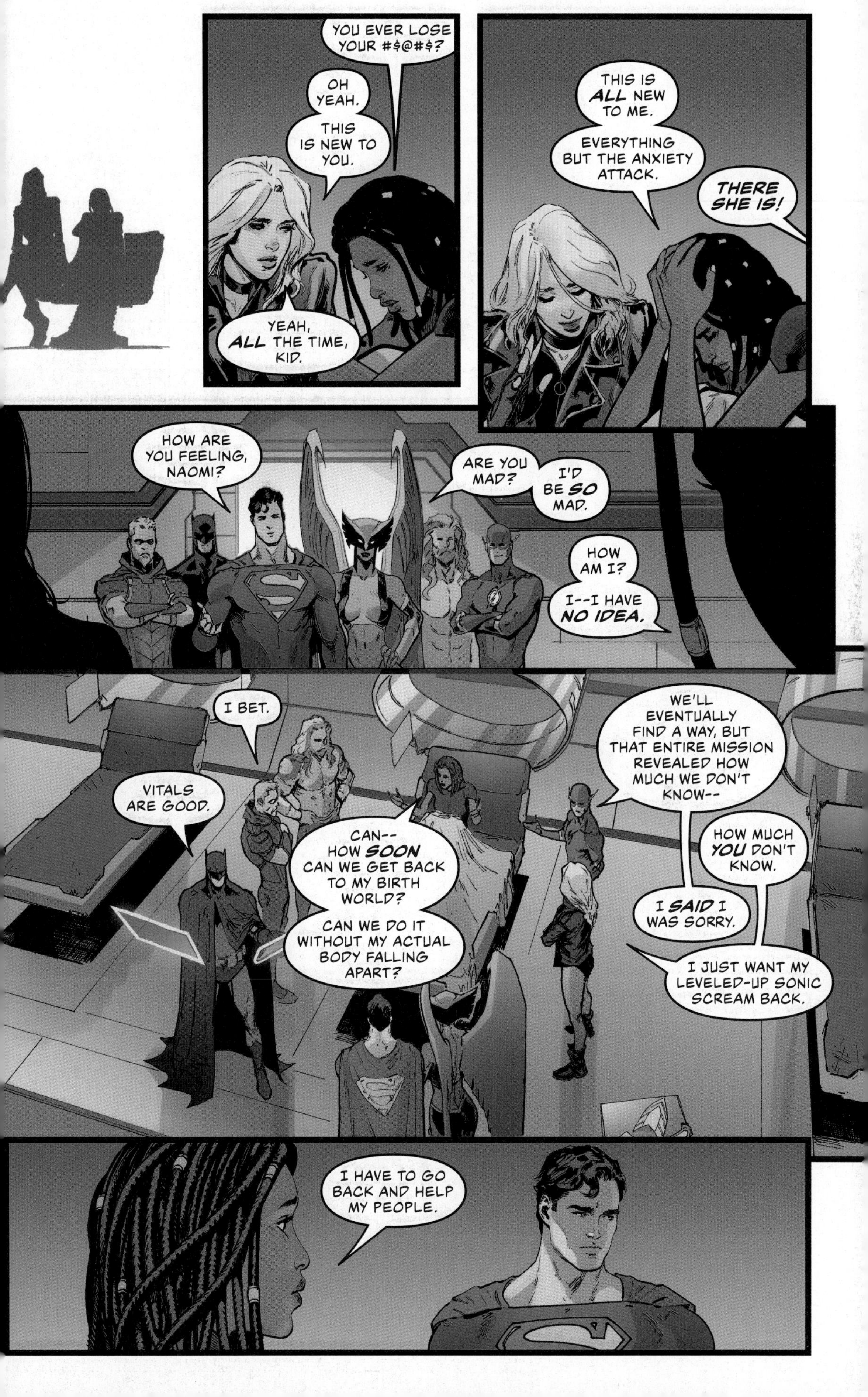
YOU EVER LOSE YOUR #$@#$?
OH YEAH.
THIS IS NEW TO YOU.
YEAH, ALL THE TIME, KID.
THIS IS ALL NEW TO ME.
EVERYTHING BUT THE ANXIETY ATTACK.
THERE SHE IS!
HOW ARE YOU FEELING, NAOMI?
ARE YOU MAD?
I'D BE SO MAD.
HOW AM I?
I--I HAVE NO IDEA.
I BET.
VITALS ARE GOOD.
CAN-- HOW SOON CAN WE GET BACK TO MY BIRTH WORLD?
CAN WE DO IT WITHOUT MY ACTUAL BODY FALLING APART?
WE'LL EVENTUALLY FIND A WAY, BUT THAT ENTIRE MISSION REVEALED HOW MUCH WE DON'T KNOW--
HOW MUCH YOU DON'T KNOW.
I SAID I WAS SORRY.
I JUST WANT MY LEVELED-UP SONIC SCREAM BACK.
I HAVE TO GO BACK AND HELP MY PEOPLE.

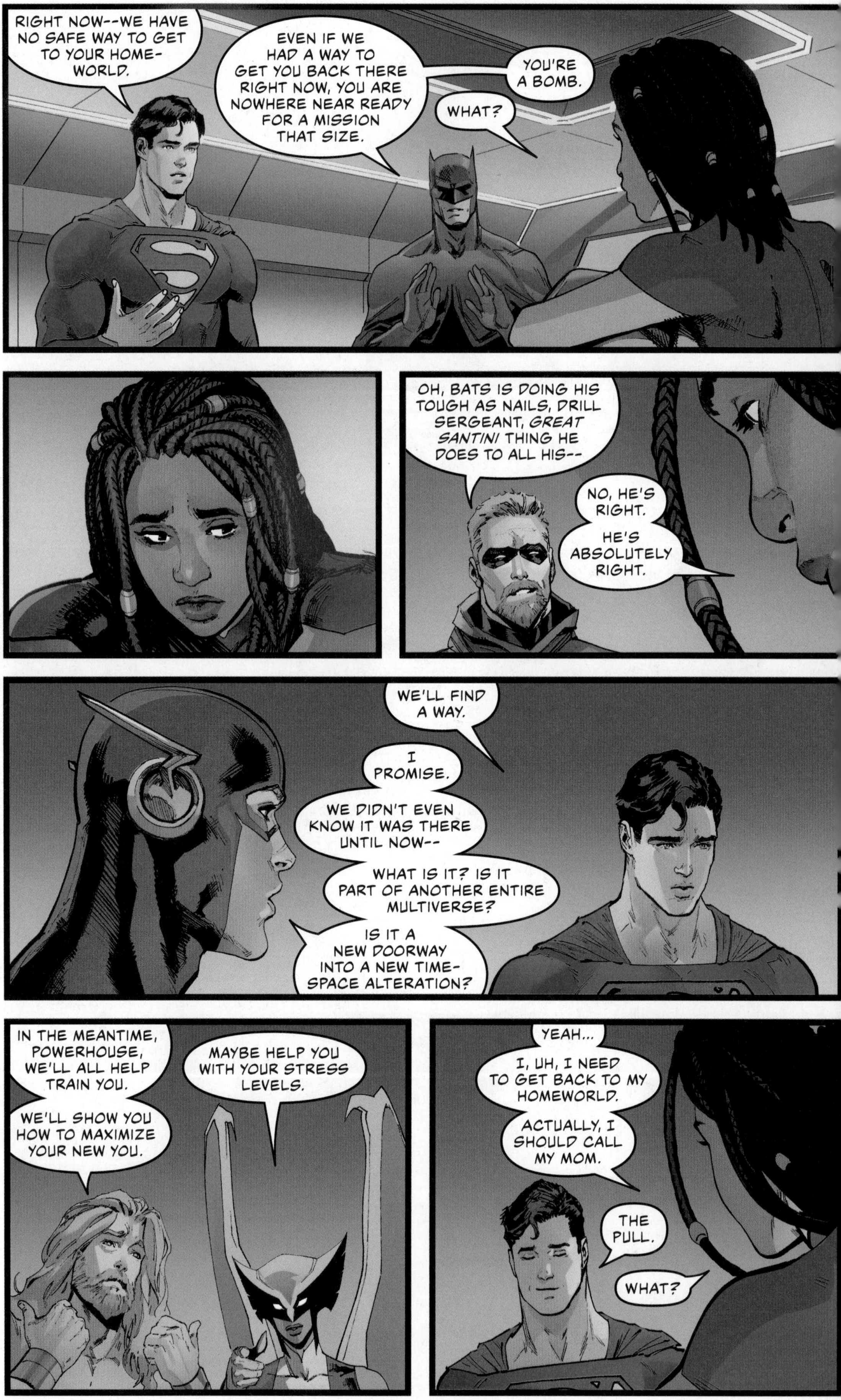
RIGHT NOW--WE HAVE NO SAFE WAY TO GET TO YOUR HOME-WORLD.
EVEN IF WE HAD A WAY TO GET YOU BACK THERE RIGHT NOW, YOU ARE NOWHERE NEAR READY FOR A MISSION THAT SIZE.
YOU'RE A BOMB.
WHAT?
OH, BATS IS DOING HIS TOUGH AS NAILS, DRILL SERGEANT, *GREAT SANTINI* THING HE DOES TO ALL HIS--
NO, HE'S RIGHT.
HE'S ABSOLUTELY RIGHT.
WE'LL FIND A WAY.
I PROMISE.
WE DIDN'T EVEN KNOW IT WAS THERE UNTIL NOW--
WHAT IS IT? IS IT PART OF ANOTHER ENTIRE MULTIVERSE?
IS IT A NEW DOORWAY INTO A NEW TIME-SPACE ALTERATION?
IN THE MEANTIME, POWERHOUSE, WE'LL ALL HELP TRAIN YOU.
WE'LL SHOW YOU HOW TO MAXIMIZE YOUR NEW YOU.
MAYBE HELP YOU WITH YOUR STRESS LEVELS.
YEAH...
I, UH, I NEED TO GET BACK TO MY HOMEWORLD.
ACTUALLY, I SHOULD CALL MY MOM.
THE PULL.
WHAT?

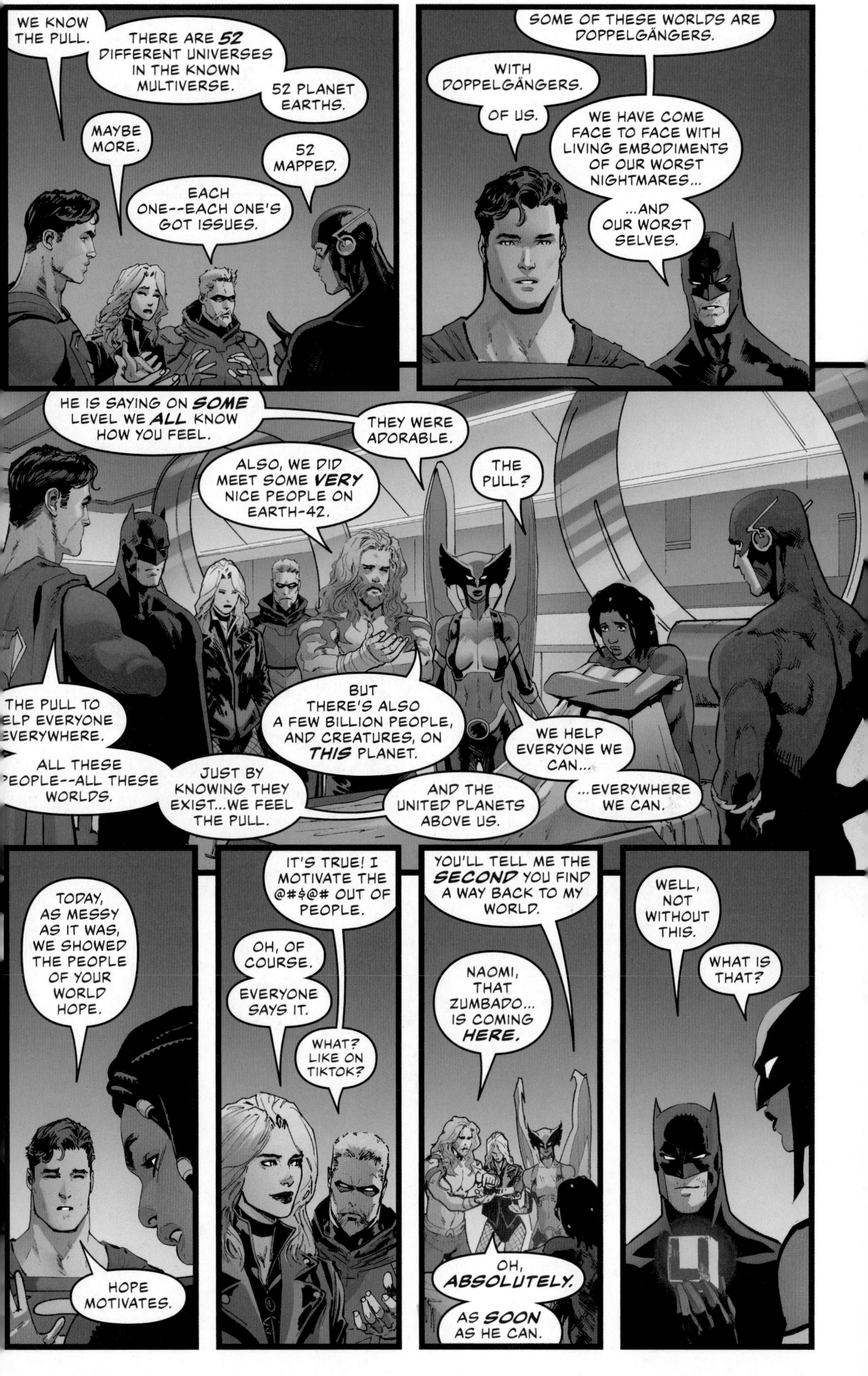
WE KNOW THE PULL.
THERE ARE 52 DIFFERENT UNIVERSES IN THE KNOWN MULTIVERSE.
52 PLANET EARTHS.
MAYBE MORE.
52 MAPPED.
EACH ONE--EACH ONE'S GOT ISSUES.
SOME OF THESE WORLDS ARE DOPPELGÄNGERS.
WITH DOPPELGÄNGERS.
OF US.
WE HAVE COME FACE TO FACE WITH LIVING EMBODIMENTS OF OUR WORST NIGHTMARES...
...AND OUR WORST SELVES.
HE IS SAYING ON SOME LEVEL WE ALL KNOW HOW YOU FEEL.
THEY WERE ADORABLE.
ALSO, WE DID MEET SOME VERY NICE PEOPLE ON EARTH-42.
THE PULL?
THE PULL TO ELP EVERYONE EVERYWHERE.
ALL THESE EOPLE--ALL THESE WORLDS.
JUST BY KNOWING THEY EXIST...WE FEEL THE PULL.
BUT THERE'S ALSO A FEW BILLION PEOPLE, AND CREATURES, ON THIS PLANET.
AND THE UNITED PLANETS ABOVE US.
WE HELP EVERYONE WE CAN...
...EVERYWHERE WE CAN.
TODAY, AS MESSY AS IT WAS, WE SHOWED THE PEOPLE OF YOUR WORLD HOPE.
HOPE MOTIVATES.
IT'S TRUE! I MOTIVATE THE @#$@# OUT OF PEOPLE.
OH, OF COURSE.
EVERYONE SAYS IT.
WHAT? LIKE ON TIKTOK?
YOU'LL TELL ME THE SECOND YOU FIND A WAY BACK TO MY WORLD.
NAOMI, THAT ZUMBADO... IS COMING HERE.
OH, ABSOLUTELY.
AS SOON AS HE CAN.
WELL, NOT WITHOUT THIS.
WHAT IS THAT?

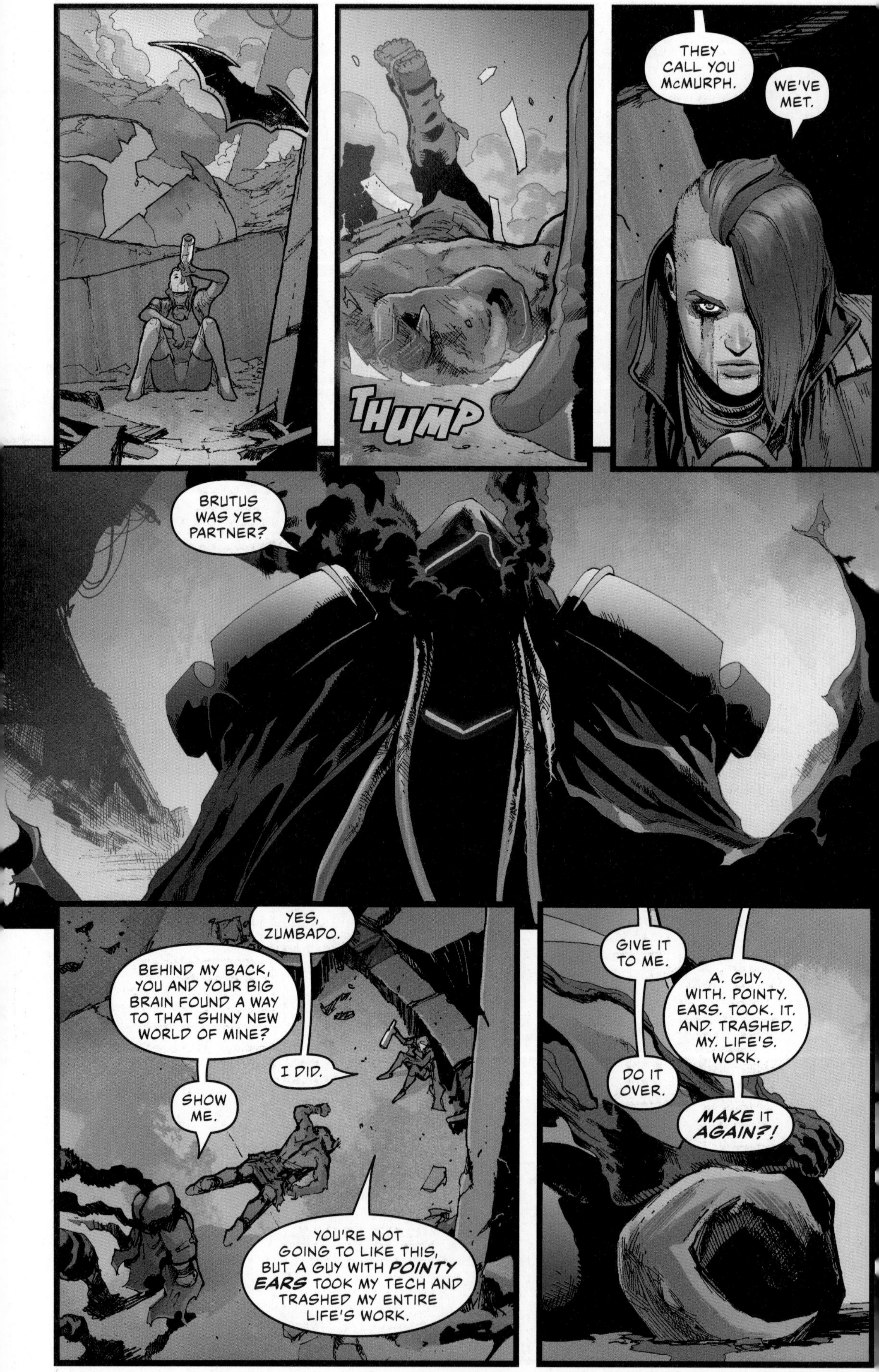
THUMP
THEY CALL YOU McMURPH.
WE'VE MET.
BRUTUS WAS YER PARTNER?
YES, ZUMBADO.
BEHIND MY BACK, YOU AND YOUR BIG BRAIN FOUND A WAY TO THAT SHINY NEW WORLD OF MINE?
I DID.
SHOW ME.
YOU'RE NOT GOING TO LIKE THIS, BUT A GUY WITH POINTY EARS TOOK MY TECH AND TRASHED MY ENTIRE LIFE'S WORK.
GIVE IT TO ME.
A. GUY. WITH. POINTY. EARS. TOOK. IT. AND. TRASHED. MY. LIFE'S. WORK.
DO IT OVER.
MAKE IT AGAIN?!

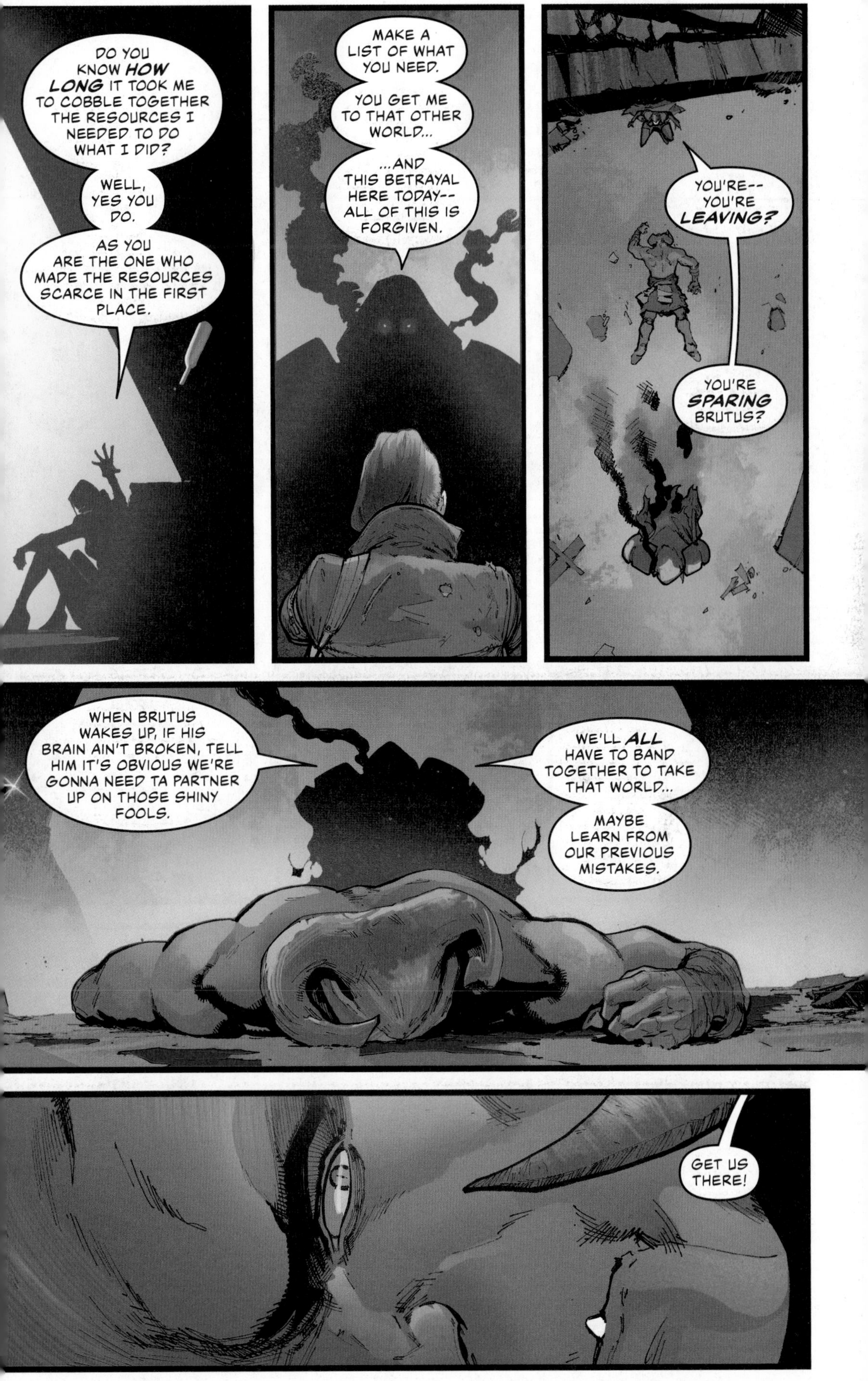
DO YOU KNOW HOW LONG IT TOOK ME TO COBBLE TOGETHER THE RESOURCES I NEEDED TO DO WHAT I DID?
WELL, YES YOU DO.
AS YOU ARE THE ONE WHO MADE THE RESOURCES SCARCE IN THE FIRST PLACE.
MAKE A LIST OF WHAT YOU NEED.
YOU GET ME TO THAT OTHER WORLD...
...AND THIS BETRAYAL HERE TODAY-- ALL OF THIS IS FORGIVEN.
YOU'RE-- YOU'RE LEAVING?
YOU'RE SPARING BRUTUS?
WHEN BRUTUS WAKES UP, IF HIS BRAIN AIN'T BROKEN, TELL HIM IT'S OBVIOUS WE'RE GONNA NEED TA PARTNER UP ON THOSE SHINY FOOLS.
WE'LL ALL HAVE TO BAND TOGETHER TO TAKE THAT WORLD...
MAYBE LEARN FROM OUR PREVIOUS MISTAKES.
GET US THERE!

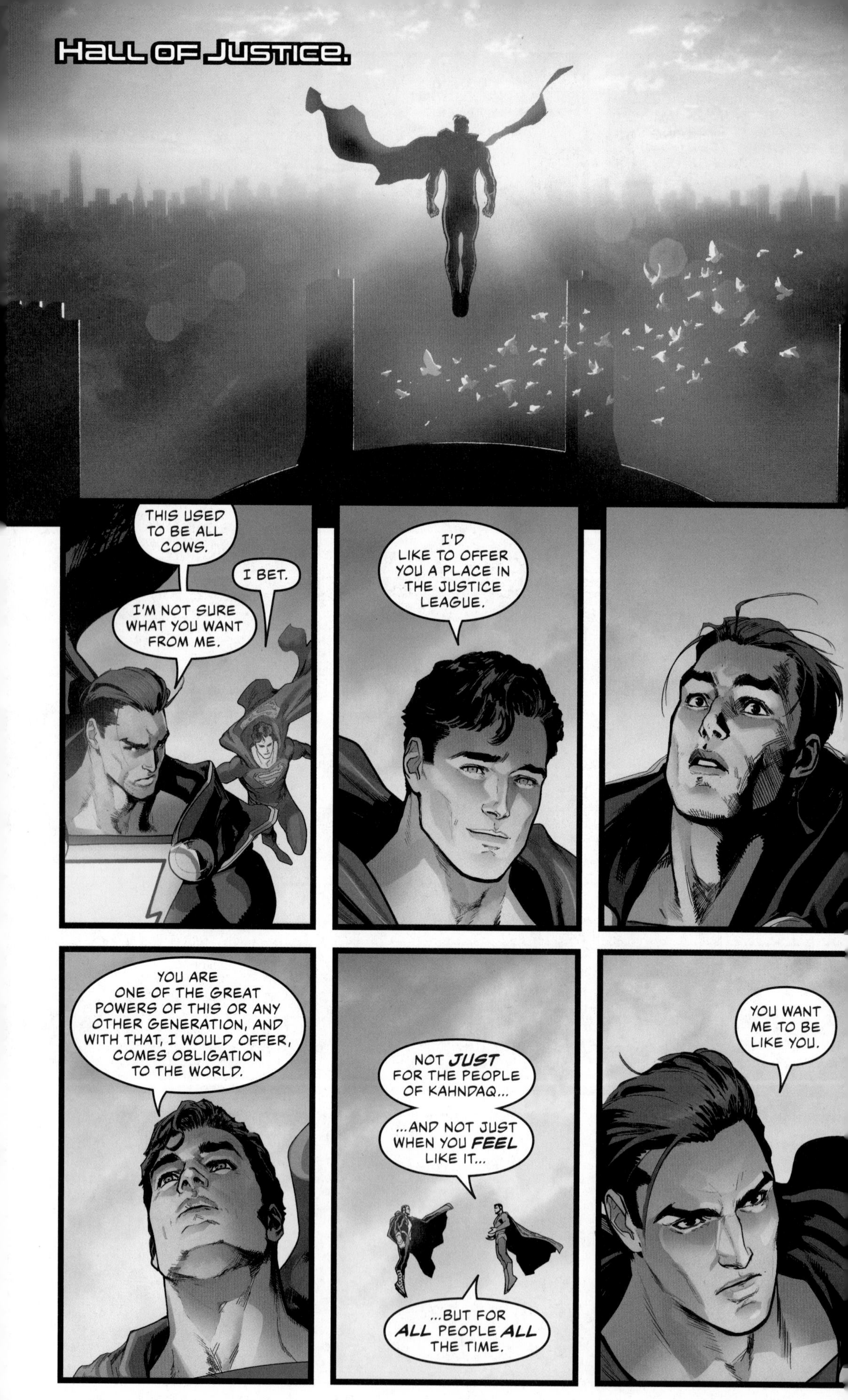
HALL OF JUSTICE.
THIS USED TO BE ALL COWS.
I BET.
I'M NOT SURE WHAT YOU WANT FROM ME.
I'D LIKE TO OFFER YOU A PLACE IN THE JUSTICE LEAGUE.
YOU ARE ONE OF THE GREAT POWERS OF THIS OR ANY OTHER GENERATION, AND WITH THAT, I WOULD OFFER, COMES OBLIGATION TO THE WORLD.
NOT JUST FOR THE PEOPLE OF KAHNDAQ...
...AND NOT JUST WHEN YOU FEEL LIKE IT...
...BUT FOR ALL PEOPLE ALL THE TIME.
YOU WANT ME TO BE LIKE YOU.

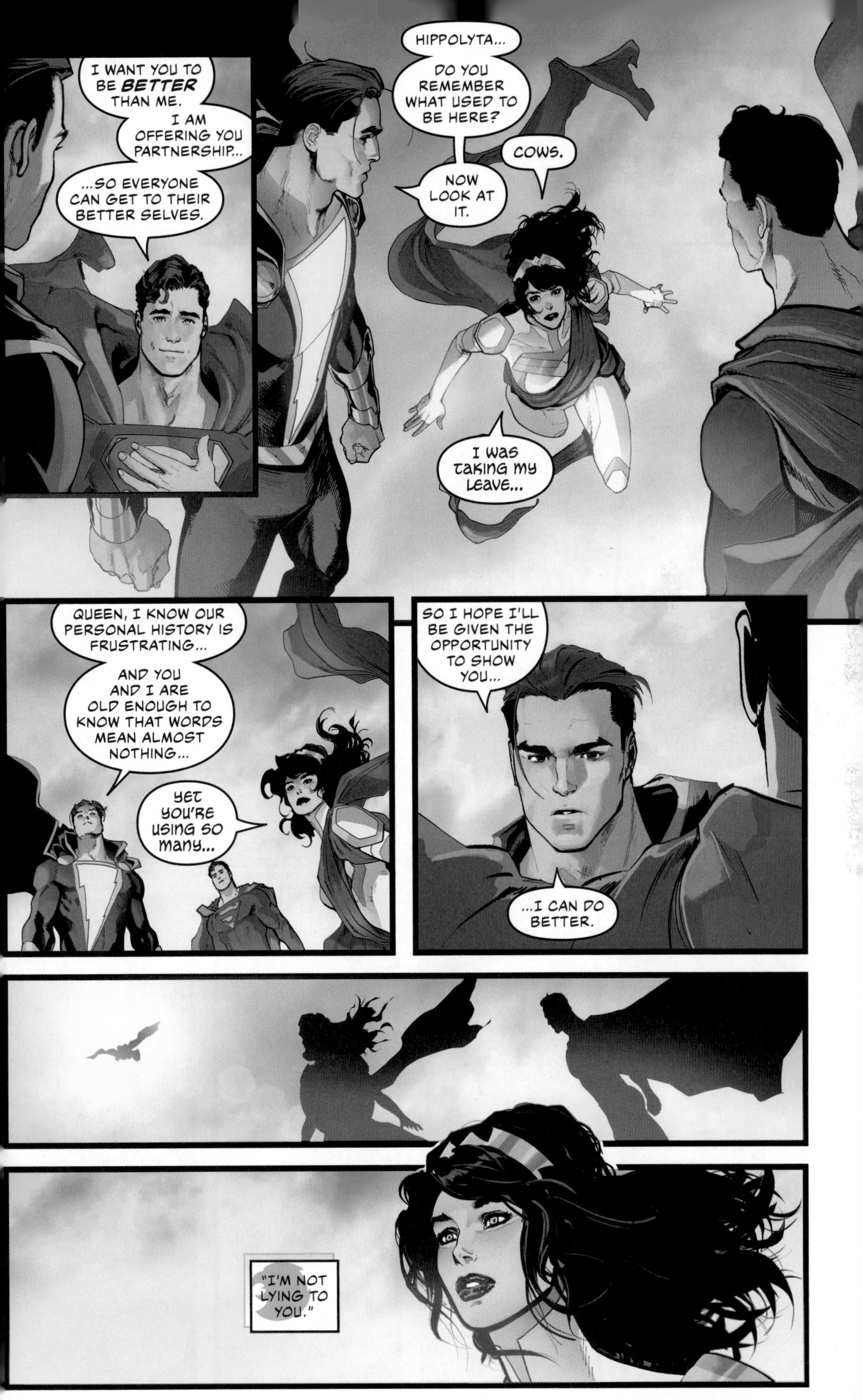
I WANT YOU TO BE BETTER THAN ME.
I AM OFFERING YOU PARTNERSHIP...
...SO EVERYONE CAN GET TO THEIR BETTER SELVES.
HIPPOLYTA...
DO YOU REMEMBER WHAT USED TO BE HERE?
COWS.
NOW LOOK AT IT.
I WAS TAKING MY LEAVE...
QUEEN, I KNOW OUR PERSONAL HISTORY IS FRUSTRATING...
AND YOU AND I ARE OLD ENOUGH TO KNOW THAT WORDS MEAN ALMOST NOTHING...
YET YOU'RE USING SO MANY...
SO I HOPE I'LL BE GIVEN THE OPPORTUNITY TO SHOW YOU...
...I CAN DO BETTER.
"I'M NOT LYING TO YOU."

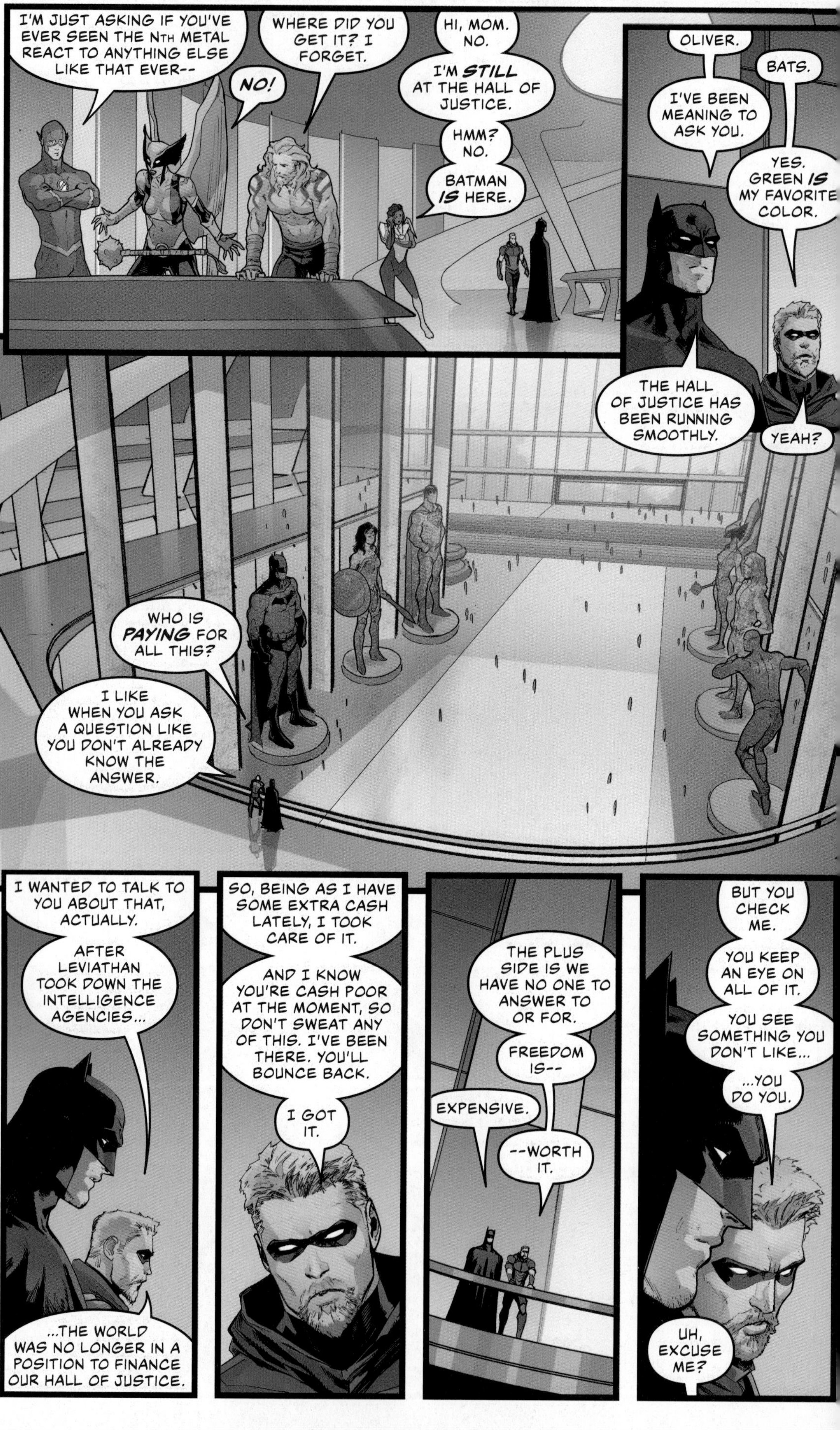
I'M JUST ASKING IF YOU'VE EVER SEEN THE NTH METAL REACT TO ANYTHING ELSE LIKE THAT EVER--
NO!
WHERE DID YOU GET IT? I FORGET.
HI, MOM. NO.
I'M STILL AT THE HALL OF JUSTICE.
HMM? NO.
BATMAN IS HERE.
OLIVER.
I'VE BEEN MEANING TO ASK YOU.
BATS.
YES. GREEN IS MY FAVORITE COLOR.
THE HALL OF JUSTICE HAS BEEN RUNNING SMOOTHLY.
YEAH?
WHO IS PAYING FOR ALL THIS?
I LIKE WHEN YOU ASK A QUESTION LIKE YOU DON'T ALREADY KNOW THE ANSWER.
I WANTED TO TALK TO YOU ABOUT THAT, ACTUALLY.
AFTER LEVIATHAN TOOK DOWN THE INTELLIGENCE AGENCIES...
...THE WORLD WAS NO LONGER IN A POSITION TO FINANCE OUR HALL OF JUSTICE.
SO, BEING AS I HAVE SOME EXTRA CASH LATELY, I TOOK CARE OF IT.
AND I KNOW YOU'RE CASH POOR AT THE MOMENT, SO DON'T SWEAT ANY OF THIS. I'VE BEEN THERE. YOU'LL BOUNCE BACK.
I GOT IT.
THE PLUS SIDE IS WE HAVE NO ONE TO ANSWER TO OR FOR.
FREEDOM IS--
EXPENSIVE.
--WORTH IT.
BUT YOU CHECK ME.
YOU KEEP AN EYE ON ALL OF IT.
YOU SEE SOMETHING YOU DON'T LIKE...
...YOU DO YOU.
UH, EXCUSE ME?

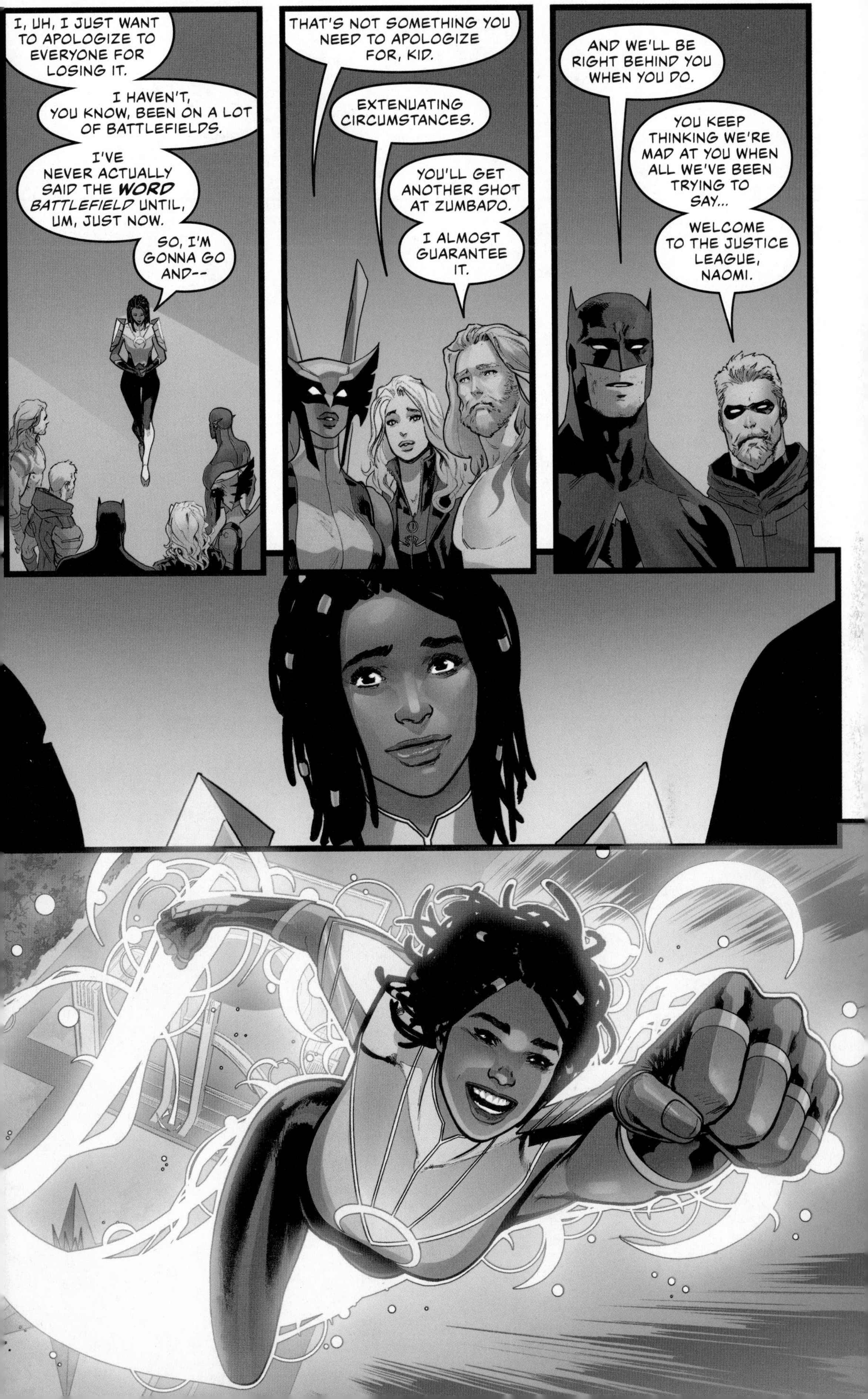
I, UH, I JUST WANT TO APOLOGIZE TO EVERYONE FOR LOSING IT.
I HAVEN'T, YOU KNOW, BEEN ON A LOT OF BATTLEFIELDS.
I'VE NEVER ACTUALLY SAID THE WORD BATTLEFIELD UNTIL, UM, JUST NOW.
SO, I'M GONNA GO AND--
THAT'S NOT SOMETHING YOU NEED TO APOLOGIZE FOR, KID.
EXTENUATING CIRCUMSTANCES.
YOU'LL GET ANOTHER SHOT AT ZUMBADO.
I ALMOST GUARANTEE IT.
AND WE'LL BE RIGHT BEHIND YOU WHEN YOU DO.
YOU KEEP THINKING WE'RE MAD AT YOU WHEN ALL WE'VE BEEN TRYING TO SAY...
WELCOME TO THE JUSTICE LEAGUE, NAOMI.

Justice League #59 variant cover art by **David Marquez & Tamra Bonvillain**

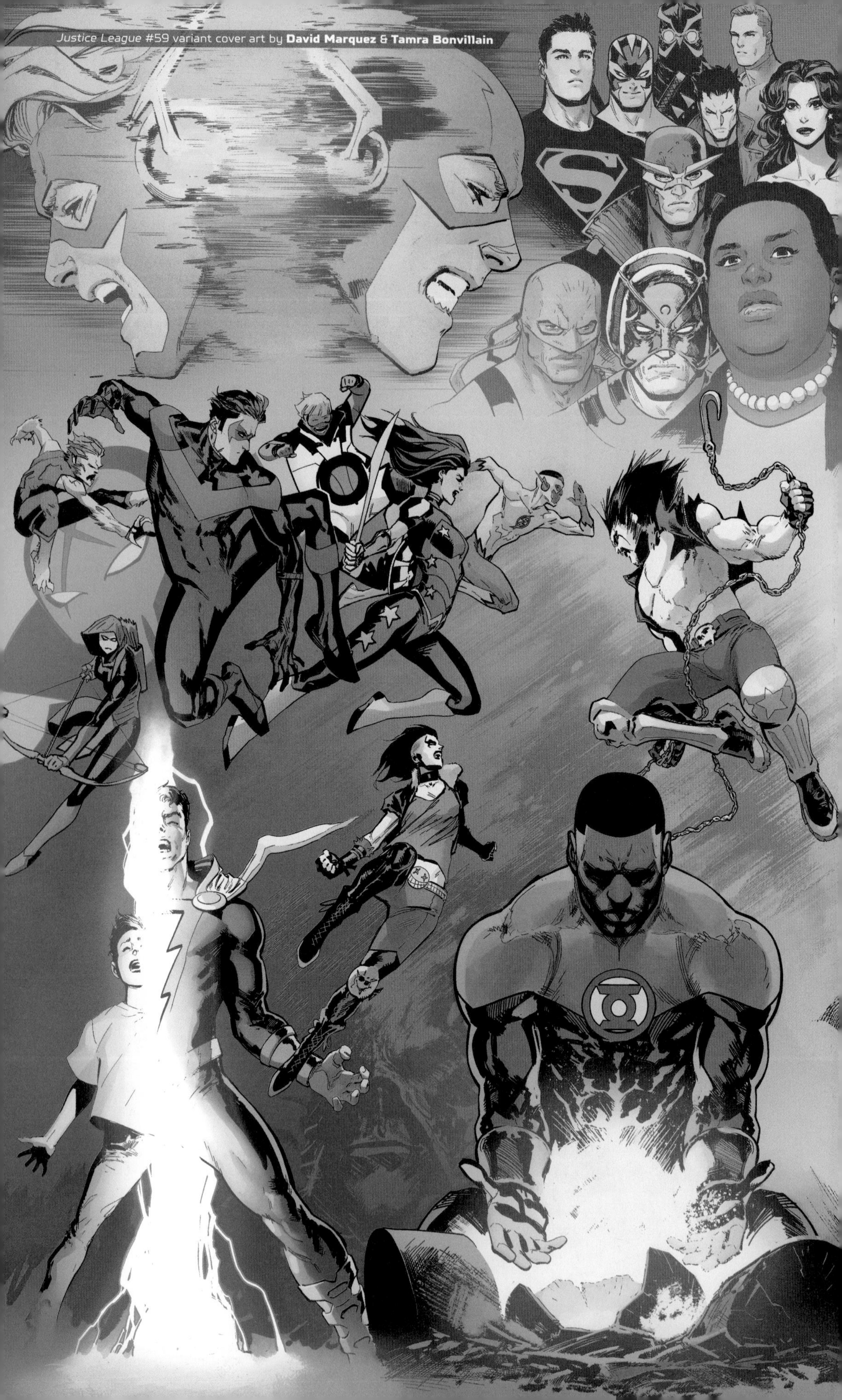

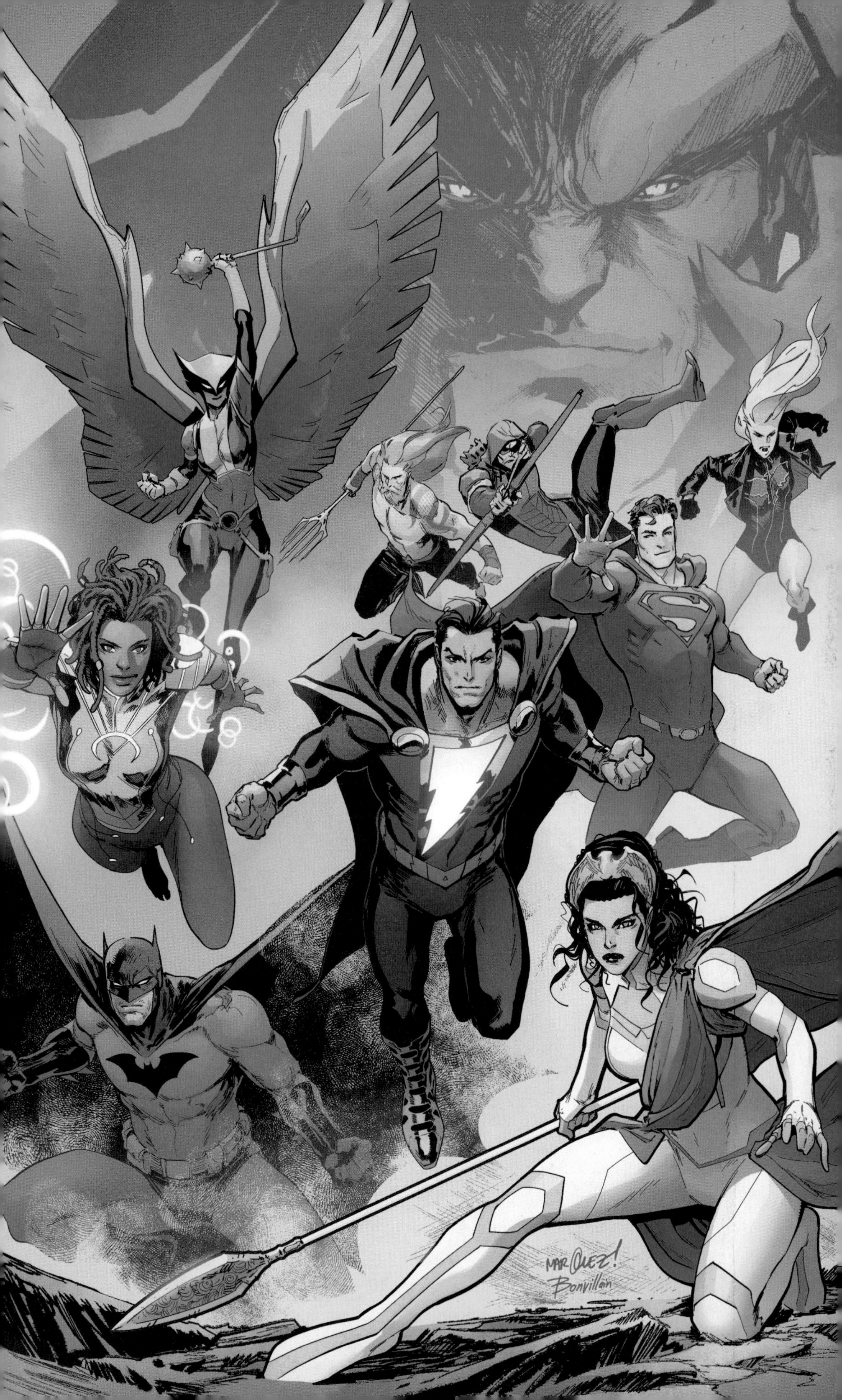
MARQUEZ!
Bonvillain

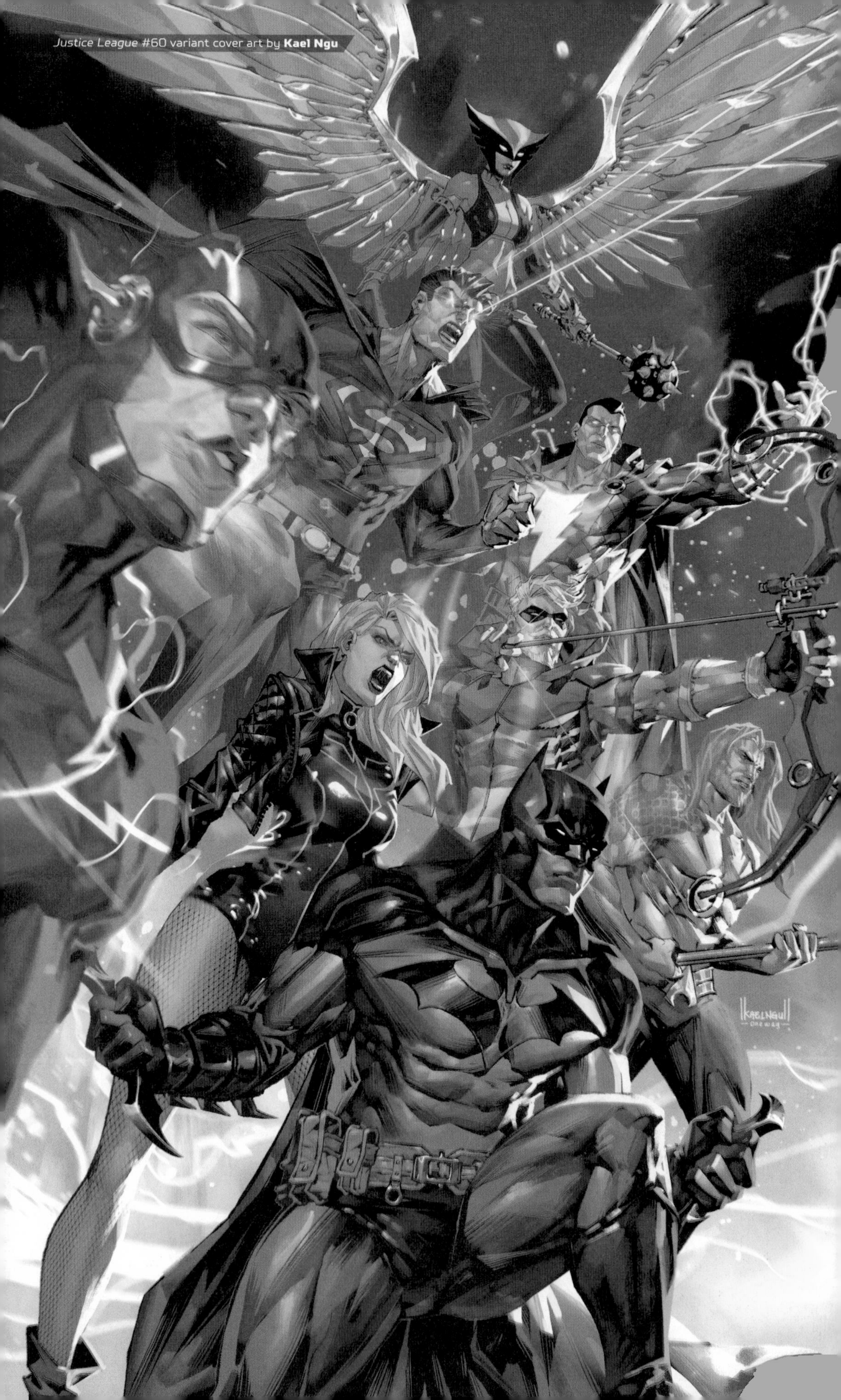

Justice League #60 variant cover art by **Kael Ngu**

Justice League #61 variant cover art by **Kael Ngu**

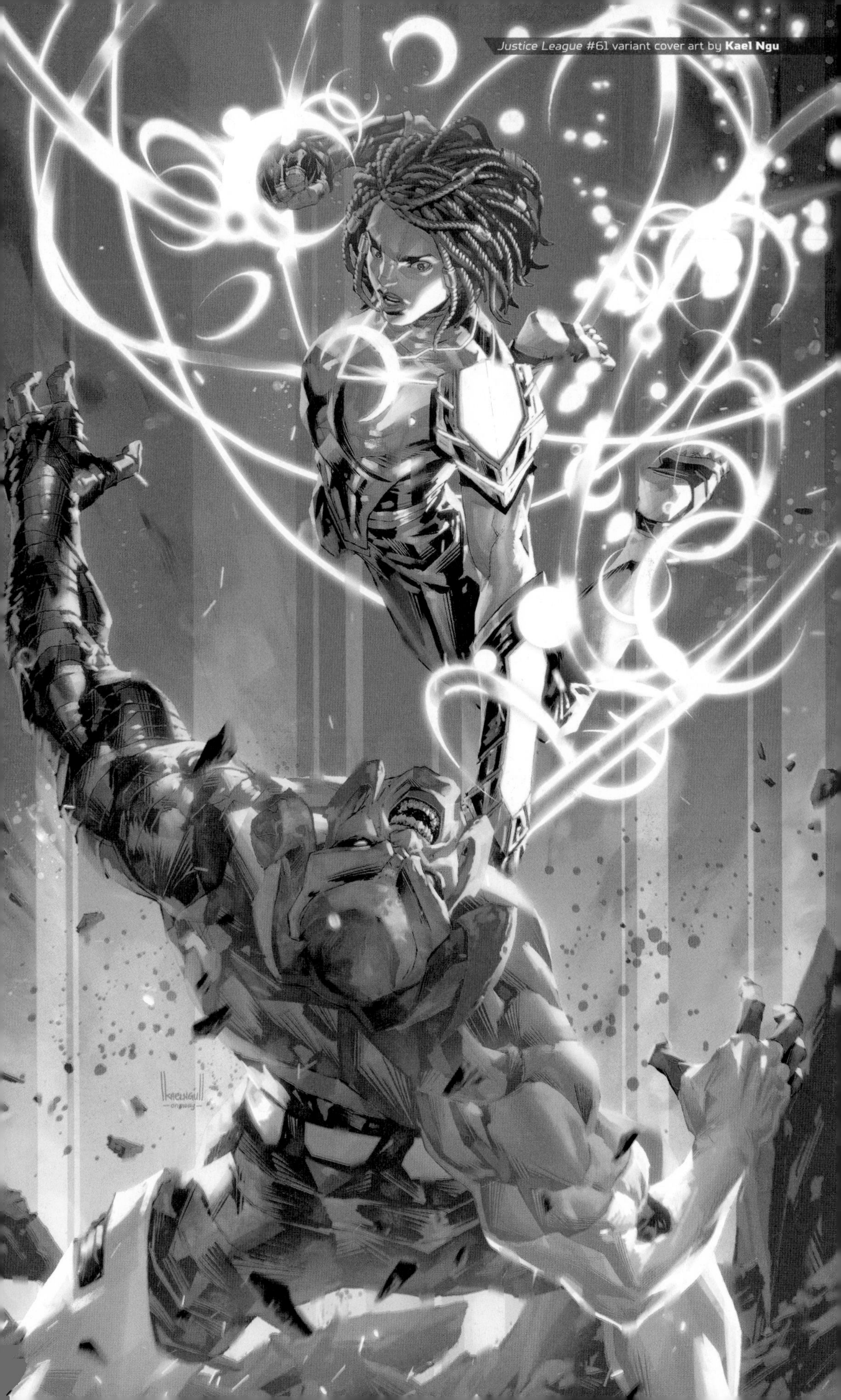

Justice League #62 variant cover art by **Howard Porter** & **Hi-Fi**

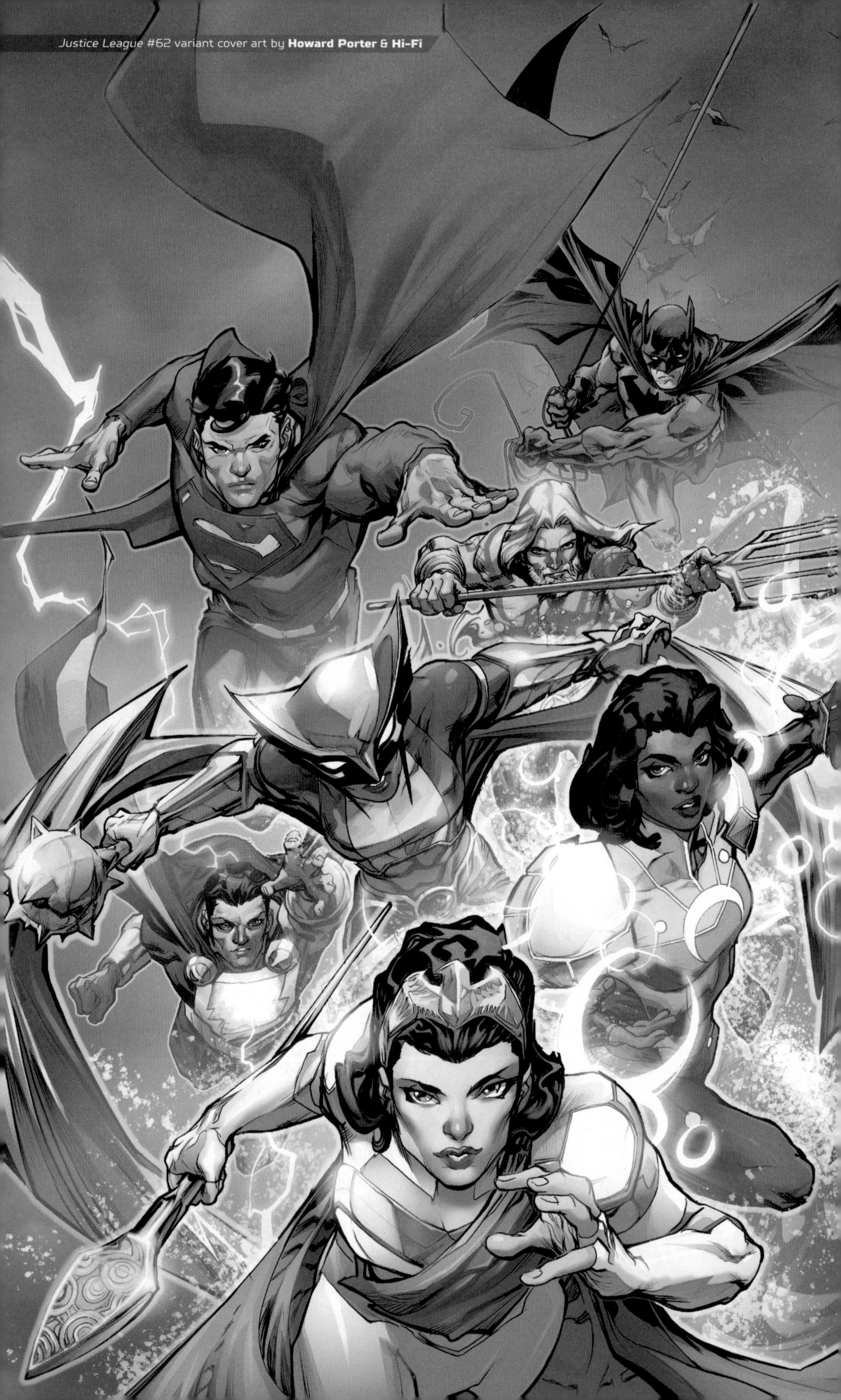

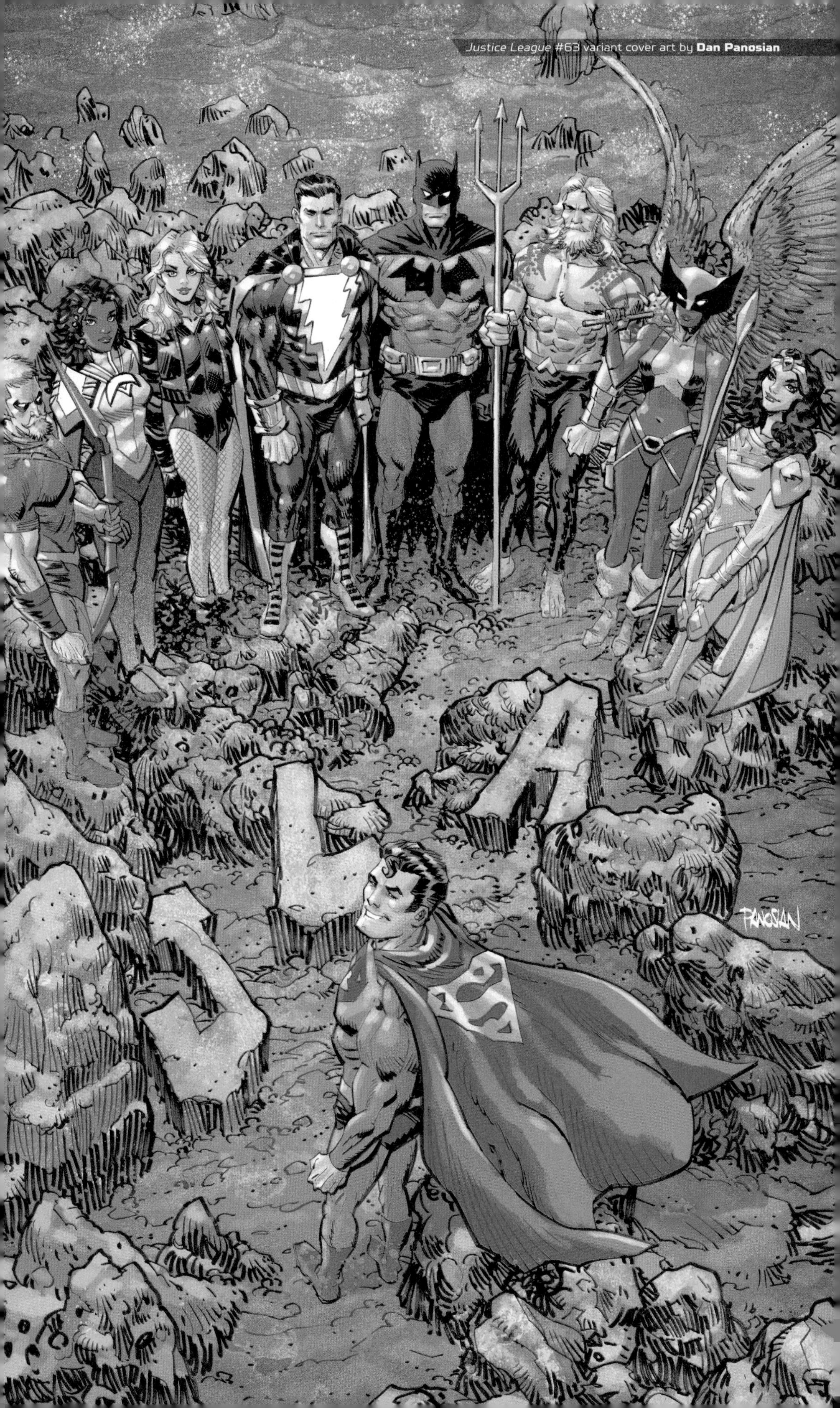

JLA
PANOSIAN

Justice League #63 variant cover art by **Dan Panosian**

Zack Snyder's Justice League variant cover art for *Justice League* #59 by **Jim Lee & Alex Sinclair**

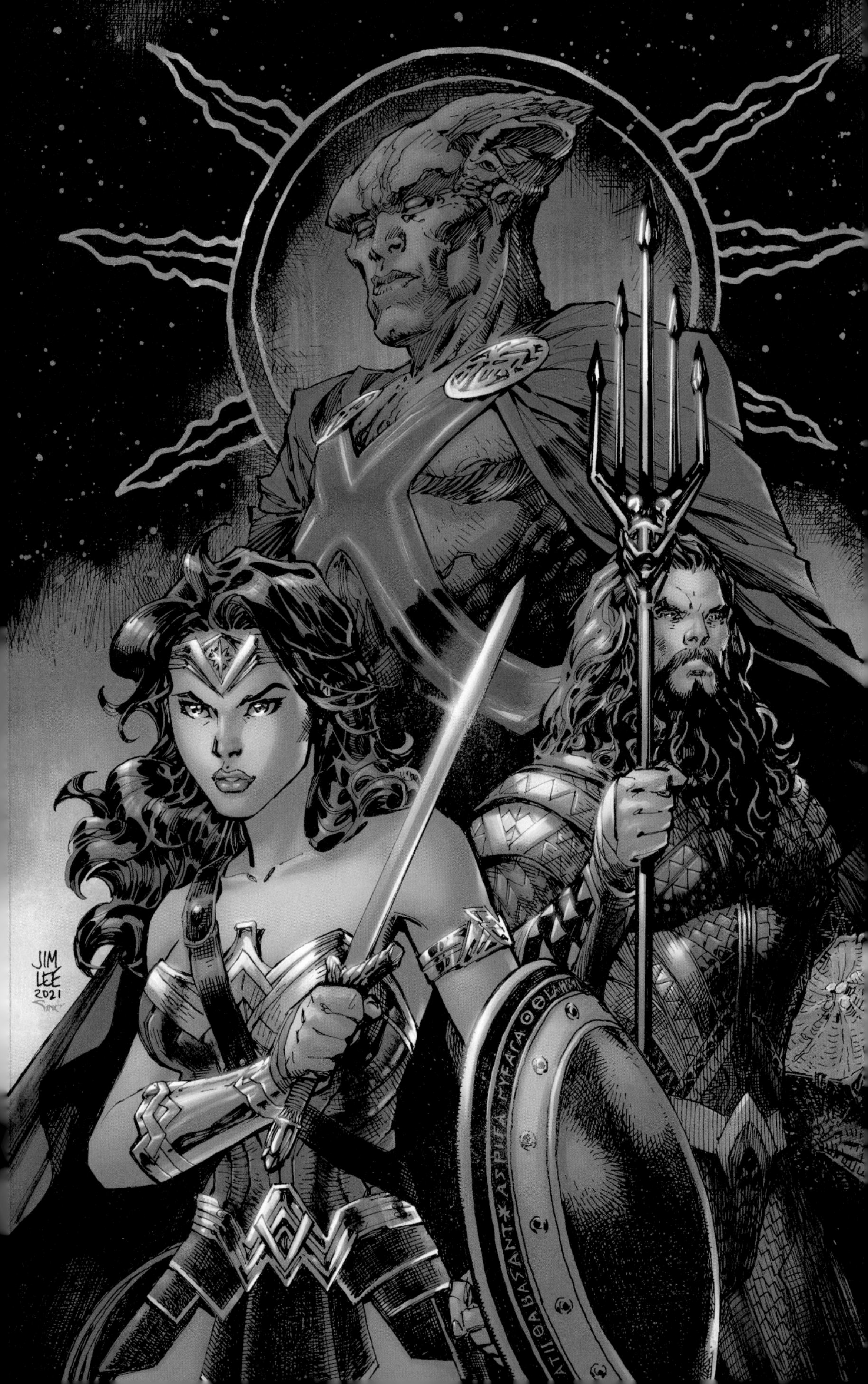
JIM
LEE
2021

BONUS SKETCHBOOK BY
DAVID MARQUEZ

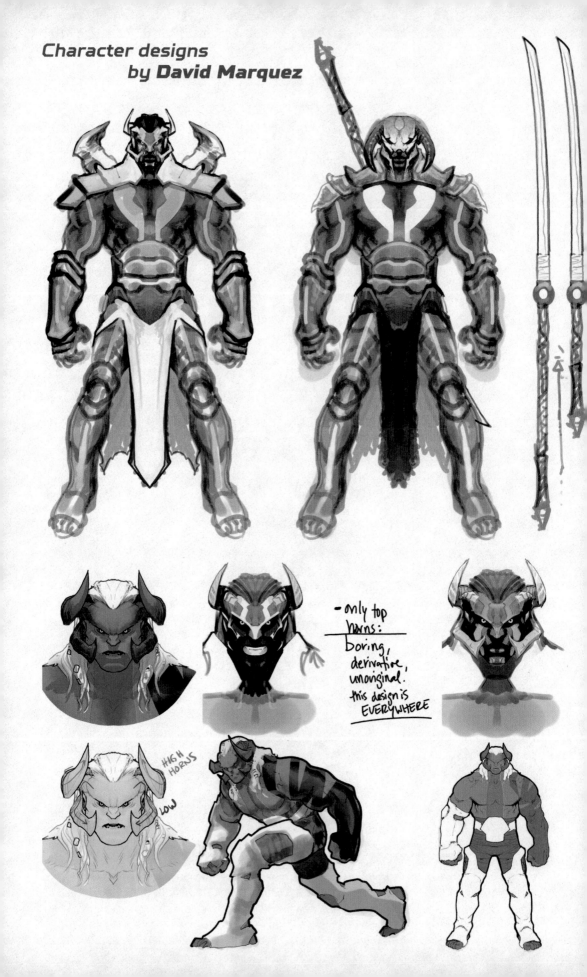

Character designs
by **David Marquez**

- only top horns: boring, derivative, unoriginal. this design is EVERYWHERE

HIGH HORNS

LOW

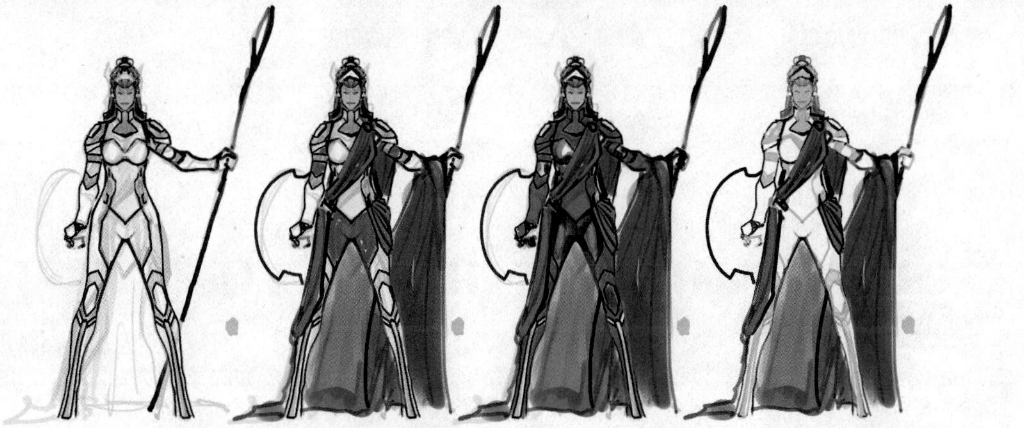

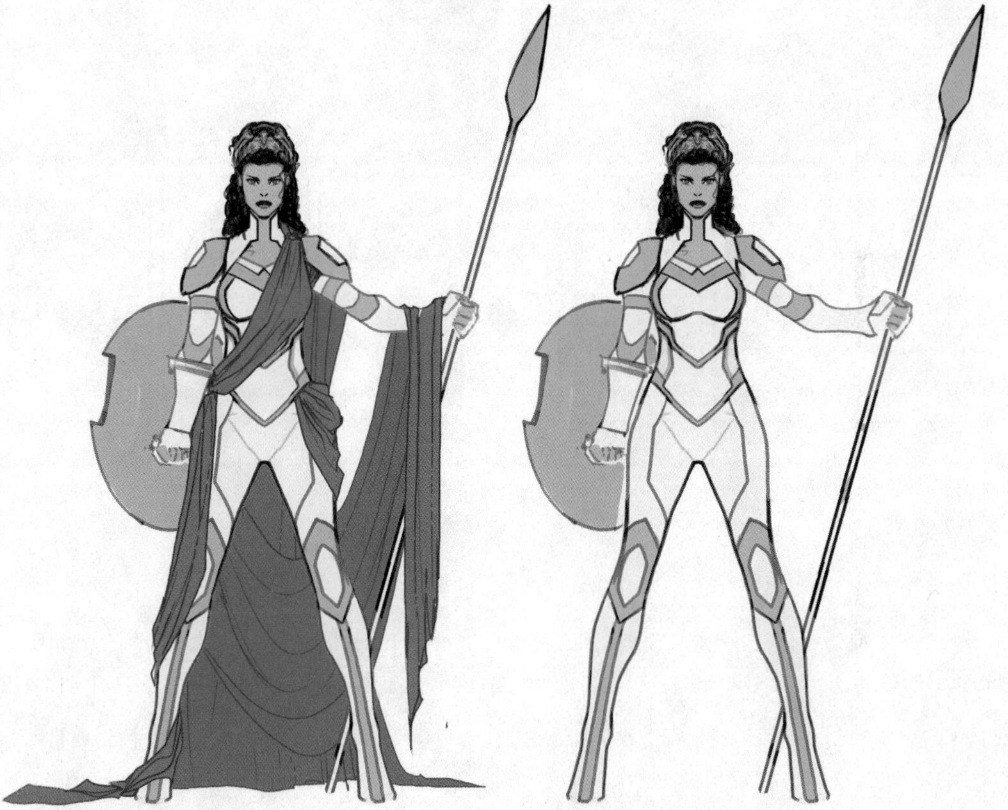

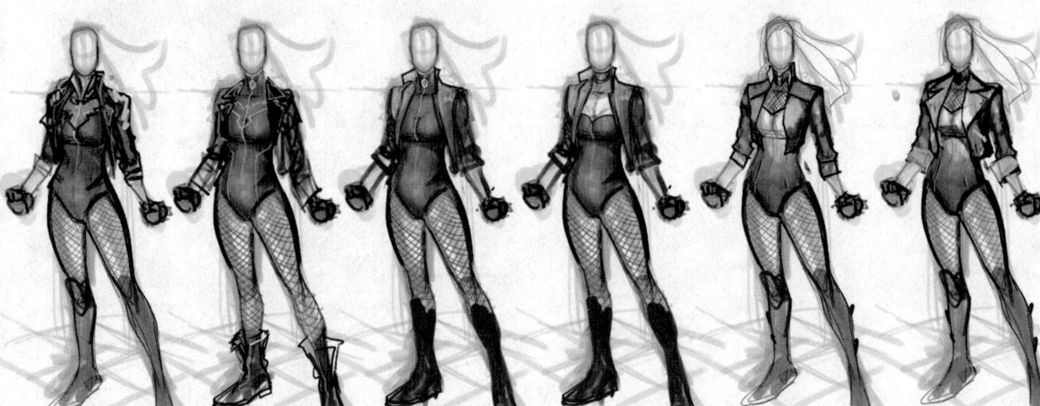
A
B
C
D

Pencils and inks by ***David Marquez***

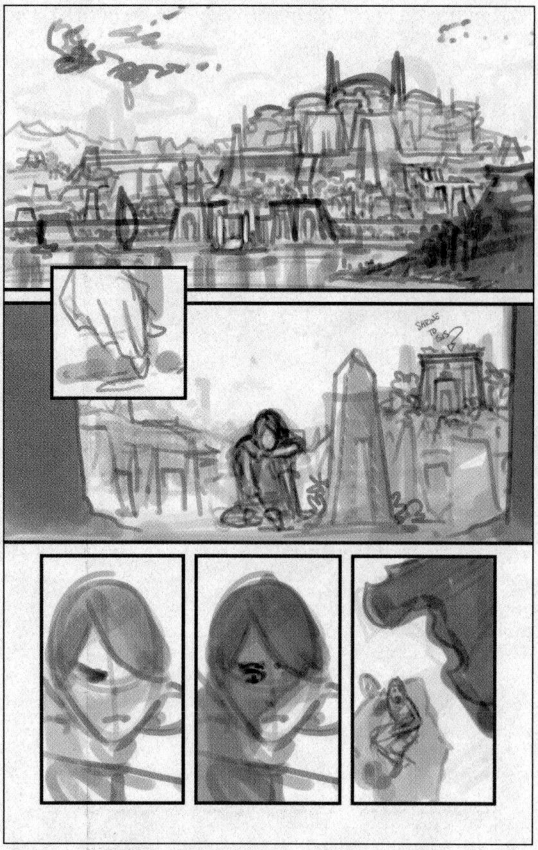

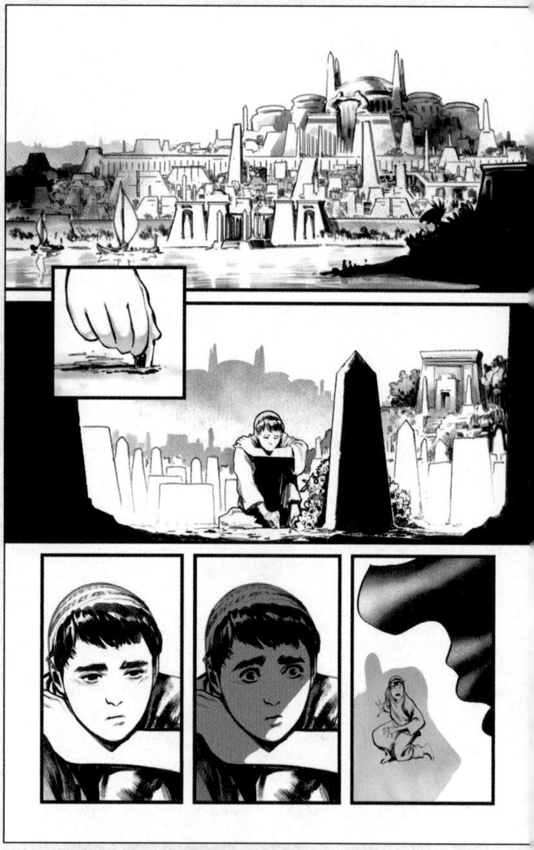

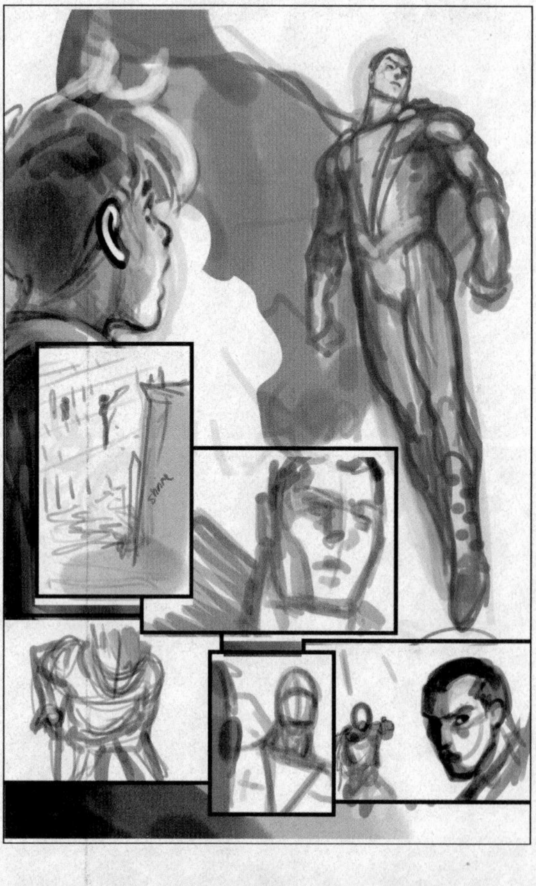

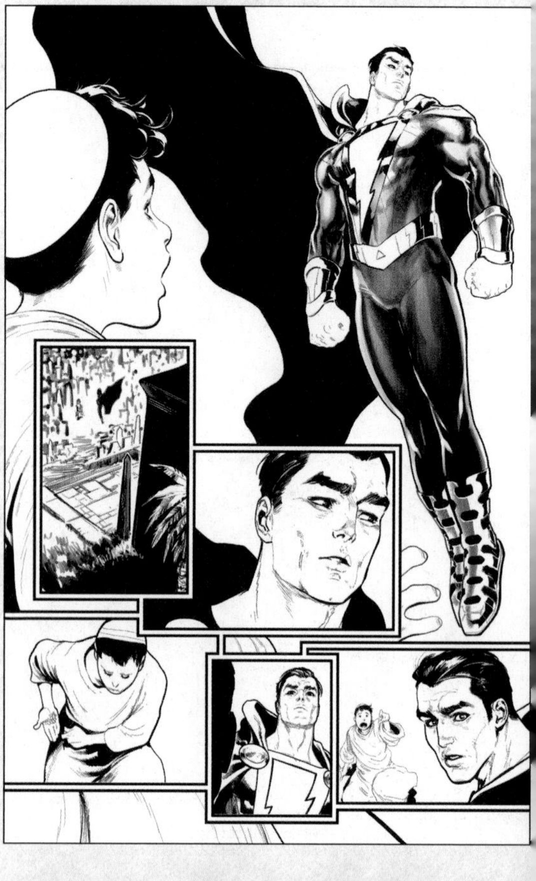

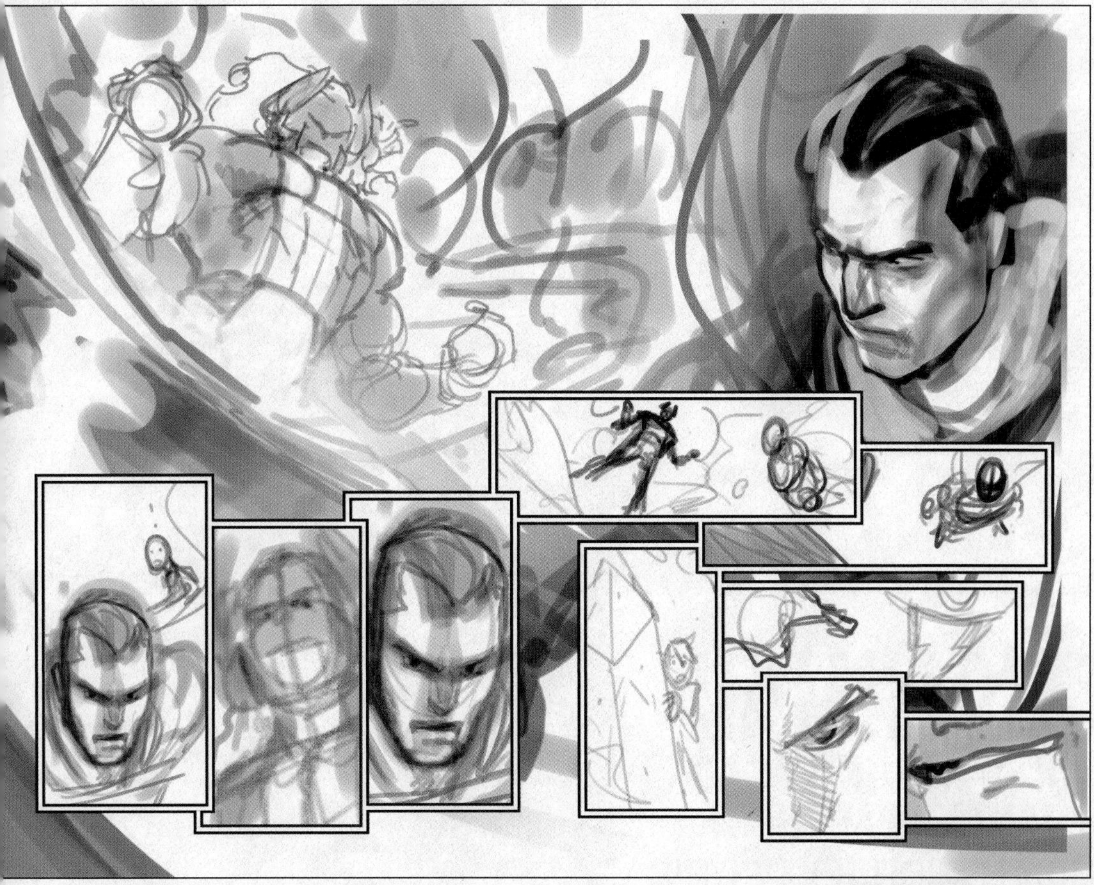

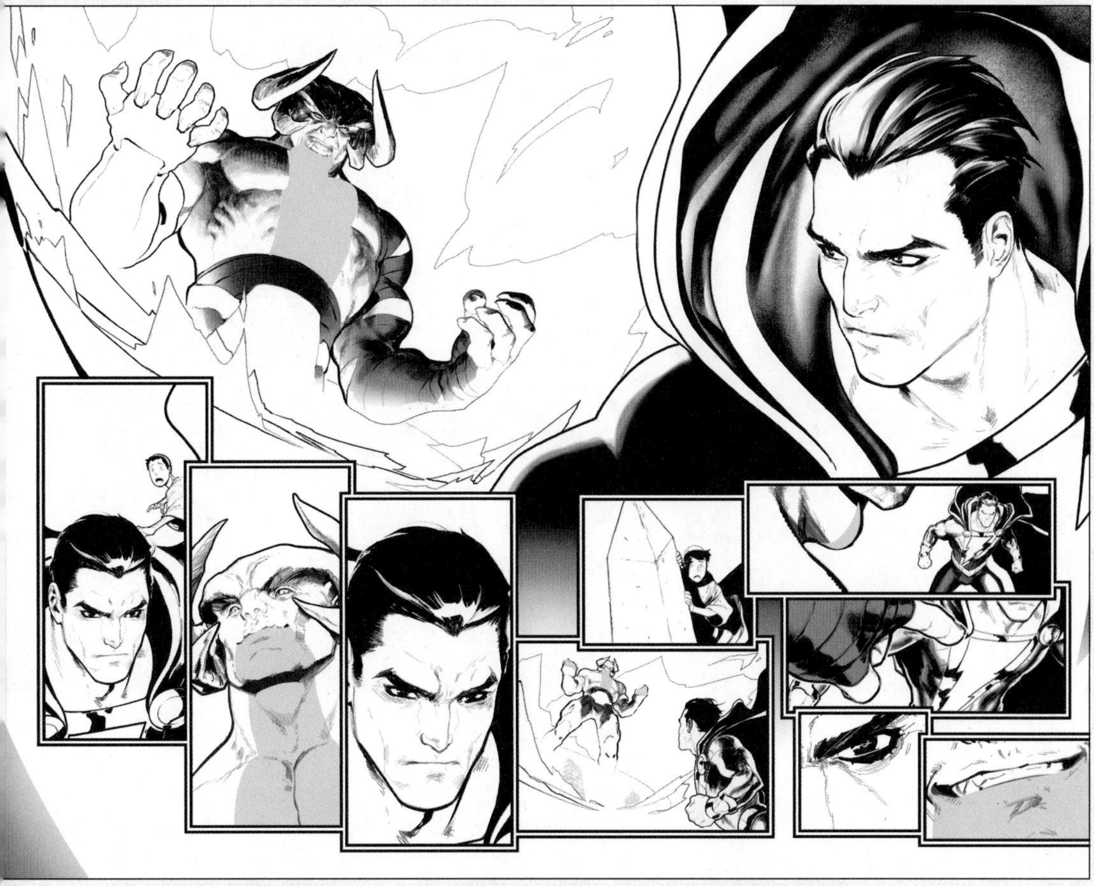

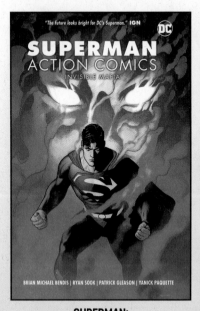
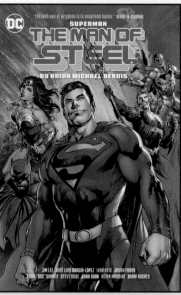

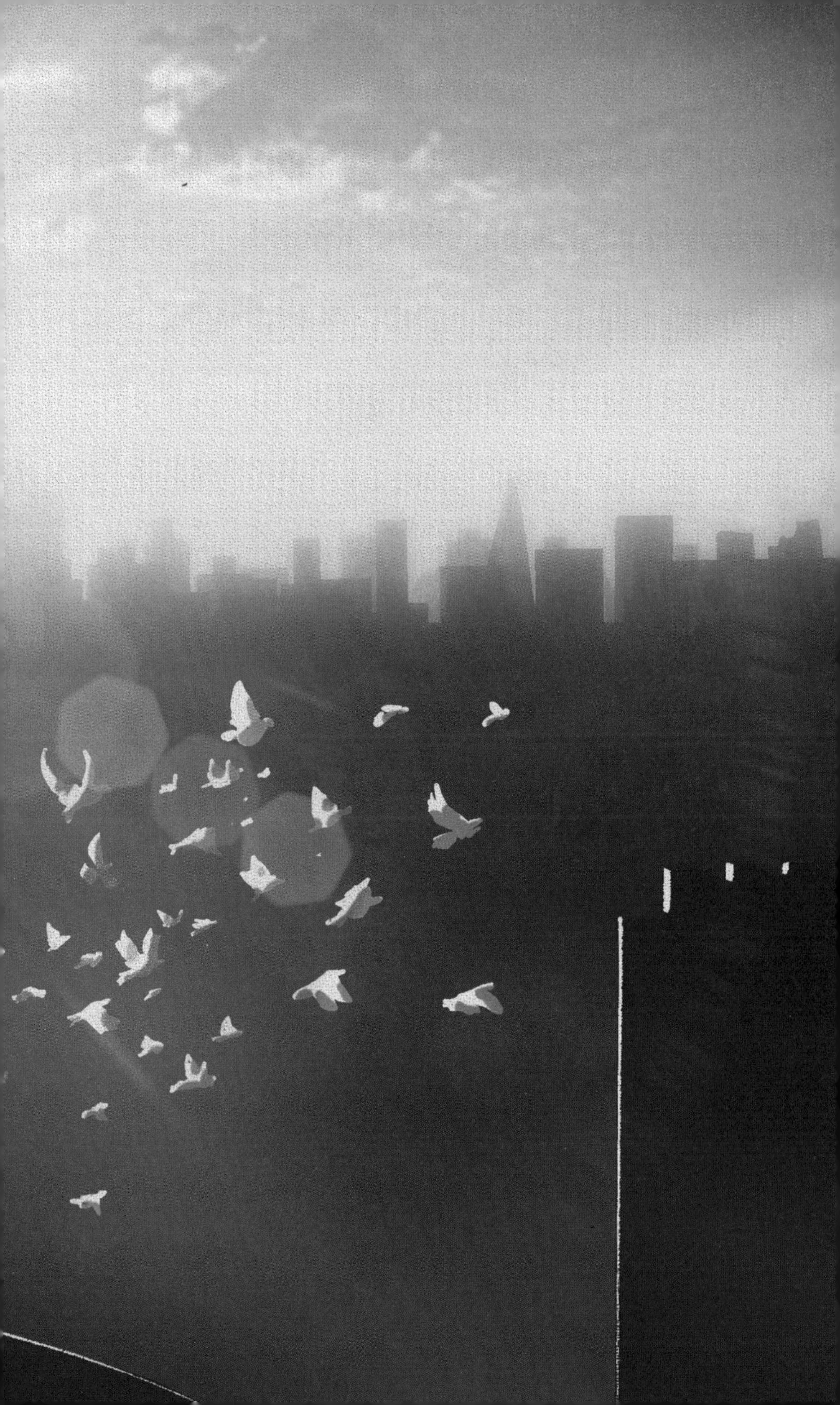

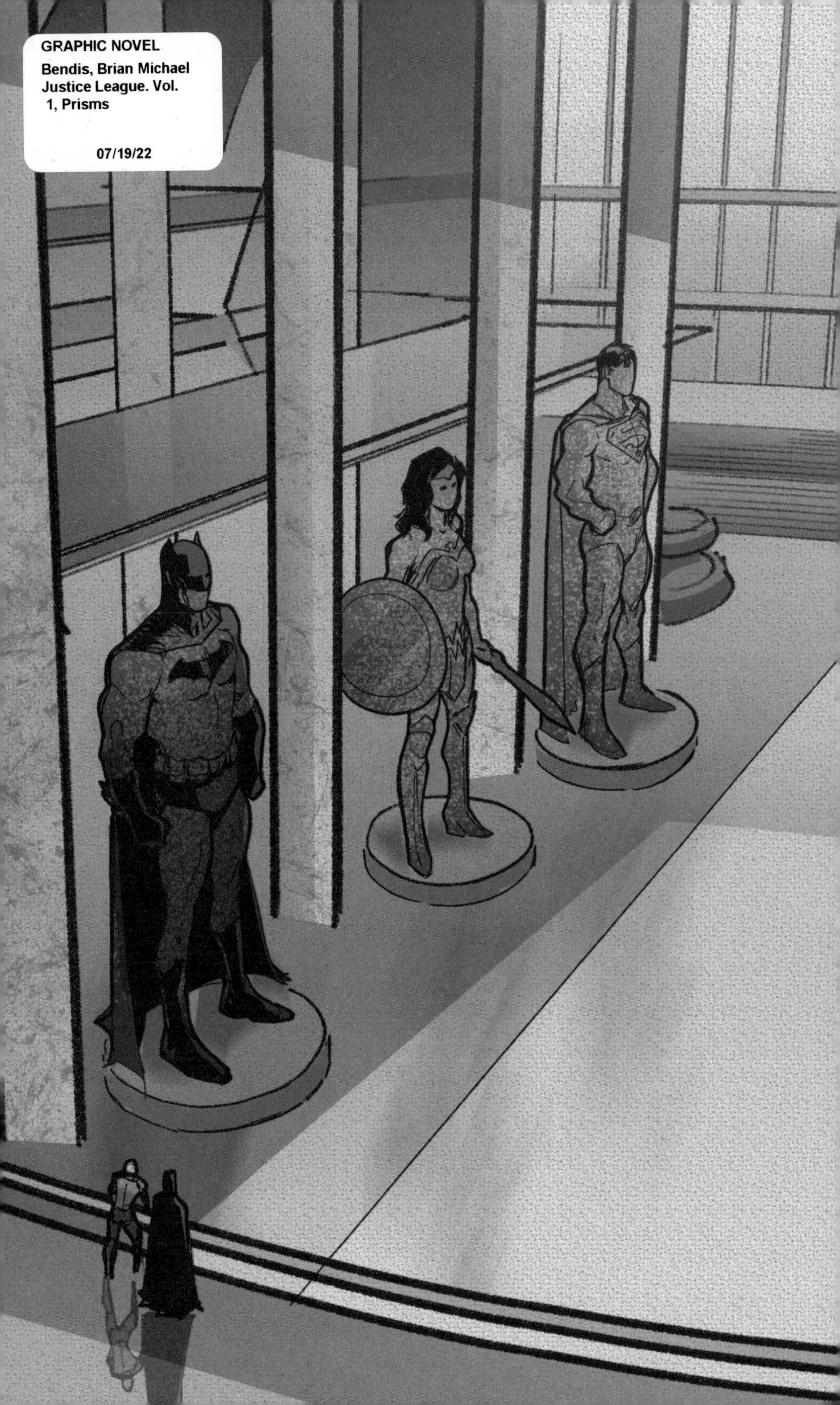